Palgrave Studies in European Union Politics

Following on the sustained success of the acclaimed European Union Series, which essentially publishes research-based textbooks, Palgrave Studies in European Union Politics publishes cutting edge research-driven monographs. The remit of the series is broadly defined, both in terms of subject and academic discipline. All topics of significance concerning the nature and operation of the European Union potentially fall within the scope of the series. The series is multidisciplinary to reflect the growing importance of the EU as a political, economic and social phenomenon. To submit a proposal, please contact Senior Editor Ambra Finotello ambra.finotello@palgrave.com.



More information about this series at
http://www.palgrave.com/gp/series/14629

Florian Bieber • Roland Bieber

# Negotiating Unity and Diversity in the European Union

palgrave
macmillan

Florian Bieber
Centre for Southeast European Studies
University of Graz
Graz, Austria

Roland Bieber
University of Lausanne
Lausanne, Switzerland

ISSN 2662-5873 ISSN 2662-5881 (electronic)
Palgrave Studies in European Union Politics
ISBN 978-3-030-55015-8 ISBN 978-3-030-55016-5 (eBook)
https://doi.org/10.1007/978-3-030-55016-5



Cover illustration: Magic Lens/Shutterstock

This Palgrave Macmillan imprint is published by the registered company Springer Nature Switzerland AG.
The registered company address is: Gewerbestrasse 11, 6330 Cham, Switzerland

# Acknowledgments

This book approaches the European Union and the fundamental challenge of how to balance diversity and unity within it from different perspectives. First, it is based on the collaboration of a legal scholar and a political scientist, trying to bring both disciplines to bear on the discussion. Second, it incorporates literature and debates on the EU and European Law, as well as those on diversity and multinational states. It thus seeks to bring different disciplines, literatures, and debates together, convinced that this allows for fruitful academic engagement that both adds to the understanding of the European Union and advances research and debates on how to accommodate diversity in multinational states.

Florian Bieber began developing ideas for this book as Luigi Einaudi Chair in European and International Studies at Cornell University in 2009. Roland Bieber's contribution to this project has matured since 2011, when he enjoyed the hospitality and the extraordinary research opportunities at the European University Institute in Florence as a Fernand Braudel Senior Fellow. His research also benefited from a generous grant from the Swiss National Science Foundation.

We would like to thank Sarah Kutz for proofreading the manuscript and Fynn Morten-Heckert for helping with formatting the text. We would also like to thank Emma Lantschner and Patricia Morris for their constructive feedback on sections of this book.

This book was conceptualized jointly, and then the draft chapters were written and commented upon by both authors of this volume.

Florian Bieber is the primary author of the Introduction and Chaps. 2, 3, and 8. Roland Bieber is the primary author of Chaps. 4, 5, 6, and 7. The conclusion and the epilogue was written jointly.

To close on a personal note: this book is not just the collaboration of a legal scholar and a political scientist; it is also the collaboration between a father and a son. As such, the book is the result of a much longer conversation and shared life experience. This book cannot begin to express this, but it is an attempt to give intellectual shape to the academic dialogue between a father and son, reflecting in a microcosm the potential of combining unity and diversity.

Graz and Bonn
May 2020

Florian Bieber
Roland Bieber

# Contents

CHAPTER 1

# Introduction

The European Union is often understood through its motto 'united in diversity,' adopted in 2000 and in use for years earlier. Yet the primary focus has often centered on unity or the policies that bring together the divergent populations of the Union. Diversity is self-evident and obvious. However, this diversity is at the core of the European integration project and the novel ways in which the EU has been recognizing difference and incorporating it into its institutions and modus operandi constitutes an often-neglected aspect of EU integration.[1]

For over a decade, the European Union appears to be lost in an endless series of crises, beginning with the global economic crisis of 2008, the subsequent Eurozone crisis, the migration crisis, Brexit, and the COVID 19 crisis. These have constituted the most serious challenges to the European Union since the establishment of the European Community of Coal and Steel more than half a century earlier. The integration project has seen periods of economic stagnation and political conflict, including President de Gaulle's "Non" to British Membership, the period of 'Eurosclerosis' during the oil shock of the 1970s, and political stagnation of the Community. Even during the decades preceding the current crises, there have been serious setbacks, including the French and Dutch rejection of the European constitution, the Danish referendum in which the

[1] A similar argument has been made by Prügl and Thiel (2009), p. 9.



F. Bieber, R. Bieber, *Negotiating Unity and Diversity in the European Union*, Palgrave Studies in European Union Politics,
https://doi.org/10.1007/978-3-030-55016-5_1

Maastricht Treaty was temporarily rejected, and other setbacks to European integration.

The past decade, with its recession and the ensuing debt crisis in recent years, has raised a question of economic and financial collapse and tested the solidarity of the Union to its limits. In addition to the difficulties of the EU in responding effectively to the economic crisis and its subsequent debt and currency crises, the difficulties in persuading German citizens to support the economies in Europe's South, particularly Greece, demonstrated the constraints of the EU. Solidarity is always a fragile good; many modern states suffer from the difficulty of convincing their citizens of the need for solidarity with co-citizens. In addition, the European project has been challenged by populist parties. Combining anti-elite rhetoric with hostility toward migration and global cooperation, these parties have been successful in elections in recent years and have found copycats among mainstream parties. Some mainstream parties, British conservatives in particular, have challenged the usefulness of the European integration project and some of its basic premises. The 'Brexit' referendum in June 2016 resulted in a majority of citizens in a Member State voting to leave the European Union. Thus, the European integration project finds itself in the most serious crisis since its beginnings in the 1950s. Yet it has also succeeded in establishing an unprecedented level of cooperation and integration on the European continent. In core areas of EU politics, for example environment, transport, internal market, and consumer protection, it has established a web of rules, which apply to more than 400 million people. In fact, despite or because of the crisis, the EU has increased in popularity among its citizens, and record numbers identify themselves as Europeans. This paradox between a high level of integration—often invisible to most citizens or taken for granted—and its challenges merits a revaluation of the European Union as a polity that has sought to accommodate difference. Diversity is inherent in any social group as a result of the multitude of its composing identities. Unless oppressed by authoritarian rule, diversity is intrinsically in permanent tension with the unity of the respective group.

Crisis and resilience shine a light on a core challenge and achievement of the EU, namely its ability to accommodate diversity. We argue that the EU has developed a set of unique responses to the challenges of diversity throughout its existence. A union of not just diverse states but citizens with divergent understandings of citizenship, solidarity, and a variety of national identities has had to find novel ways to incorporate difference.

Rather than a ready-made plan, the European project gradually built up institutions and instruments to mediate and incorporate this diversity. We will argue that this experience also offers insight into how states can engage with diversity. As such, we analyze the European Union through the lens with which one might view a state and argue that its policies contain lessons for other states.

The European Union since its founding has been defined by its diversity in terms of languages, religions, historical experiences, and traditions. While observers often note that the EU has become more diverse with the enlargement toward post-Communist countries, they may easily downplay the variety among (and within) the Member States of the 'old' EU.[2] In response, the EU has developed a careful web of institutions and policies that seek to accommodate this diversity while allowing the EU to function and evolve. The recent crises highlighted not only the tenuous nature of these structures, but also the mechanisms that the EU has developed to weather the crises.

This is not to argue that the EU with all its institutions and structural particularities constitutes a role model for countries seeking to accommodate diversity around the world, or that the EU offers a set blueprint—in fact, its ability to respond through creative ambiguity to challenges of diversity offers greater insight than the formal institutions themselves. In general, the transfer of institutions without accounting for different contexts has not served the process of state-building and democratization. Yet, understanding how one polity addresses a particular feature of its social structure, be it inequality, size, or diversity, can help draw broader lessons.

The core argument of this book is that the EU has developed implicit and explicit forms of addressing the diversity that extend beyond merely acknowledging the diversity of its Member States. These range from offering a distinct layer of European citizenship, to prohibiting discrimination, to developing institutional mechanisms that ensure a balance of the majority while giving a voice to smaller Member States. This development was piecemeal and gradual, rather than being based on a grand design of how to accomplish 'unity through diversity.' We argue that an essential feature of the EU's approach to diversity has been not by design, but by confronting particular challenges over time, thus creating an evolving and growing

[2] For example, the difference in wealth within Germany (East/West) and Italy (North/South).

response to diversity. What evolved is not a unified, coherent set of laws or policies, but a complex, multi-layered, and asymmetric web. The result is by no means comprehensive or perfect. National minorities are often marginalized both nationally and in the EU, including the large pan-European Roma community. Racial diversity and migration are often marginalized, as numerous EU Member States still refuse to recognize their own diversity through migration.

What the EU is, was, or should be has been one of the most difficult questions to answer. It has been variously called an 'empire' (Zielonka 2005, pp. 11–14), a 'small power' (Toje 2010, pp. 5–10, 182–184), a community of values (Richardson 2002–2003), a system of governance (Jordan 2001), a trading power (Meunier and Nicolaïdis 2006), a normative power (Diez 2005), and much else. The variety of labels often reflects different perspectives. Seen as a foreign policy power, it gains a different shape than as an actor upon and together with the Member States.

The multitude of ascriptions is also a result of the EU itself having been notoriously elusive in its self-definition (Zielonka 2005, pp. 4–7). This evasion has been largely an exercise in survival and adaptability. The creative ambiguity of the EU has been a core feature of the Union and also what has kept it going. In fact, this conundrum itself is already a response to the challenges of diversity. The EU could be understood as an 'incompletely theorized agreement,' a term coined by the American constitutional lawyer Cass Sunstein. He notes that agreement on overarching concepts might be elusive. Ambiguity and abstraction—rather than great detail—can provide accommodation for otherwise conflicting positions (Sunstein 2001, p. 56). While such an approach might be criticized for avoiding confrontation on key issues in a society, 'incompletely theorized agreements' have clear benefits in divided societies: "Especially in a diverse society, silence—on something that may prove false, obtuse, or excessively contentious—can help minimize conflict…and save a great deal of time and expense" (Sunstein 2001, p. 58). As such, these types of agreements not only reduce "the political cost of enduring disagreements" (Sunstein 2001, p. 60), but might also provide for the necessary institutional stability. Had the European Union at its foundation as European Economic Community been defined as a confederation or as a federation, the project would have alienated a number of Member States and political actors. It is unlikely that any subsequent treaty would have been signed, not to mention ratified, had it contained such a clear definition of what the EU was. In fact, the creative ambiguity of what the European Union is has not only spurred vivid debate for decades among scholars, but has in many ways been the foundation of the European Union.

Just like a state that calls itself a 'Democratic People's Republic' should not be taken at face value (but rather the opposite), a polity that refuses to call itself anything should not mean that scholars should refrain from naming it.

Jiří Přibáň has observed that "the Union's complexity, polycentric structure and functionally differentiated pluralism represent a departure from the nation-state and its sovereignty as a unified system of representative authority in full territorial and political control" (Přibáň 2009, p. 30). Indeed, much of the literature on the EU notes its distinct and unique character.[3] Michael Walzer in his discussion of toleration, to which we will return in the next chapter, argues that, in addition to different regimes of toleration, the European Union "isn't an empire or a consociation but something different from both and perhaps new in the world" (Walzer 1999, p. 48). Yet this distinction risks leading to a conceptual dead end by arguing and reinforcing the EU's approach as unique and incomparable. Of course, the EU—with its institutional structure and historical trajectory—is unlike any other state or international organization, and is thus unique. However, the ghost of uniqueness renders comparison futile and limits inquiry. Social sciences and law thrive from comparison and the ability to identify broader trends and typologies. If taken as a case sui generis, it cannot serve as a case to be compared with other polities, nor can politics of diversity or any other domain be applied to it. Neither it is productive. Whereas the combined features of the EU are particular and not easily compared, if taken individually they are not immune to comparison.

Populations diverse in terms of national identity, ethnicity, language, and religion inhabit polities around the world and very few states are homogenous. While the 'nation-state' remains widely used and is deeply ingrained in the language and understanding of inter*national* relations (United *Nations*, *Völker*recht), it is largely a fiction. The classic definition of nation-states with well-delineated borders and peoples applies to few states and is adopted either by default or as an aspirational goal that nation and state ought to be congruent (Gellner 2006). This ideal type of state is often associated with the Peace of Westphalia of 1648, but is in fact a product of later centuries (Zielonka 2005, p. 10).

[3] See, for example, Börzel (2012), and comments in Caporaso et al. (1997).

Once confronted with diversity, the state can respond in multiple ways. The first choice centers on whether the state seeks forms of accommodation, or rejects the diversity. Rejecting diversity includes a wide range of policies, from assimilation or ignoring the particular group, to repressive measures, such as expulsions, 'ethnic cleansing,' and genocide. While there is a large difference between a state that forces its minorities to change their names or discourages (or prohibits) the use of their mother tongue and one that expels its minorities or kills them, they are all based on rejecting diversity. This may be because the majority considers itself the rightful and sole owner of the state, or because minorities are associated with past grievances or current threats. States might also confront different minority groups in a variety of ways. These repressive policies have been widespread since the emergence of the modern nation-state in the nineteenth century and can be found around the globe. In addition to the profound moral problems that rejecting diversity implies, the policies of eliminating diversity have generally failed (McGarry and O'Leary 1993). The continued attempts by some self-proclaimed nation-states to reduce diversity through assimilation, integration, and more odious policies such as expulsions and genocide are offset by large streams of migration and previously voiceless groups 'remembering' or inventing their group identity. Genocides and expulsions often remain 'incomplete,' as significant parts of the target population survive. The normative cost is high, as state policies do not merely violate the human rights of those targeted, but usually such state policies also make majorities complicit in mass violence or at least repression, and repressive policies toward minorities often go hand in hand with authoritarianism. More gradual assimilation might entail less repression, but unless the population subject to assimilation does not hold a strong national identity, as might have been the case in the nineteenth and early twentieth centuries, resistance and resentment are common responses.

Accommodating diversity thus seems like the obvious state response. Even if states opt for this response, it entails a wide range of different approaches. These might be weak multicultural policies that accept the diversity of a society without actively preserving or promoting it, as is the case in many European countries that confront migration. Fully recognizing and including the voice of different groups takes a range of policies, from minority rights to power-sharing and ethnic federalism. Yet strategies remain contested; and where identity matters, institutions that seek to incorporate different groups are often fragile and might risk reinforcing the lines of fragmentation they seek to overcome. There is no universal policy to address the very different needs of communities around the world. While policies such as minority rights and political inclusion of different groups—especially through power-sharing—have seen widespread adoption in post-conflict settings, they are not without their challengers in practice and theory, and there is no blueprint that could be adopted across the world without considering local context and demands.

Debates on accommodating differences, especially in divided societies, have focused on a set of institutional responses. At the center of most academic debates has been power-sharing. Power-sharing describes divergent institutional responses that aim to include different identity groups in the decision-making process. Power-sharing institutions come in a variety of shapes and forms. Some might be temporary arrangements, as in post-election coalitions to bridge high levels of polarization, while others are long-lasting and constitutionally prescribed, as in Belgium or South Tyrol. Another line of distinction is between corporate and liberal power-sharing. Liberal power-sharing describes power-sharing institutions that allow for considerable flexibility and give priority to individual over collective rights, whereas corporate power-sharing is rigid and subordinates the citizen to the collective ethnic group, as in, for example, Bosnia and Herzegovina (McCulloch 2014). Critics of power-sharing have advocated more inclusive and cross-community institutions that challenge the notion of group representation altogether (Roeder and Rothchild 2005). Separate, but not disconnected, are other debates on institutional design focused on federalism, in particular federal or territorial autonomy along ethnic lines. Here, a key question is the balance of power between the units and the center, as well as the degree of homogeneity or diversity within the territorial units (Erk and Anderson 2009). Finally, minority rights constitute the third pillar of debates on institutional responses to diversity, centering on the balance between human rights, non-discrimination, and group-based minority rights (Kymlicka 2007).

The different institutional options include different underlying concepts of integration and distinctiveness, that is, how members of identity-based groups should be part of a larger integrated society versus the preservation of the distinctive features of the community. The second large debate framing the variety of options centers on the balance between recognizing and institutionalizing groups and the potential risks of reinforcing group boundaries. There is no clear-cut conclusion to the debates, but rather state policies toward diversity need to balance these different considerations. If the institutions are too rigid and based along the lines of ethnicity or other collective markers, they restrict individual choice and reproduce divisions in society. If they neglect deeply rooted differences, they might not address disputes over identity and political representation, and often inadvertently favor a particular actor (Marko 2019).

Bringing the European Union into this debate will thus enrich the options of accommodation, as well as show their limitations based on the experience of the EU. Literature on diversity and state strategies to accommodate different groups has drawn on 'successful cases' for decades. Every resolved ethnopolitical conflict suggests itself as a model for others, from more recent settlements in South Tyrol and Northern Ireland to Switzerland, Canada, or the United States (Gagnon et al. 2003; Schneckener 2002; Watts 2002). Failed or difficult cases, such as Iraq or Bosnia and Herzegovina, serve as examples of the difficulties in accommodating difference as well (McCulloch and McGarry 2017; Hartzell and Mehler 2019; Bieber and Keil 2009).

Bringing the EU in adds an important case for studying policies of diversity. While not a state, the Union has established institutions and practices that not only resemble a state, but also offer insight into how states and sub-state units might confront diversity. This book does not propose the EU as a generalizable model for diverse societies around the world, as in fact no state or sub-state unit can be used as such. Yet, understanding the approaches and experience of addressing diversity in the EU can be useful for greater comprehension of the EU itself, and helps shed new light on other cases.

The obvious and immediate challenge to discussing the EU in conjunction with states is that the EU is not a state. "What is the EU?" is the question that has been bedeviling research on the EU for decades (Fabbrini 2017; Hooghe and Marks 2019; Jordan 2001; Schmitt and Thomassen 1999). Indeed, there is no consensus on what the EU actually is. The EU has been studied as an international organization or a regional grouping. Others have focused more on its processes, whereas many others consider the EU to be a distinct and unique structure. However, as Olson and McCormick have suggested, "we could also try to understand the EU as a political system in its own right and compare its structure and operating principles with those of conventional national political system" (McCormick and Olsen 2018, pp. 76–77). And indeed, we do not argue that the EU is a state. Yet many states lack key features associated with statehood as well. The EU explicitly refrains from understanding itself as a state, and integration has only been possible because it did not claim to strive to *become* a state.

While the EU is not a state, it shares many features with states, such as external borders and shared political institutions, including elections, common laws and courts, citizenship, and symbols. These co-exist and interact with its Member States and have given rise to the notion of the EU as part of a multi-level governance, that is, to not separate the EU from the Member States, but instead to consider the complex and intrinsic rules and institutions that link both. In this sense, the EU is certainly not a state in the conventional sense, but its framework allows it to be comparable to states.

It is important to consider that many states do not function as the ideal type of state that consists of a polity with a fixed boundary, a steady population, independence, and international recognition. Many states also maintain the fiction of being nation-states, despite being inhabited by a diverse population. There are states that exceed the EU in terms of diversity, with small Papua New Guinea displaying far greater linguistic diversity than the EU, and Nigeria being home to both greater religious and linguistic differences. Some political arrangements are as complex as the EU, such as Belgium and large federations such as India, Canada, or Russia (in the case of the latter, mostly on paper). Numerous countries exercise less control over their political sub-units, or have less authority over their external borders—not just failed states such as Somalia, but also Bosnia and Herzegovina.

What sets the EU apart from these states is the non-hierarchical relationship between the constituent units and the whole, as well as the absence of the EU's claim to statehood, which facilitates the symbiotic relationship with states.

While the study of the EU has emerged as a distinct and separate field of research from both international relations and national politics, it is not helpful to limit the study of the EU to a sui generis phenomenon. This is not to deny the particularities of the Union that set it apart. However, overemphasizing the particularities undermines key principles of social science, namely generalizability and comparability. This book does not seek to offer an answer to whether or not the EU should or should not be considered a state. First, the answer to such a question will not only vary depending on the normative perspective, but also on the disciplinary standpoint. Second, the distinguishing line between the EU and conventional states has become blurred in recent decades, as the EU gained competences and institutions and the weakness of many states increased, both due to the rise of international regimes and to sub-national challenges. Third, we can find numerous states around the world that de jure or de facto have less state-like competences than the European Union. In the developing world, many states might have great ambitions, but often only limited means to exercise control.

Rather than positing the EU in one category and states in another, this book proposes to understand them all as part of a continuum with the ideal type of a classic nation-state at one end—centralized, with one center of power and authority—and anarchy at the other—the absence of any central authority. Between two such ideal types, polities would cluster in distinct groups: from centralized, relatively homogenous states such as Japan, to federal systems like Germany or the United States, to multinational federal systems like Bosnia or Belgium, and to failed and very weak states, such as Somalia or South Sudan. This clustering highlights the distinction between the voluntary and regulated fragmentation of authority, as in the EU or federal systems, and involuntary and non-consensual fragmentation as in failed states.

While one might want to distinguish a polity that is no longer a state from those that are, they are still part of the same continuum and thus can be understood in this framework of polities. Therefore, irrespective of where the line is drawn, polities grouped together more closely on this continuum might have more in common than those at its far ends. Thus, there is little doubt that multinational federations are more suitable for comparison among themselves than comparing Canada with, say, Iceland.

As a result, this book argues that the EU can be compared with states and understood in the context of states. Thus this book is an effort to understand the EU with the tools applied to diverse and complex states, rather than to international organizations, and to understand the EU as a sui generis construct; its findings aim to speak to our understanding of accommodating diversity in complex states.

In addition to exploring the tools of diversity accommodation, this book will also draw on the literature that explores how states construct a sense of shared identity and citizenship among their inhabitants. While the EU, to take Eugen Weber's powerful metaphor of "Peasants into Frenchman" (Weber 1976), does not strive to transform "Frenchmen into Europeans," European identity has emerged as a layer of identification in addition to French or any other national identity. The multiplicity of identity, as will be discussed later in this book, constitutes a reflection of the multiple layers of the institutional structure. Europeanness is a supplement to national identity—be it identified in civic or ethnic terms—and a large number of Europeans identify as such. According to the 2018 Eurobarometer 2% of Europeans feel exclusively European, a seemingly small number, but equal to the percentage of Greeks or Czechs in the EU, and representing a larger number than citizens of 16 smaller EU Member States. Considering the possibility of multiple identities, most Europeans see themselves as both citizens of their country and of the European Union (European Commission 2018, p. 36).

Understanding how the EU reflects and manages diversity also requires us to move beyond institutions alone. Scholarship on post-conflict state-building and institutional accommodation, be it power-sharing or federalism, has focused extensively on institutions, while devoting less attention to questions of symbols or citizenship. In contested polities, of course, symbols are often particularly contested and mediators either seek to avoid the questions, if possible, or propose new, 'neutral' symbols, such as the flags of countries that map its shape (Kosovo and Cyprus) or adopt generic pro-European stars in blue and yellow (Bosnia). State symbols and the identities they promote are crucial questions for diverse polities with strong, competing identities. Though the mechanisms used in nation-states seeking to build a shared identity and understanding are instructive, even they cannot be replicated in the same manner in multinational, diverse polities such as the EU.

## 1.1 The Argument and Approach

This book argues that the European Union has developed a unique set of tools, policies, and approaches toward diversity that are best understood in the context of states' similar efforts to cope with diversity, from ethnicity to religion and language. Rather than exploring the EU as either an international organization or a sui generis system, seeing the EU as part of the same continuum of polities that includes more conventional states can help us understand the EU better and also provide for valuable pointers toward broadening state tools of diversity management. The EU, by virtue of its 'unfinished' structure, its expansion, and its size, clearly differs from most states. However, we argue that one can examine the EU through the analytical lens of a state. As such, the argument is about establishing a dialogue between two schools of scholarship, namely scholars of the EU and those studying diversity and divided societies.

This study is the product of the meeting of different disciplines—law and political science—and fields of inquiry—EU and diversity management. The book approaches the topic out of the conviction that this dialogue is fruitful and can contribute both to the scholarship of the EU and to that of diversity.

The multiple crises the EU has been confronted with in recent years, from the economic crisis to the COVID-19 pandemic, coupled with challenges to European solidarity and the Brexit referendum, show that the EU is struggling to find a response to external shocks and internal difficulties of solidarity and legitimacy. We thus do not propose the EU as a model, but as a creative and organically grown effort to mitigate and manage difference on the European continent. Whether these strategies will ultimately prevail in the face of the crises remains open at the point of writing. Irrespective of the outcome, an understanding of these approaches is important and provides insights for other complex state structures that are set up to govern complicated societies confronted with high levels of diversity.

## 1.2 Structure of the Book

This book will first outline how the experience of diversity fits into the context of other cases and how diversity in the EU can be best understood. It will then explore how the Union has understood itself and the balance between unity and diversity, before exploring how it has negotiated these in key fields, from institutions, to symbols, citizenship, and minorities. In conclusion, it will discuss the underlying principles of solidarity and the applicability of these features and strategies for other diverse states.

In Chap. 2, we will place the EU in the context of other multinational polities—historical and contemporary. The historical and global comparison helps locate the EU among regimes of diversity and will illustrate that the EU does not fit a clear typology, as it shares key features with a number of polities that have sought to negotiate diversity. It will explore five different types of polities seeking to balance unity and diversity: (1) early modern multipolar regimes; (2) early modern federal systems; (3) early modern complex empires; (4) multinational federalism; and (5) ethnonational power-sharing.

Next, Chap. 3 will discuss how this diversity has shaped the European Union and its construction. Mapping the diversity of the EU is more than merely listing the working languages of the EU, its regions, religions, and nations. In addition, we explore the relevance and salience of the EU's diversity, the diversity of diversities. In as large a space as the one encompassed by the EU, some forms of diversity primarily touch regions of Member States, while others are not limited to just one or several Member States, such as the Roma minority, with some six million EU citizens hailing from this community (more than Danes or Finns in the EU), or migrants and EU citizens who live outside their own Member States.

Chapter 4 in this section will explore how the EU has understood the concepts of unity, the will and ability to work together, and diversity, as well as the intrinsic recognition that difference is at the core of the European project, and how it has negotiated the tension between cooperation and hierarchy.

In the second section, the book explores *EU strategies toward diversity*. As with other states, diversity is not a choice, but a reality, and can be met with a variety of responses. The EU cannot afford to deny diversity as states have often sought to do, but not all forms of diversity in the EU are recognized equally and by the same approaches. As the four chapters in this section will highlight, these strategies and approaches did not emerge out of a single deliberate choice, but rather grew and adapted over time.

Chapter 5 discusses the institutional responses to diversity. Perhaps most obviously, the EU is often defined and studied through its institutions. As they emerged to represent the Member States, the EU institutional architecture incorporated into its DNA the balance between unity and diversity, namely with the goal to represent the Member States in their diversity while ensuring the ability to function as a unified institutional system and acknowledging the diversity of Member States in terms of size.

Symbols are the focus of Chap. 6. The chapter outlines how the symbols of the EU emerged and how they are central to reflecting both the diversity in the EU and creating shared symbolic markers. Take the euro: its bills contain stylized examples of architectural features found in Europe. However, no bill displays statesmen or women of the EU or its Member States, nor can you find anywhere a real building. Such a display of neutrality stands in contrast to the state-centered coins of the EU, full of heroes, artists, rulers, and national symbols. Thus, even money has two different responses toward difference, one that underlines symbolic difference based on Member States, and another that places greater emphasis on a vague communality.

In Chap. 7, citizenship will be the focus, namely the emerging European citizenship and how it co-exists with the citizenship of Member States and the implicit assumptions about representation and inclusion. In particular, it will focus on how a shared citizenship provides the basis of solidarity.

Finally, in Chap. 8, we will examine the EU policies toward minorities. As the EU itself has few competences in the field and only limited tools to promote and integrate minorities, it has drawn extensively on the emerging minority rights framework of the Council of Europe. The emerging European minority rights regime will be at the center of this final chapter.

In conclusion, the book will identify the broad lessons from the EU experience for diverse and divided states, and reflect on what the diversity management of the EU tells us about the EU and its ability to overcome crises that have shaped European integration or disintegration over the past decade.

The EU, as this book argues, has been constantly re-negotiating diversity. It emerged without a clear commitment to which kind of diversity it should reflect and incorporate, besides the cooperation of Member States that are intrinsically different. Instead, it has evolved as diversity and the understanding of it changed within it. The continuous evolution brings along its own challenges and inconsistencies, as this book also highlights. Tensions between diversity and unity, as they emerge, are rarely resolved, but usually managed, postponed, and renegotiated. European integration does not provide a template for other complex and diverse polities, but instead, the process of negotiating diversity and also accepting the tension is a central lesson from the EU. We will return to the question of solidarity and responsibility in the conclusion, yet the idea of negating diversity is premised on the solidarity of the participants and the responsibility toward the shared project. This is often a neglected feature of accommodation in diverse societies: without a basic commitment to seeking compromise and engaging in mutual solidarity, difference cannot be negotiated.

## References

Bieber, F., & Keil, S. (2009). Power-sharing revisited: Lessons learned in the Balkans? *Review of Central and East European Law, 34*(4), 337–360.

Börzel, T. A. (2012). The European Union: A unique governance mix? In D. Levi-Faur (Ed.), *The Oxford handbook of governance* (pp. 613–627). Oxford: Oxford University Press.

Caporaso, J. A., et al. (1997). Does the European Union represent an *n* of 1? *ECSA Review, 10*(3), 1–5.

Diez, T. (2005). Constructing the self and changing others: Reconsidering 'normative power Europe'. *Millennium: Journal of International Studies, 33*(3), 613–636.

Erk, J., & Anderson, A. (2009). The paradox of federalism: Does self-rule accommodate or exacerbate ethnic divisions? *Regional & Federal Studies, 19*(2), 191–202.

European Commission. (2018). *Eurobarometer 90: European citizenship*. https://ec.europa.eu/commfrontoffice/publicopinion/index.cfm/ResultDoc/download/DocumentKy/86438. Accessed 20 Mar 2020.

Fabbrini, S. (2017). Intergovernmentalism in the European Union: A comparative federalism perspective. *Journal of European Public Policy, 24*(4), 580–597.

Gagnon, A. G., et al. (2003). *The conditions of diversity in multinational democracies*. Montreal: Institute for Research on Public Policy.

Gellner, E. (2006). *Nations and nationalism*. Ithaca/New York: Cornell University Press.

Hartzell, C. A., & Mehler, A. (Eds.). (2019). *Power sharing and power relations after civil war*. Boulder: Lynne Rienner.

Hooghe, L., & Marks, G. (2019). Grand theories of European Integration in the twenty-first century. *Journal of European Public Policy, 26*(8), 1113–1133.

Jordan, A. (2001). The European Union: An evolving system of multi-level governance ... or government? *Policy & Politics, 29*(2), 193–208.

Kymlicka, W. (2007). *Multicultural odysseys: Navigating the new international politics of diversity*. Oxford: Oxford University Press.

Marko, J. (Ed.). (2019). *Human and minority rights protection by multiple diversity governance: History, law, ideology and politics in European perspective*. London: Routledge.

McCormick, J., & Olsen, J. (2018). *The European Union: Politics and policies*. Boulder: Routledge.

McCulloch, A. (2014). Consociational settlements in deeply divided societies: The liberal-corporate distinction. *Democratization, 21*(3), 501–518.

McCulloch, A., & McGarry, J. (Eds.). (2017). *Power-sharing. Empirical and normative challenges*. London: Routledge.

McGarry, J., & O'Leary, B. (1993). Introduction: The macro-political regulation of ethnic conflict. In J. McGarry & B. O'Leary (Eds.), *The politics of ethnic conflict regulation* (pp. 1–40). Abingdon: Routledge.

Meunier, S., & Nicolaidis, N. (2006). The European Union as a conflicted trade power. *Journal of European Public Policy, 13*(6), 906–925.

Přibáň, J. (2009). Legal flexibility, governance and differentiated integration: On functional differentiation of EU law and politics. In K. Dyson & A. Sepos (Eds.), *Which Europe? The politics of differentiated integration* (pp. 24–38). London: Palgrave Macmillan.

Prügl, E., & Thiel, M. (2009). Understanding diversity in the European Integration Project. In E. Prügl & M. Thiel (Eds.), *Diversity in the European Union* (pp. 3–20). Basingstoke/New York: Palgrave Macmillan.

Richardson, J. (2002–2003). The European Union in the world: A community of values. *Fordham International Law Journal, 26*(12), 12–35.
Roeder, P. G., & Rothchild, D. (Eds.). (2005). *Sustainable peace: Power and democracy after civil wars.* Ithaca/New York: Cornell University Press.
Schmitt, H., & Thomassen, J. (Eds.). (1999). *Political representation, and legitimacy in the European Union.* Oxford: Oxford University Press.
Schneckener, U. (2002). Making power-sharing work: Lessons from successes and failures in ethnic conflict regulation. *Journal of Peace Research, 39*(2), 203–228.
Sunstein, C. R. (2001). *Designing democracy: What constitutions do.* New York: Oxford University Press.
Toje, A. (2010). *The European Union as a small power: After the Post-Cold War.* Basingstoke/New York: Palgrave Macmillan.
Walzer, M. (1999). *On toleration.* New Haven: Yale University Press.
Watts, R. (2002). Models of federal power sharing. *International Social Sciences Journal, 53*(167), 23–32.
Weber, E. (1976). *Peasants into Frenchmen: The modernization of rural France, 1870–1914.* Stanford: Stanford University Press.
Zielonka, J. (2005). *Europe as empire: The nature of the enlarged European Union.* Oxford: Oxford University Press.

CHAPTER 2

# Regimes of Diversity

Today and throughout history, diversity, be it linguistic, religious, ethnic, or national, has been the norm. States, which have also been confronted with difference, have found various responses. However, not all differences matter, and diversity can be socially and politically irrelevant. Politics based on difference and diversity might matter, such as women's rights or the recognition of LGBTQ people, yet these distinctions, gender and sexual orientation, are often temporary political dividers and do not permanently structure political divisions. Similarly, linguistic, religious, and ethnic differences do not inherently translate into conflict or even politically relevant diversity. In this chapter, we are interested in polities that have had to respond to diversity as a politically and socially salient issue throughout the modern period. In the next chapter, we will explore the nature of diversity and even the 'diversity of diversity' in the European Union.

On the most fundamental level, O'Leary and McGarry have argued that regimes pursue policies of either managing diversity or denying diversity. This fundamental choice results in a range of state policies: for governments who do not accept diversity they range from the most radical response, genocide, to assimilation; for governments who do accept diversity, they range from illiberal control to multiculturalism (McGary and O'Leary 1993). Often governments pursue both identity-affirming and identity-denying policies, based on the particular group in question or their location, and thus the approaches often co-exist, even if they are



F. Bieber, R. Bieber, *Negotiating Unity and Diversity in the European Union*, Palgrave Studies in European Union Politics,
https://doi.org/10.1007/978-3-030-55016-5_2

conceptually distinct. Here, however, we are interested in state policies that acknowledge politically and socially relevant divisions along identity lines. Michael Walzer categorized five regimes of toleration: multinational empires, international society, consociations, nation-states, and immigrant societies (Walzer 1999). Nation-states are inherently hostile to identities other than that of the dominant nation, especially if these extend to a collective, yet they might tolerate difference. Considering that nation-states are centered on a single dominant nation, they also provide an ill-fitting comparison with the European Union, which stands out in not having a singular nation at its core. International society is a regime not bound by sovereignty and thus inherently removed from the state and therefore from our focus. This leaves three regimes of toleration that we consider relevant for identifying the link between state and nation:

*a) Empire*
The empire is not concerned with self-rule and thus does not have to face the conceptual dilemma of a diverse population. Pre-modern empires cannot be considered as multinational, as national identity was not a defining feature of their populations, and when it did exist as a term to define groups, it was usually restricted to small groups of elites without much political relevance for most of the population. The term 'multinational empire' conjures up the inherent difficulties and tensions of an imperial project that does not organize itself along national lines. Imperial rule can both suppress and accommodate difference. As empires are less concerned with creating formal equality, "it tolerates groups and their authority structures and customary practices" (Walzer 1999, p. 16). Walzer argues that empires have greater ease in accommodating groups than individuals (Walzer 1999, p. 18). At first, empires could respond to modernity by creating states that exercised control and administered the country.

Yet the former regime of toleration through which the empires allowed for autonomous enclaves stood in inherent tension with these modernizing and centralizing efforts. The Hungarian lands of the Habsburg Monarchy, for example, maintained Latin as their official language until the 1840s. However, its predominance was reduced in favor of German in the late eighteenth century and Hungarian in the nineteenth century. The use of German in the time of absolutism was largely driven by the fact that it was then the dominant language. Hungarian emerged later with the rise of national identity in the Hungarian lands. Each language choice, while more practical than Latin, alienated others: the use of German increased Hungarian nationalism, while the increased preference for Hungarian created opposition among Croats and other groups whose mother tongue was not Hungarian (Inglehart and Woodward 1967, pp. 34–36).

Similarly, the Ottoman Empire in its effort to modernize and secularize government reduced the autonomy of the millets, the non-Muslim communities that had a high degree of self-administration, in the mid-nineteenth century. As Bernhard Lewis noted, "[w]hile non-Muslims in general were willing to accept the benefits of equality, they opposed its price" (cited from Shaw and Shaw 1977, pp. 128). In particular, the equality when it came to military service—from which non-Muslims had been historically exempt—was fiercely opposed.

Empires with diverse populations could accommodate different identities, as the common unifying feature of empires was not a single national identity, or even a coherent centralized political system. As a consequence, they were able to tolerate diversity and difference to a greater degree than modern nation-states. This quality eroded when empires came under pressure from nation-states and sought to follow the seemingly more successful model of statehood; they began—with varying degrees of success—to transform themselves into nation-states, as the Ottoman and Russian Empire endeavored to do in the early twentieth century. As the aforementioned vignettes from the Habsburg Monarchy and the Ottoman Empire highlight, empires could not be neutral to questions of linguistic, national, or religious diversity that often resulted in groups wielding privileges over others. In recent years, there has been renewed interest in Empires (Kumar 2017). This reflects a more critical perspective on the nation-state and national narratives that have often dismissed empires as pre-modern and flawed. Furthermore, they have served as points of comparison to contemporary polities. At times, the term has served to underline continuity, such as by the United States during the Cold War and the post-Cold War period as imperial, Sometimes, also the EU has been compared, although for differnent reasons with an empire, as Jan Zielonka has (Zielonka 2006). He had less the expansionist, colonial empires in mind when comparing the United States with the British or French Empire, and more the medieval and early modern empires that sought to balance different groups or territories in a complex superstructure. Empires are thus multifaceted, and when exploring the case studies in this chapter, we will return to empires as a form of regime of toleration.

*b) Multinational States*

Multinational states encompass different political systems that explicitly recognize and empower different group-based national, ethnic, or religious identities. The state is not neutral, but rather based on the recognition of diversity. This recognition requires affirmative policies by the state for particular identity groups, be they identified by language, national belonging, religion, or otherwise. The two most common strategies of accommodation are multinational federal arrangements and consociational/power-sharing systems. In the case of the former, the power is decentralized primarily along territorial lines wherein units do not represent mere administrative units, as in German or American federalism, but also grant groups self-government through decentralization, such as in Canada or Belgium (Gagnon and Seymour 2012).

Consociations primarily focus on group representation at the center, and ensure that decision-making is inclusive through grand coalitions and veto rights. They are thus not intrinsically territorialized, but rather focus on joint decision-making (McEvoy and O'Leary 2013; Lijphart 2008).

Both types of accommodation represent the most common form of group inclusion around the world today, and can be found on all continents and in both post-conflict settings and states that have avoided identity-based conflict.

*c) Multicultural States*

Multicultural states recognize diversity without the explicit recognition of groups. Instead, the state surrenders the right to define a dominant culture and withdraws as much as possible from any attempt to impose a particular culture and its different expressions on a society, be it religion, history, or language. Furthermore, multicultural states are expected to positively affirm diversity and provide support for expressions thereof (Taylor 1994). The term has been rendered problematic for its generous usage to describe the factual existence of diversity, as well as any state policy of toleration. Critics have often dismissed it as a recipe for segregation, yet without disentangling different approaches to multiculturalism. Furthermore, this approach leaves some key challenges unaddressed, in particular the question of language, especially when a dominant group speaks a different language than most of the other communities. While the state might allow for the use of a multitude of languages, languages of instruction in schools, or those used by the public administration, still require the recognition of some, and the non-recognition of others. It is thus unsurprising that multicultural policies remain closely associated with diversity as a result of migration, rather than with established minority communities who make a stronger claim for preserving their mother tongue in public life.

The three types of states—empires, multinational states, and multicultural states—engage with diversity differently. They are, however, not inherently mutually exclusive. Empires have historically been agnostic toward diversity and bound their subjects through channels other than loyalty—through a shared dynasty justified through divine rule or later through military might and diplomatic success. Multinational and multicultural states both offer equal citizenship; while the former offers a high level of joint and self-rule, the latter is concerned more with state affirmation of markers of difference than with those representing the groups.

In relation to his categories of toleration, Walzer argued that the European Union "isn't an empire or a consociation but something different from both and perhaps new in the world" (Walzer 1999, p. 48). However, our starting point for this study is that the EU is not a unique creature among polities that defies any comparison, as outlined in the introduction. This is not to deny the particularities of the EU. We posit that it remains comparable and, if unique, at least includes recognizable features of existing state regimes of toleration. Central here is not whether the EU looks like a particular state, but whether its approach to diversity is comparable with other polities today or historically.

By including past polities, we are able to substantially increase the number of potential points of comparison. The glance toward the past reflects what one could describe as the recent "temporal turn" in social sciences (Pierson 2004). By taking time and the past into account, social scientists expand their horizons (and cases) and acknowledge the importance of historical processes. However, a note of caution is due. If we just look back to increase the number of cases, we risk reducing historical context. An electoral democracy functioned very differently in the mid-nineteenth century than it does today, over 150 years later. Not only has the social and legal understanding of who can vote (women, citizens without property, etc.) changed, but so have norms, technology, and the global context. Thus, uprooting a case from its historical context might deplete it of its meaning. On the other hand, bringing in history can run the opposite risk, that is, by asserting that history matters and that a long range of historical experiences shape current political systems, one risks sliding into historical determinism: where history shapes the present and thus today's institutions, states, and structures seem to be little more than pre-determined reflections of the past, immune or at least not easily amenable to change. In such a context, comparisons become nearly impossible, as every case becomes unique and historically determined.

Here, we explore how the EU fits in with previous "regimes of toleration," to draw upon Walzer's terminology. We are interested in polities that accommodate diversity and which are not defined as nation-states that have complex and multi-layered structures of government. Thus, we preclude minority rights regimes that many modern nation-states afford to small, often territorially defined minorities, for example as Italy does in South Tyrol/Alto Adige to the German and Ladino speakers of the region, or as Finland grants cultural rights to Swedish-speakers and territorial autonomy to the Åland Islands. Nation-states that provide minority rights tolerate minorities, but do not give up the dominance of the majority, nor are they overall complex polities—even if they might resort to structures of accommodation at the local or regional level. The localization to a particular region or minority means that most citizens are unaffected by the complexity of the regime of toleration.

Instead, we are interested in comparing the EU to polities that are complex in structure and do not assert the dominance of a particular group, and are thus inherently built around multiple identities—be they defined as nations, religions, or 'cultures.'

We will now explore the following five regime types and a key example, as well as discussing their appropriateness for the EU's regime of toleration:

1. Early modern multipolar regimes: The Holy Roman Empire
2. Early modern federal systems: The early United States
3. Early modern complex empires: The Habsburg Monarchy
4. Multinational Federalism: Socialist Yugoslavia
5. Ethnonational Power-sharing: Belgium

All five models offer points of comparison that highlight some shared features with the European Union, as well as some of the specificities of the EU that we will explore in greater detail in the rest of the book. Again, the comparison is to highlight not just the 'comparability' of the EU, but also to point to specific institutional features that can be found elsewhere, across time and space.

## 2.1 Early Modern Multipolar Regimes: The Holy Roman Empire

At first glance the Holy Roman Empire might seem like an odd structure for comparison. This loose grouping of principalities, cities, and kingdoms is today largely forgotten or considered irrelevant. However, it represents a type of political system without a clear center and multiple governing structures that were at times cooperative, and at times competing. The Holy Roman Empire is one of the longest-lasting political structures in the history of the western world, enduring for nearly a millennium from 962 until its final abolition under Napoleon in 1806. It claims not just continuity with the Roman Empire, but also with the short-lived Carolingian Empire headed by Charlemagne in the early ninth century, often evoked by the EU as a historical point of reference (Wilson 2016, pp. 1511–1513).

The term 'Holy (Roman) Empire' only dates to the twelfth and thirteenth centuries, and the suffix 'of the German Nation' was used only from the sixteenth century onwards. So strange was this polity—neither a state nor really an empire—that Voltaire famously quipped that "[t]his organism which was called and which still calls itself the Holy Roman Empire was neither holy, nor Roman, nor an empire"[1] (Voltaire 1877–1885, p. 542). The view of the Empire implicit in Voltaire's assessment reflected a common perception of the Holy Roman Empire. It became widely described as a messy hold-over from medieval times that failed because it delayed decisions—or to use the German metaphor derived from the Empire, '*auf die lange Bank schieben*,' literarily to push onto the long bench, referring to the trunks used by delegates in the *Reichstag* to place documents (and forget them). However, this view is shaped very much by the dominant nineteenth-century perspective that saw the sovereign, bounded nation-state as the natural and desirable way of organizing government. This has been reflected in historiography that mocked the Holy Roman Empire after it was abolished in 1806 as Napoleon's armies brought a new idea of the state to the continent and the French Revolution linked the ideas of sovereignty, nation, and state (Stollberg-Rilinger 2009, p. 8–9).

[1] "Ce corps qui s'appelait et qui s'appelle encore le saint empire romain n'était en aucune manière ni saint, ni romain, ni empire."

Although Voltaire could easily state what the Holy Empire was not, it is hard to define what it was, not unlike the European Union itself. It was neither a federation nor just an association of states. It lacked a constitution, a unified legal system, or clear borders. Its duration of 844 years—from the early Middle Ages to the modern period—meant that it changed its shape and structure over time. Even within its name, the references to Holy, Roman, and German were changed, added, or dropped. The institutions emerged only slowly, mostly in the late fifteenth and sixteenth centuries, and extended to the mostly German-speaking parts of the Empire that had earlier included parts of France and Northern Italy, as well as to Switzerland and the Netherlands. In its early modern form, it included some 200 principalities, some 50 imperial cities, and 7 (later 10) *Kurfürsten* (prince-electors), the princes with the right to elect the emperor. As the historian Karl Härter argues, the multiple levels of law and the lack of a unified legal system meant that the legal system of the empire was "heterogonous, polycentric and diverse," yet one can speak of a constitutional system nevertheless (Härter 2015, p. 328). The legal orders were based on Roman law, imperial law, and the specific laws of the constituent units. These laws were not in a clear hierarchy, as was the case in other early modern empires.

A highly decentralized elective monarchy meant that the 'emperor' had limited ability to impose his will on the many rulers. The Reichstag, established after 1663 as a permanent assembly of the jurisdictions of the Empire, can be compared to the upper chamber representing regions in federal systems, or the Council of Ministers of the EU. Unsurprising for its time, a lower, representative chamber did not exist. The main administrator of the empire was the *Reichserzkanzler*, who organized the elections of the emperor and strongly shaped the common administration.

A crucial feature of the state, especially after the Peace of Westphalia of 1648 following the Thirty Years' War, was the relatively high level of toleration and diversity within the Holy Roman Empire in comparison to other polities of its time. While Catholics (58%) dominated the Empire, it included a sizable Protestant population (around 40%) and a small Jewish minority in the late eighteenth century. The Catholic rulers did not dominate or exclude the Protestants in the ways in which both Protestant and Catholic monarchies elsewhere in Europe tended to do. In matters pertaining to religion, as the German historian Peter Claus Hartmann notes, a Catholic and a Protestant college were established among the representatives and neither could impose a majority decision, but consensus was required. Proportionality requirements in the administration and the army ensured that one religion was not permanently outvoted (Hartmann 2005).

The laws passed in the *Reichsrat* were largely consensus-based agreements or contracts that included a number of key laws from the *Constitutio Criminalis Carolina*, the penal code of 1532, to answer questions of religious freedom and the regulation of established professions. Overall, legislation focused on regulating the empire and its administration and less on imposing detailed laws on all its units. The consensus requirements made this impossible and, consequently, the legislative process could be likened to the principle of subsidiarity that would enter the vocabulary only much later. The laws were to be implemented by the principalities and cities, and thus the executive institutions of the Holy Roman Empire were minimal. Over time, however, the common laws, especially penal law, necessitated the emergence of imperial courts, the *Reichskammergericht* and the *Reichshofrat*. The courts became active in a broad range of instances, including when rulers appeared to have violated the established rights of their subjects (Härter 2015, pp. 336–338). This legal system curtailed the absolutist power of the rulers and created a complex legal structure that extended across the empire. The consensus-based system and indirect application meant that it was less flexible and could not adapt as quickly as the legal and institutional systems in neighboring monarchies that began emerging as nation-states. Thus, its power and legislative capacity declined well before it abolished itself in 1806.

The empire came to an end after the princes of the Rhine Confederation, under pressure from Napoleon, left the empire; subsequently, the last emperor, Francis II, abdicated and dissolved the Holy Roman Empire. Already in the years running up to its formal dissolution, it had stopped functioning for all intents and purposes, as some princes joined Napoleon, and as the Habsburgs—who had held the imperial post since 1745—were increasingly squeezed out of the lands of the empire (Stollberg-Rilinger 2009, pp. 111–115). The witnesses of the end of the Empire were in shock, but amid the Napoleonic wars, it was hard to judge the significance of the event. Only later would the end of the empire be seen as the logical victory of the nation-state over the Empire (Burgdorf 2012), a process that would continue for at least another century. However, some saw it already in the eighteenth century as a model for future European integration, exemplified by Abbé de Saint-Pierre's plan for perpetual peace in Europe (1713).

The Holy Roman Empire only reentered debates on Europe and the EU rather recently, in particular in the context of the crisis of the EU in recent years. Already in the 1970s, more conservative advocates of European unity had drawn parallels to the Holy Roman Empire, including Otto von Habsburg (Wilson 2016, pp. 1514–1515). At first glance this might seem obvious considering the 'holy' qualifier of the empire, yet it is also odd, as the complex and overlapping jurisdictions do not fit into a contemporary conservative understanding of clear hierarchies and sovereignty. For the noted British historian Brendan Simms, the similarities between the Holy Roman Empire and the EU are mostly negative. In his view, the quasi-confederal structure of both polities inherently leads to endless futile debates, while being unable to contain or constrain the larger powers among them, in the former Prussia and Austria and in the latter presumably Germany. The conclusion for Simms is more federal structures, arguing that the failed Articles of the Confederation in North America after the War of Independence offered similar lessons, as we shall see in the next section (Simms 2013, June 10, p. A23).

However, others, including *The Economist*, have taken a less glum view of the analogy. The ability of the empire to be a forum of conflict resolution and peaceful cooperation among some 300 different principalities, kingdoms, cities, and other political units can be viewed as a success story (*The Economist* 2012, December 22).

This interest can also be seen as part of a larger imperial turn that has led scholars to look at early modern empires less dismissively than earlier generations had done. In particular, the Ottoman Empire has been salvaged from the view of just being the 'sick man in Europe' as the popular image had it in the nineteenth and twentieth century, and now its sophisticated and for its time often fairly advanced mechanism of religious toleration is also considered. As with the Ottoman Empire, a similar reevaluation has also occurred in regard to the Habsburg Monarchy, as we will discuss in one of the following sections, and to the Holy Roman Empire.

While it would not be productive to just swap a negative for a positive stereotype given to the empire, a more nuanced comparison could be useful. In effect, the comparison of the Empire for our contemporary understanding of the EU fits into the larger 'neo-medievalist' view. In international relations, this perspective is less a longing for the Middle Ages than the argument that the era of national sovereignty—often closely associated with the Westphalian Peace and the rise of the modern state—is over. Some argue that this development, matched by the rise of non-state actors from terrorist groups, to private security contractors, to influential individuals, is akin to a new dark age (Khanna 2009, September 17). However, a more useful view is to take the medieval era as a metaphor to illustrate a phenomenon in current international relations, a "system of overlapping authority and multiple loyalty, held together by a duality of competing universalistic claims" (Friedrichs 2001, p. 482). The comparison does not argue that a new medieval period also brings with it the Black Plague or the universalism based on divine authority for government (although even this is not absent today). The decline of the primary actor of international relations in the nineteenth and twentieth centuries, namely the nation-state, is key. It is not, as its advocates among scholars of international relations argue, replaced by a clear alternative source of authority, but rather by competing multiple layers of authority and loyalty.

It is within this context that we can best locate the Holy Roman Empire as a metaphor. It is a system that reflected and responded to the structure of power and loyalty during the medieval and early modern period, not unlike the Venetian republic, whose lifespan ran parallel to the Holy Roman Empire, ending nine years prior to the latter, also as a consequence of the Napoleonic Wars. Thus, their decline reflects a larger shift of the international system. Today, we might see another such shift with the EU being the harbinger of this neo-medieval world, for lack of a better word. Jan Zielonka has made this argument, suggesting that the EU is best understood in the context of the medieval empires, and in fact makes a normative argument that it should embrace this structure: "I have no hesitation in concluding that Europe should embrace a neo-medieval EU. A neo-medieval empire would be in a good position to stabilize the external environment, manage the presence of overlapping structures of power, and facilitate the flow of goods, services, and people throughout the EU's borders" (Zielonka 2006, p. 166). For Zielonka it is the diversity of the Union, especially after 2007, that precludes it from becoming a Westphalian super state; it is thus best served by aiming for a new medieval empire that can co-exist with alternative sources of authority and loyalty.

A challenge of such complex systems without a clear hierarchy and (formal) delineation of authority and its overlap with legitimacy is that it might suffer from a lack of democratic control. While the polycentric nature provides for some in-built means of checks and balances, democratic legitimacy remains a concern that Zielonka, too, acknowledges as a risk: "informal rather than formal controls of complex rather than simple governance networks make it particularly difficult for ordinary citizens to feel in charge of daily policies" (Zielonka 2006, p. 185). The challenge might be perceptional. If we accept the global environment as being characterized by neo-medievalism, then the idea of a clearly structured hierarchy is largely an illusion.

The comparison with the Holy Roman Empire provides for a number of useful insights. First, it suggests that to capture the political structure of the EU, we might be best served not to only look at states, and in the absence of easy comparisons declare the EU a creature sui generis. Second, it highlights that complex polycentric systems of government need not be temporary or provisional, and that they can prove to be fairly enduring. When the comparison is embedded, it also draws our attention to consider a polity such as the EU not separate from its international context. The nature of the 'state' will depend on the system in which it is embedded. This also means that a comparison to an era several centuries ago needs to be taken with a grain of salt.

## 2.2 Early Modern Federal Systems: The United States

The United States is in many ways the obvious case of comparison for the EU. As Fabbrini notes, the United States is the first modern attempt to combine democratic governance with representation of territorial units, creating a "compound republic" (Fabbrini 2005, p. 4). As an ongoing federal experiment, it would also seem a more normatively desirable comparison than a long-collapsed unwieldy Holy Roman Empire. However, the United States does not offer just one polity to serve as a comparison with the EU, but in fact several, depending on which period is chosen (Elazar 2001).

Among the nearly 240 years since independence, there are several points in time that can and have served as a comparison with the EU today. One could consider the Articles of Confederation (1777–1789) that established a loose (and eventually doomed) confederation among the original 13 states (Cuyvers 2013), or the original federal constitution that came into force in 1789 and its formative period until the end of the Civil War (1861–1865) (Moull 2004) and settled the question over the relationship between the federal state and the constituent states of the Union. Finally, one might also consider the subsequent evolution of the United States that strengthened its federal structure over two centuries as a point of reference (Fabbrini 2007).

The comparison with the United States crucially highlights the dynamics of change in the institutional setup. Thus, the *longue durée* of the American federal experiment allows the gradual building up of Federal competences and structures—among others—to be highlighted through decisions of the Supreme Court[2] that any comparison with a younger federal structure would not allow for. Unlike the Holy Roman Empire, the Habsburg Monarchy, or Yugoslavia that moved toward eventual demise and disintegration, the story of the United States is that of a centripetal system.

If we focus the comparison on the Articles of Confederation and Perpetual Union, which governed the United States for most of the 1780s, the emphasis is on the formation of a functional federal system against the background of the original confederal structure. The confederation only had limited competences when it came to war and peace, as well as mediating in conflicts among its members. Its institutions were limited to a congress composed of state delegates with equal votes for all states, and enforcement required state consent, while funding was granted by the states, leaving the congress and the army constantly short of funds. There were no executive institutions, and thus the confederation had little to no ability to act on its own. The argument for a federation was also an argument for more representative government, for federalists realistically worried about state power being a cover for authoritarian rule. Thus, the creation of a stronger, larger polity was viewed as a tool for democratization. The short experiment with a loose confederation in the United States could be viewed as a failure, although the ability to transform itself into a federal system through the new constitution, which came into force in 1789, also highlighted that it was not a fixed and stagnant polity. The new federal constitution shifted the power from the states to the federal center, yet the question as to where ultimate power rested and whether states could leave the federation was not determined until the Civil War. Thus, in many ways the most fruitful period of comparison is the half-century between the promulgation of the US constitution and the outbreak of the Civil War (Tortarolo 2005, pp. 81–89). In fact, Backer argues that "the European Union has restarted a conversation about the nature and elasticity of federalism which was cut off in the United State in 1865" (Backer 2001, p. 177).

[2] See Moull on comparing the ECJ and the Supreme Court.

A crucial question in the comparison is one of democracy and the democratic legitimacy of the Union. In 1819, the Supreme Court ruled on McCulloch v. Maryland, stating that "[t]he government of the Union… is, emphatically, and truly, a government of the people. In form and in substance it emanates from them. Its powers are granted by them, and are to be exercised directly on them, and for their benefit" (McCulloch v. Maryland 1819). It is this question of legitimacy through being a government of the people that has also shaped the adjudication of the ECJ and the German Constitutional Court in recent years, as Moull (2004) notes.

Backer argues that the EU debate over federalism challenges the prevailing presumption that a federal system has to be based on a nation and that it is exclusively a system of domestic law, rather than also international law: "…federal systems have emerged which may not be nations, as conventionally understood. These non-nation federal systems are also governed by constitutions. The constitutions are derived from international law, yet they perform the core functions traditionally reserved for the basic internal law of nations" (Backer 2001, p. 178).

A crucial difference between the United States—in whatever incarnation is chosen—and the EU is the nature of the constituent units. While the diversity of its citizens has been a defining feature of the United States, especially following the large migration from the nineteenth century onward, this diversity did not coincide with the territorial units. Even if there were some geographical concentrations of some groups, these have not defined the states. The only relevant divide that followed state lines and was defined by states was between North and South. By the first half of the nineteenth century, the economic modes of the North and the South created a distinct identity, which associated the North with industrialization and economic success, and the South with stagnation and slavery. Thus for many Northerners, the South stood in conflict with the values of the United States, and often the term 'United States' itself was used synonymously with the North (Cobb 2005, pp. 36–38). The divergent identities and mutual stereotyping, however, were not the cause of the Civil War; rather, it was the conflict over economic and social perspectives. Importantly, the South did not frame the secession from the United States as the process of creating a new state, but instead of re-claiming the original republic. Thus, the conflict was less a classic group-based conflict over independence, and rather about the nature of the polity (Cobb 2005, pp. 55–56). The war and the defeat of the South led to a postbellum period, which reinforced the distinct Southern collective identity of victimhood (Schievelbusch 2004). This distinctive identity continues to be relevant today, and has shaped US politics (Cobb 2005, pp. 318–328). The differences are overlaid by numerous other regional economic and social differences in the United States; yet, they do not amount to distinct identities that are reinforced through overlapping markers of difference and thus do not amount to clear political differences.

The Civil War is significant for another reason in the comparison of the United States with the EU. Because the war was between the Union and the secessionist states, the United States settled the question over the possibility of its units leaving the common state. In the case of the EU, Article 50 of the EU Treaty clarifies that "[a]ny Member State may decide to withdraw from the Union in accordance with its own constitutional requirements." The Civil War led to a different answer for the United States—unilateral secession was not possible and would bring about the intervention of the federal state.

The formative years of the United States thus might offer a useful point for comparison, yet the more permissive approach of the EU toward its Member States should not automatically be interpreted as a lower level of integration.

In conclusion, the comparison with the United States sheds light on the changing nature of the institutional system and its need to adapt. Furthermore, the United States offers insight into the difficulties of establishing a balance between the center and the units over a century. Even after the Civil War, the balance changed, most notably during the New Deal era and once more during the Civil Rights movement. Thus, this relationship is not settled, but subject to constant recalibration, often over issues that are not directly related to the power of the federal government or the states, but rather other issues which require a determination of who would pursue these new policies. The diversity of states, although not a function of clear national, ethnic, or religious diversity coinciding with territorial boundaries, did shape the federation, and the United States is not a multinational federation like Canada, nor are its units purely administrative boundaries of an otherwise homogenous population. Thus, the diversity of diversity in the United States is an important example for the EU—as discussed in the next chapter—of how the units and the center intersect, and not necessarily overlap, with different forms of diversity.

To understand the challenges of diversity where it was defined along linguistic and national lines in a historical comparison, we need to move away from the United States, a pioneer of a modern republican state, to a 'survivor' of the medieval and early modern state system, the Habsburg Monarchy.

## 2.3 Early Modern Complex Empires: The Habsburg Monarchy

For a long time, multinational states and empires were seen as anachronistic in the modern age, as noted in the earlier discussion of the Holy Roman Empire. While the Ottoman Empire became 'the sick man of Europe,' suggesting the inevitable decline of this form of government and the intrinsic incompatibility with modernity, the Habsburg Monarchy was subsequently viewed by many contemporaries and scholars with marginally more sympathy, but no less doomed. The title of the Habsburg Emperor Franz Joseph I after 1867, when Italy had just become a nation-state and Germany was to emerge within a few years, was "*Francis Joseph I, by the grace of God Emperor of Austria; Apostolic King of Hungary, King of Bohemia, Dalmatia, Croatia, Slavonia, Galicia, Lodomeria, Illyria; King of Jerusalem, etc.; Archduke of Austria; Grand Duke of Tuscany, Crakow; Duke of Lorraine, Salzburg, Styria, Carinthia, Carniola, the Bukovina; Grand Prince of Transylvania; Margrave of Moravia; Duke of the Upper & Lower Silesia, Modena, Parma, Piacenza, Guastalla, Oswiecin, Zator, Cieszyn, Friuli, Ragusa, Zara; Princely Count of Habsburg, Tyrol, Kyburg, Gorizia, Gradisca; Prince of Trent, Brixen; Margrave of the Upper & Lower Lusatia, in Istria; Count of Hohenems, Feldkirch, Bregenz, Sonnenberg, etc.; Lord of Triest, Kotor, the Wendish March; Grand Voivode of the Voivodship of Serbia etc. etc.*" (Trost 1969, p. 360). Some titles were outlandish (King of Jerusalem), others were dated (Lusatia, a region close to the core of Prussian power), and still others were quaint (Hohenems on the Swiss border, with a population of 4191 in 1869).

While nation-states claimed to represent a people and its rulers had to build their legitimacy based on popular rule, Franz Joseph's title betrayed the supposed divine origin of his right to rule. Even more so, the list of titles reflects history: it is a collection of domains which mattered for power, historical provenance, or fiction, making for an eclectic collection of regions, large lands, and little towns that even at the time few could have found on a map. This list of lands was neither a modern federal state nor a collection of regions that had a strong sense of identity—although some doubtlessly did. The list was oblivious to nations or even the structure in which the regions were governed at the time. Instead, it reflected the historical growth of the empire and the importance of these titles as the foundation of rule. It was less the divine and more the historical gain of the title that secured the rule. One might thus argue that the empire was intentionally anachronistic, as this was the only justification for its existence. However, this was not all. As the penultimate emperor governed the lands for more than six decades, the empire was confronted with the rise of nations that made competing claims within the Habsburg domain. The monarchy oscillated between repression and reform in tackling these challenges. Ultimately, it would not find a solution to provide it with the legitimacy necessary to endure World War I. Nevertheless, it took a global war—and even then four years of it, which included the repressive policies of the monarchy toward its own subjects whose loyalty it doubted, and its inept handling of the war—to extinguish Austria-Hungary. Holding together the complicated amalgam of regions, nations, religions, and domains, all with different languages and reasons for having ended up the country was a constant exercise in compromise and improvisation.

At the beginning of *Sleepwalkers*, his controversial study of the origins of World War I, Chris Clark draws an explicit connection between the EU and the Habsburg Monarchy: "From the perspective of today's European Union we are inclined to look more sympathetically—or at least less contemptuously—than we used to on the vanished imperial patchwork of Habsburg Austria-Hungary" (Clark 2014, p. xxviii).

The grounds for comparison are clear: both the EU and Austria/Hungary were complex, multi-layered polities that had to find institutional answers to competing demands of diversity. As Robert Cooper, a senior EU official, has argued, the two share a multinational elite—in the Habsburg times centered on the officer corps, and in the EU on the civil service—and the association was voluntary, in the EU through the association of states and in the Habsburg lands (at least at the level of elites) through marriage, as embodied by the famous saying "*Bélla geránt alīī, tú felix Áustria nūbe*" *(Others might lead wars, you, lucky Austria, marries)* (Cooper 2012). It is easy to note the parallels to the EU not in terms of enlargement through marriage, but in terms of the peaceful association and the tools of foreign policies that emphasize peaceful conflict resolution, which so upset the American neocons in the aftermath of 9/11. The second line of praise for Austrian rule, *Nám quae Márs alīīs, dát tibi díva Venūs (For those kingdoms Mars gives to others, Venus gives to you)*, mirrors

Robert Kagan's claim that "Americans Are From Mars, Europeans From Venus" (Kagan 2003).

Yet, the differences are also clear. The Habsburg Monarchy was never a voluntary state of its citizens, or even of the domains it brought together. They found themselves in this state due to historical serendipity that cast together a mountain farmer close to the Swiss border with a Muslim landlord in Bosnia and Herzegovina and Jewish tailor in Galicia. Democracy—within the restrictions of its era—came late to the monarchy. Universal suffrage for men was only introduced in 1907, and the emperor retained powers that restricted popular will. The hierarchies of an aristocratic society placed emphasis on social class and provided little space for equal political access, especially in the regions of the empire that experienced less modernization.

Cooper also argued that ultimately the Habsburg Monarchy, unlike the EU, was a state. Although the imperial and royal halves of the empire, that is, the joint government of the Austrian and the Hungarian halves, only had three ministries—war, foreign affairs, and finance (which was also the administrator of Bosnia and Herzegovina after 1878)—it was able to mobilize its army and be a single actor in dealing with other powers (Cooper 2012). The difference in terms of statehood is relative, however. While indeed the Habsburg Monarchy acted as such in times of war and the monarchy had the ultimate authority, this mattered little in everyday life. During times of peace, the differences between the monarchy and the EU were less pronounced.

Furthermore, the monarchy had multiple levels of diversity that interacted and conflicted. The *Ausgleich* or 'compromise' between Hungary and the monarchy in 1867 created a state comprising two units, the imperial Austrian half known as *Cisleithanien* on one side of the Leitha (the small river that separated the two east of Vienna), and *Transleithanien*, the lands beyond. The name betrayed its Viennese perspective but also created two regions that were internally very diverse. The Austrian lands included Galicia and Dalmatia, but also the German-speaking lands that are now part of Austria. The Hungarian half was more coherent, centering on the Hungarian-populated lands. While the Austrian lands comprised 35.6% German speakers, Hungarians constituted 48.1% of the population in *Transleithanien* in 1910 (Wandruszka and Urbanitsch 1980, pp. 39, 414). Both groups dominated their respective parts of the empire through a combination of the electoral system (at least until 1907), dominance in parties, official languages, and historical patterns. Yet, the preeminence of the two language groups/nations was not a given or secure, as the fact that their share of population was below an outright majority suggests, and only the Hungarian half engaged in open assimilationist policies. Thus, the other lines of diversity existed within the two larger units with a plethora of nations and language groups vying for recognition and rights. The sites of dispute were often towns and regions that were bilingual and thus the linguistic dominance of one disadvantaged the other, especially as language became a vehicle of identity, whereas earlier in the early modern period it was less closely intertwined with personal or collective identity (Anderson 1991).

For example, in the small town of Cilli/Celje in lower Styria (today in Slovenia), Slovenes, who were a minority and mostly lived outside the city, gradually became dominant and caused many local Germans to fear for the political and social dominance they had long enjoyed. In 1895, the Slovenes' demand for more teaching of Slovenian in local schools and the resistance of Germans in Cilli/Celje became a flash point in the monarchy in which the German fear of rising Slavic nationalism articulated itself. Similar disputes emerged throughout the monarchy, both in the Austrian territories as well as in the Hungarian lands, where the dominant Hungarian elite pursued a more forceful assimilation campaign. Tensions ran particularly high in Bohemia and Moravia between Germans and Czechs (Judson 2007; Suppan 1998). The 1905 Moravian compromise constitutes a key moment in the monarchy's efforts to settle disputes among different language groups and thus nations. It assigned seats in the Moravian diet (parliament) to Czech and German representatives, voted for by citizens of the respective national identities, also forcing voters to register as belonging to either group. The school system was also segregated into separate German and Czech schools. This was later replicated in Bukovina and Galicia in 1910 and 1914, respectively (Kelly 2003, p. 279). The compromise rendered decision-making in Moravia more effective than in other contested regions, such as Bohemia, where no such compromise was reached. However, as Kelly argues, it also reinforced the language divide and "appear[ed]...to be little more than a final and fatally flawed attempt of the nineteenth-century aristocratic and middle-class political leaderships to hold on to their political authority" (Kelly 2003, p. 283).

While it might not have been the solution for the monarchy's nationality problems, compromise inspired the development of cultural autonomy, as articulated by the Austrian Marxist Otto Bauer. Bauer argued that rather than territorial autonomy, as advocated by Russian Marxists including Stalin, the most appropriate solution for a country such as the Habsburg Monarchy would be cultural autonomy. According to Bauer, this meant the transformation of nations into legally recognized corporations in public law that would give them legal protection and self-government (Bauer 2000, pp. 311–312). The Austrian Marxist concept of cultural autonomy owed its ideas to the diversity of the monarchy, where few nations lived as large majorities in distinct territories, and the conflicts emerged in places where different nations competed over territory, rights, and recognition. The concept of cultural autonomy, implemented more fully in other countries in the twentieth century, such as Finland and Estonia, ignores or sidelines the question of territory, which is often at the core of national movements' claims.

The final layer of diversity of the monarchy was the regions that had become part of the monarchy over time, as reflected above in the title of the emperor. Within Hungary after 1867, the kingdoms of Croatia and Slavonia enjoyed a distinct status, whereas in Cisleithania, 15 crownlands (Kronländer) reflected historical regions. Finally, Bosnia and Herzegovina had a special status, being a type of condominium, associated with neither of the two units of Austria-Hungary. In some cases, these lands were meaningful units that could mobilize national or subnational identity, such as Tyrol, but for most of the different nations those regions were a political framework with little ability to generate loyalty across national lines.

In the next chapter, we will explore the features of the EU's diversity. Yet, in comparison with the Habsburg Monarchy we can note that on one level, the EU is less complex, as its constituent units are states, and the diversity at the state and sub-state level has only an indirect and mitigated effect on the Union overall. In the Habsburg Monarchy the dispute over language rights in a small lower Styrian town would shape the politics and coalitions throughout at least the Austrian half of the empire. In the EU, subnational disputes within Member States only affect the overall Union if they touch upon secession—that is, if a unit secedes from a Member State, it also leaves the larger Union. This was of course a crucial aspect of the argument over Scotland, when it was given the opportunity to vote over leaving the United Kingdom in 2014.

The closest the Habsburg Monarchy came to the EU was limited to the world of ideas, for example in the vision of Aurel C. Popovici, who proposed in 1906 the establishment of the "United States of Greater Austria." The Romanian politician suggested the transformation of the monarchy into a federal state with its federal units reflecting the different nations. It would include a predominantly German-speaking region that is largely identical to today's Austria; the regions inhabited by the Sudeten Germans, coinciding with Deutschösterreich, the territories claimed by German-Austrian politicians in 1918–9; Slovakia, Hungary, Croatia, and Carniola (todays Slovenia), all largely congruent with the successor states today; as well as Vojvodina, Transylvania, the Hungarian-inhabited Szeklerland, Trento, and two Galician regions. In addition, multilingual regions and cities such as Prague would enjoy further autonomy. While the vision certainly followed the Romanian preference to reduce the power of the Hungarian control over its half of the monarchy, the congruence with the states that emerged after 1918 points to the relevance of Popovici's proposal (Neumann 2002). The features of the state, as envisaged by Popovici, mirror many features of the United States' constitution, which he took as a model. Parallels can also be drawn with the constitutional foundations of the European Union. As Isac notes, his ideas are tainted, however, by strong racist and anti-Semitic thinking and the fundamental assumption that the separation of nations is the most desirable approach to the management of differences (Isac 2007).

## 2.4 Multinational Federalism: Socialist Yugoslavia

The eminent historian of Europe, A.J.P. Taylor, once described Tito as the last Habsburg: "ruling over eight different nations, he offered them 'cultural autonomy' and reined in their nationalist hostility" (Taylor 1976, p. 260). A decade later in 1991 on the eve of the country's dissolution, the Bosnian comedians of *Toplista Nadrealista* (Top chart surrealists), drew a different parallel. In their skit, weary EU observers gaze down at the Yugoslav wars from a high wall separating united Europe from the fighting Yugoslavs. As the EU welcomes the last Yugoslav survivor of the wars into its midst, an argument breaks out among the EU members over who is to blame for the Yugoslav wars. As the last Yugoslav discreetly makes off with food back to his Yugoslavia, fighting breaks out in the EU, and in the end the Yugoslav observers peek over the wall to monitor the fighting in the EU (Top Lista Nadrealista & Slozna Braca 2015). For Taylor, socialist Yugoslavia was an empire in the era of the nation-state, a potentially successful reincarnation of an earlier era. This view sees Tito as an emperor who would be the ultimate, largely respected arbiter of the conflicts within the state (Jović 2009, pp. 30–31).

For the surrealists from Sarajevo, Yugoslavia was the EU's future. Their skit was not based on the idea that the diversity of both would invariably lead to conflict, but rather that ill-will and bad leadership pave the road to war. However, it is not only historians and comedians who have drawn parallels. Most prominently in recent years, the Slovenian economist and minister of the economy during independence, Jože Mencinger, has repeatedly argued that the EU is going down the same path as Yugoslavia, drawing parallels between the period of economic crisis in Yugoslavia during the 1980s and in the EU today (Kerbler 2014, May 3). However, before turning to potential parallels in terms of crisis, we will look at the structural differences and similarities.

The Yugoslav project has its origin in the nineteenth century as an emancipatory, supranational state project. However, it coincided with the emerging nation-state-building projects among South Slavs and was variously competing and overlapping with Croatian and Serbian nationalisms. Before its establishment in 1918, the Yugoslav idea was thus conceived as a broad roof under which multiple nations would share statehood, or as a shared nation with multiple sub-identities. The first Yugoslavia during the interwar period came about under dominance of the Serbian state and monarchy, and was a highly centralized and dysfunctional state. The centralization triggered opposition from different groups, most prominently the largest Croatian Peasant Party that rejected the centralist Yugoslav state. The state itself oscillated between the idea of a tri-national state of Slovenes, Croats, and Serbs and a Yugoslav nation-state with the three nations being 'tribes' rather than distinct nations. Belatedly, and after a failed experiment with a royal dictatorship that sought to break up national particularisms, Yugoslavia moved toward more decentralization, granting territorial autonomy to a Croatian *banovina* (province) in 1939. The second Yugoslavia came about against the odds due to a successful partisan campaign that not only sidelined collaborationist forces and other resistance groups, but also offered a vision of a post-war state. At first, Yugoslavia closely followed the Soviet model of formal federalism with a strongly centralized communist party in charge, a model that has little in common with the EU or any democratic federal system. The break with the Soviet Union and the challenge to find appropriate and legitimate governing structures for a highly diverse polity with developed and competing national projects triggered the transformation of the state from formal federalism to a complex federal—and as some argue, confederal—arrangement. Until the eve of its dissolution, Yugoslavia was an authoritarian state based on single-party rule. However, as the party and the state decentralized, it became a polycentric polity, no longer dominated by a monolithic party, but rather shaped by a largely federal League of Communists that had rival groups in the different republics competing over different visions of economic policy, politics of accommodation, and liberalism.[3]

The political scientist Dejan Jović has argued that the structure of the state that emerged was not just a pragmatic response of the communist elite to the domestic and external challenges of Yugoslavia, but had ideological underpinnings. Its key ideologist and author of the 1974 (and earlier) constitution, Edvard Kardelj, conceptualized the idea of the "withering away of the state" wherein the state gradually erodes and gives way to a complex network of social actors that interact through common rules, but without a strong state. The state structures would essentially be limited to arbitration, rather than governing the polity (Jović 2009). The 1974 constitution, the longest in the world and highly complex, as well as the 1976 Law on Associated Labor, created an intrinsic system of small units that would interact horizontally rather than in a hierarchy. However, sociologists of the time note that the reality was more mundane, with party officials and managers holding greater sway than 'ordinary' workers. Thus, the experiment of a horizontal fragmented state was never complete, but by the 1970s, the power had certainly shifted from the federal state to the constituent units: the six republics and two autonomous regions.

The trajectories of Yugoslavia and the EU are clearly different: while Yugoslavia moved from a highly centralized and purely formal federal structure to a loose federal or even confederal state, the EU has taken the opposite road, moving from an international organization with some competences to a complex state-like structure that features powers and institutional mechanisms in a wide range of domains. Both lack a clear *finalité*: the EU's aspiration to an 'ever-closer union' is sufficiently ambiguous to not offer a single final structure, and the constant reworking of the treaties over the decades suggests mostly a continuous work in progress. Yugoslavia similarly had four constitutions (1946, 1953, 1963, and 1974) and underwent several large-scale constitutional reforms. The constant

[3] Discussed in greater detail in Bieber (2013).

constitutional tinkering reflected the experimental nature of the Yugoslav state and the evolution of the party's views on the country. In its final constitution, the goal was defined less elegantly than in the ever-closer union as the "development of the Yugoslav community as a whole, to ensure the development of socialist self-governing democratic relations on the road to liberate labor and to build a communist society" (Ustav SFRJ 1974, Preamble). Thus, both the EU and Yugoslavia were in the eyes of their builders 'works in progress,' which were shaped and re-shaped, yet had different overall directions for their reconfiguration.

Robert Cooper's assessment of the Habsburg Monarchy could also apply to Yugoslavia. It was also a state with an army (or, as some would argue, toward the end it was an army with(out) a state), unlike the EU. However, here we can see the circular argument of the distinction. Of course, Yugoslavia was a member of the UN, it had one of the largest standing armies in Europe, and its red passport was widely respected around the world. However, if we reduce statehood to classic markers such as passport, armies, and membership in international organizations, we miss out on the parallels between a quasi-state structure such as the EU and complex states such as Yugoslavia. Although the army and foreign policy as well as the common currency were all competences of the state—not unlike the Habsburg Monarchy—the main power brokers were the republics. Politicians made their careers in the republics, and owed their loyalty to the parties of the republics and to state authorities. The ultimate test of the balance of power came at the moment of crisis. When Yugoslavia encountered intersecting economic, political, and social crises that provided the fertile ground on which elites could use nationalism to gain support, it was the republics—not the federal state—that proved more resilient. The first multiparty elections in 1990 were held in each of the republics, yet not at the federal level, delegitimizing the federal state over its (more) democratic federal units. The collective head of state was the state presidency in which each republic and province was represented. This ensured that there would not be a single Yugoslav source of authority after Tito's death in 1980, but instead a collective body that sought to represent the units, rather than replacing Tito with another unifying figure.

As a result, the institutions designed to protect the federal state became tools of the republics; primarily Serbia and its allies were able to pursue largely their own interests until the federal state ceased to exist. This was hardly the 'withering away of the state' as envisioned by the party during its heyday. Yes, the state did wither away, but only to be replaced by the new proto-states in waiting.

Arguably, a key distinction between the EU and Yugoslavia is the voluntary nature of association. While Yugoslavia reemerged in the aftermath of World War II through the victorious partisans who, with some legitimacy, could claim to represent most nations and people of Yugoslavia, the authoritarian nature of the state, in particular in its initial years, meant that the new state was never put to a democratic test (until it was too late). Thus, its legitimacy rested on the reality and myth of partisan warfare and self-liberation from Nazi occupation—not a vote or the choice of a democratic government of either its constituent units or the overall population. This foundation made the country vulnerable to nationalist counterclaims and the debates of the 1980s. These prepared the ground for the country's dissolution by focusing on the disadvantages the different republics (and by extension, nations) faced within Yugoslavia. Formally, the nations of Yugoslavia enjoyed the right to self-determination, at least according to the preamble of the 1974 constitution. Yet it was clear that the authors of the constitution did not envisage the republics or nations leaving the Federation. Changes to the external borders of the Federation, that is, in the case that one republic withdrew from the state, required the consent of all republics, making this a difficult option (Ustav SFRJ 1974, Section I, Preamble, art. 5).

Thus, the key distinction between the EU and Yugoslavia, and indeed many of the complex states we are looking at in this chapter, is the voluntary nature of association in the EU and the thereby implicit ability of its members to leave. Thus, choice and voluntary submission to common rules dominate over the perceived coercion (at least in times of crisis) of the Yugoslav state. Two Serbian political scientists, Slobodan Samardžić and Bojan Kovačević, contradict this view by arguing that both polities were built by concealing their structures from their citizens: the federal ambition of the EU, and the authoritarian control of the League of Communists. Thus, according to the authors, they "lack(ed) democratic legitimacy and with the crisis their output legitimacy also faltered" (Kovačević and Samardžić 2016). While the argument is that both systems sought to conceal their goals—federalism and power—such a view remains unconvincing, as the evolution of the EU cannot be described as a gradual federalization by stealth, especially as each step of integration has been supported by governments, parliaments, and at times citizens in referenda (and sometimes rejected). Thus, the hidden expansion of EU power might only be convincingly applied to the pre-Maastricht era. Similarly, the complex decision-making structures of late Yugoslavia could only disguise the power of the League of Communists to the most naive. However, if "Yugoslav federalism's main task was to conceal power into depoliticized sphere of an endless consensus searching process" (Kovačević and Samardžić 2016), we are left with a paradox. If power is concealed through seeking consensus, is it still power? The agonies of consensus seeking during the 1980s over economic and political reform in Yugoslavia suggest that this power was no longer there, and while the party formally held a monopoly of power, it could not exercise it as a homogenous actor. Thus, the fragmentation of power was real, as was the need for consensus seeking.

In fact, it is the consensus-seeking nature of both systems that is the key to understanding their similarities. Although the League of Communists remained in charge, it was not a monolithic actor, and in the absence of a final arbiter, as Tito had been, the political system required consensus on key decisions. No single institution could break a deadlock or take a casting vote. In both chambers of parliament, all republics had equal representation and the autonomous provinces (Kosovo and Vojvodina) were also represented, even if with slightly fewer MPs. In addition, the chambers had strong consociational mechanisms. A special procedure in the lower chamber required, in essence, unanimous consent of all republics and provinces, if a vital interest of a republic, province, or nation was affected (Dimitrijević 1994, p. 20). The second chamber representing the republics and provinces was also based on consensus decision-making (Dunn 1975, p. 143; Stanković 1974, February 25), and delegations from all the republics and provinces were required to be present for decisions. Furthermore, voting took place by each delegation *en bloc*, which meant that there was no space for creating cross-cutting majorities (Dimitrijević 1994, pp. 18–19). Finally, constitutional amendments were made extremely difficult, requiring a two-thirds majority in the Chamber of the Federation and adoption by all federal units. Other procedures also required unanimous consent by the Chamber of Republics and Provinces (Koštunica 1988, p. 81). Thus, the Yugoslav systems had a higher threshold of consensus-based decision-making than the EU has acquired over the past decade.

A second feature that Kovačević and Samardžić mention in the context of the EU, but which is a shared feature of both, is the depoliticized nature of decision-making (2016). Indeed, both the EU and late socialist Yugoslavia were opting for 'technocratic government' as their defining feature. This aspect is partly the result of the consensus-based decision-making that removes or at least reduces political competition. Furthermore, the technocratic decision-making is in essence removed from direct representative politics. This is a function of the elite-driven politics of both, and the remoteness of Federal Yugoslav or EU politics for most citizens.[4]

Now let us shortly return to Mencinger's argument about the similarities of the Yugoslav and the EU crises (Dragojević Mijatović 2011, June 23). Both faced an economic crisis within one economic system with a currency union yet very uneven development. The development gap between the poorest region (Kosovo) and the wealthiest increased during socialism and resulted in a GDP per capita that came to be 5.4 to 1 by 1981 (Jović 2009, p. 177). This ratio is similar to that between the richest country in the EU, Luxembourg, and the poorest, Bulgaria (5.8 in 2014), or within the Eurozone between Luxembourg and Latvia of 4.1.[5] The economic crisis led to an increasing crisis of solidarity within Yugoslavia and the EU, and the economic arguments were quickly translated into national ones, where national stereotypes—the laziness of the Southerners, or the exploitative Northerners—provided ready-made explanations for the crisis.[6] The congruence of nation, sub-state regions, and economic discrepancies thus fueled tensions and transformed economic crisis into nationalist tensions. There is little doubt that one can observe this pattern in both cases, and literature beyond the two cases notes the combustible combination of these three features.[7] We will return to these challenges for the EU as a complex polycentric polity later in this book.

## 2.5 Ethnonational Power-Sharing: Belgium

The consensus-based, complex decision-making that marks parallels between socialist Yugoslavia and the EU brings us to the last case of comparison: the country at the center of EU institutions, Belgium. Belgium

[4] For the EU, see Wallace and Smith (1995).

[5] The numbers are misleading, as Luxembourg is small and an outlier. While Luxembourg is at 263 (with 100 EU 28 average), the next countries (Ireland, the Netherlands, Austria, Denmark, Germany, and Sweden, stand between 132 and 124). If one were to exclude Luxembourg, the gap in the Eurozone would decrease to 2.1. GDP per capita, consumption per capita and price level indices, Eurostat (2019).

[6] See also Kovačević and Samardžić (2016).

[7] This particular argument is made by scholars skeptical of decentralization along ethnonational lines. See Bakke and Wibbels (2006) and Brancati (2006).

today and in recent decades has been a key example of a country governed by complex power-sharing, namely through a range of institutions that are closely associated with consociationalism (Deschouwer 2006), including consensus-based decision-making, federalism along linguistic boundaries, cultural autonomy, and strong veto rights for different linguistic groups.

Not unlike Yugoslavia, Belgium moved toward multinational federalism and consociationalism from a high level of centralism that marked most of the first century of the country's existence. While Belgium had consociational features like the neighboring Netherlands and Luxembourg, these did not reflect the now salient linguistic divide, but rather the division between Catholics, Socialists, and Liberals. Only in the course of the twentieth century did these classic pillars of division gradually erode, as elsewhere in Europe (e.g. the Netherlands and Austria), to be replaced by the division between French- and Flemish-speaking Belgians (and a small minority of German speakers). Thus, the consensus-seeking political institutions did not disappear, but rather transformed themselves to serve different lines of diversity, or rather, division.

The economic shift from the industrialized Wallonia to Flanders brought with it greater assertiveness among Flemish speakers regarding their language after the strong assimilationist pressures of French. With the rise of linguistic divisions, the new pillars became increasingly geographic, as French- and Flemish-speakers lived in distinct regions of the country. Although the earlier ideological lines of division also had their reflection in geography, it was mostly based on urban—rural divides and less on particular regions of the country. Thus, non-territorial consociationalism came under pressure to acquire a geographic dimension in separating communities. More than a decade of gradual reforms and debates finally resulted in the 1993 constitution that recast Belgium as a federal state that inextricably links territory and language (Jones 2002). The new Belgium became a complicated state, with directly elected parliaments of the regions (Brussels, Flanders, and Wallonia), as well as of the three language groups (Flemish, French, and German) and different competences for the different units.[8]

Not unlike the EU, Belgium often appears as a continuous work in progress, always under negotiation and never completed. These negotiations and the underlying divergent views of the structure of the country

[8] The parliament of Flanders and of the Flemish community merged with the Flemish parliament.

(or whether it should exist altogether) bring with them periodical crises, such as over the formation of a government after the June 2010 election that lasted until December 2011, repeated again between the May 2019 elections and government formation in March 2020. Analogous to the EU, Belgium could be described as an 'ever more remote union,' since the institutional trajectory of the country has been centrifugal, rather than centripetal. Belgium, like most other complex states discussed in this chapter, and unlike the EU (so far), is a state confronted with the challenges of diversity and deep political divisions. In addressing these, the country radically decentralized and granted powers to groups and regions in an effort to extend its own life. It is thus a classic case of a "holding together federation" (Swenden and Maarten 2006). In addition to Yugoslavia and to some degree also the Habsburg Monarchy, Spain and India are other examples of countries that have adopted federal or quasi-federal institutions to hold the country together. There is nothing about the trajectory that would invariably argue that such efforts are doomed, but institutional responses to secessionist movements are fraught with difficulties and have to face strong challengers, unlike polities that come together through the voluntary association of their units, such as the United States or the multinational Federations of Canada and Switzerland (Stepan 2001, pp. 315–360).

In addition to the crucial distinction of the shift over time from centralized to decentralized and consociational state in the case of Belgium and the gradual strengthening of joint institutions of the EU, the number of units also differs significantly. Unlike Yugoslavia, the Habsburg Monarchy, or other earlier examples, Belgium's consociational federalism rests essentially on two actors: the Francophone and Flemish communities. The federal unit of Brussels and the German community are considerably less relevant, but even if they were considered, the complexity of the Belgium system derives not from the need to accommodate a large number of groups or units, but rather from finding multiple venues in securing a compromise that keeps the two largest communities engaged. Here, Belgium is hardly unique. Most consociational arrangements today involve relatively few units—often two or three. In Bosnia and Herzegovina, three nations are recognized—so called constituent people with particular institutional safeguards. Similarly, regional consociations, such as Northern Ireland or South Tyrol/Alto Adige, provide institutions for two main groups in both cases. Other mixed consociational and federal systems, such as Canada and Iraq, also serve to accommodate few groups: in the case of Canada mostly to protect the Francophone Quebecois, and in Iraq, the failing consociational federalism is intended to accommodate three groups—Shiites, Sunnis, and Kurds.

The institutional attempt of the EU to accommodate the Member States through complex procedures and representative structures thus stands apart through the sheer number of units and their distinctiveness.[9]

## 2.6 Conclusion

This chapter has shown that there is a rich history of complex polities over past centuries that have sought to accommodate diversity outside the nation-state framework. Thus, the European Union is hardly unique or incomparable. Of course, our five cases also highlight the specificities of the EU. By embedding it in a comparative and historical context, we can note that states and other political bodies have for centuries sought to accommodate diversity, and the model of a nation-state that might or might not grant rights to minorities is by no means the only approach. Our five cases offer insight into two multinational empires—the Holy Roman Empire and the Habsburg Monarchy—and two multinational states with varying degrees of federal arrangement—Yugoslavia and Belgium. The case of the United States fits more into the category of a multicultural regime, although here we focused on its emerging federal features and its accommodation of different visions of state, rather than identity-based differences. The only model of Michael Walzer's discussion of regimes of toleration not covered here is multicultural states, as these generally fall short of the multiple regimes of accommodating diversity that multinational states face.

If we take the comparison not as evidence of how the EU is or ought to be—federal, confederal, a loosely structured network of authority, or a consociational state—but as a point of evaluation, we can highlight the following features:

1. Political systems and regimes of accommodation are embedded in the larger state system. While the nineteenth and twentieth centuries can be considered the era of the sovereign nation-state, such a characterization would not adequately capture the global system either previously

[9] The only other polity with quasi-federal institutions that accommodates diversity and a large number of different communities is India. See Stepan et al. (2011).

or in recent decades. Thus, the EU, like the other polities discussed, has to be considered in its historical context. Although this highlights the limitations of cross-time comparison, it also highlights that an excessively narrow understanding of what constitutes a state or political system by reducing it to a nation-state—and thus excluding the EU or deeming it incomparable—misses the point.

2. Institutional arrangements change and adapt. As the discussion of the United States, Yugoslavia, and Belgium highlights, complex polities never 'are,' but constantly become. Their trajectory might move toward great centralization or toward more fragmentation and a looser union. The respective path is driven by both the institutional dynamics and the larger social and political structures that place particular demands on the institutions. There are crucial junctions when polities clearly shift from one form to another and a reversal becomes less likely, such as with the Civil War in the United States, or the enactment of the federal constitution in Belgium. As the source of power shifts, the main source of authority and legitimacy alters as well. The EU currently appears not yet to have crossed such a distinct threshold, and its developmental paths remain open.
3. All the different polities discussed in this chapter were 'unfinished.' From the Holy Roman Empire to Belgium, they sought to adapt and respond to new challenges of diversity, from emerging religious pluralism to demands for national self-determination. It would be too easy and misleading to attribute this recalibration to a failure of the polities. In fact, they could only survive by renegotiating the balance of power between different institutions by accommodating new groups and forms of difference. In as much, none of them were ever complete or ever saw themselves as finished, complete states. It might be tempting to consider this to be a state of disequilibrium, which results in a shift toward either greater centralization or disintegration. However, the 'imperfect' structures of the polities allowed them to persist for considerable periods of time—between several centuries and four decades—despite diversity and politicized difference.
4. There is a diversity of diversity in the cases examined in this chapter. Belgium, Yugoslavia, and the Habsburg Monarchy constitute classic cases of multinational states that seek to accommodate the demands of identity groups, or rather the political actors claiming to represent these groups. This accommodation has been a major contributing factor to their complexity. The Holy Roman Empire and the United States

were and, in the case of the latter, are also diverse polities, yet in the USA the institutional accommodation did not revolve to the same degree around identity lines. Yet, the two had to resolve profound differences over the nature of government either through compromise or through the imposition of one view by force. It is more productive to conceive diversity on a scale than in absolutes, defined by its existence or absence in a given polity. Thus, some countries are marked by greater diversity that is politically salient than others; but diversity interacts with institutions, and just as much as it can be accommodated by institutions, it can also be reinforced by them.

In considering the five cases and the EU, what conclusions can be drawn from their 'failure,' or rather those cases that have ceased to exist? First a note of caution: it is easy to consider a state or polity that no longer exists to have 'failed.' However, such a normative judgment is problematic. Does the fact that the Habsburg Monarchy and the Holy Roman Empire came to an end in 1918 and 1806 respectively mean that they failed, or rather should we focus on their surprising endurance, spanning more than 600 centuries and nearly a millennium in either case? Few modern states have such a long history to look back on, and thus taking the end of the states as starting points runs the risk of falling for the hindsight bias. Knowing the outcome allows us to re-interpret the facts and events in line with the final outcome. As a result, the past is interpreted through the lens of a particular event, such as state dissolution, and other factors are left aside.[10]

Instead, it is more constructive to view all polities as contingent and changing. Considering that their defining feature is pluralism and diversity, these pressures are greater, and thus the balancing act does not lead to a permanent equilibrium, but rather to an adjustable polity.

## References

Abbé de Saint-Pierre [Charles Irénée Castel de Saint-Pierre]. (1713). *Projet pour rendre la paix perpétuelle en Europe*. Utrecht: A. Schouten.

Anderson, B. (1991). *Imagined Communities: Reflections on the Origins and Spread of Nationalism*. London/New York: Verso.

[10] This phenomenon is discussed in greater detail in regard to the dissolution of Yugoslavia in Bieber (2014), p. 3–4.

Backer, L. C. (2001). The Extra-National State: American Confederalism and the European Union. *Columbia Journal of European Law, 7*(2), 173–240.
Bakke, K. M., & Wibbels, E. (2006). Diversity, Disparity, and Civil Conflict in Federal States. *World Politics, 59*(1), 1–50.
Bauer, O. (2000). *The Question of Nationalities and Social Democracy*. Minneapolis/London: University of Minnesota Press.
Bieber, F. (2013). Federalising the Federation: The Failure of the Yugoslav Experiment. In J. Loughlin & W. Swenden (Eds.), *The Routledge Handbook on Regionalism and Federalism* (pp. 513–526). London: Routledge.
Bieber, F. (2014). Introduction. In F. Bieber, A. Galijaš, & R. Archer (Eds.), *Debating the End of Yugoslavia* (pp. 1–7). Aldershot: Ashgate.
Brancati, D. (2006). Decentralization: Fueling the Fire or Dampening the Flames of Ethnic Conflict and Secessionism? *International Organization, 60*(3), 651–685.
Burgdorf, W. (2012). "Once We Were Trojans!" Contemporary Reactions to the Dissolution of the Holy Roman Empire of the German Nation. In R. J. W. Evans & P. H. Wilson (Eds.), *The Holy Roman Empire, 1495–1806: A European Perspective* (pp. 51–76). Leiden/Boston: Brill.
Clark, C. (2014). *Sleepwalkers: How Europe Went to War in 1914*. London/New York: Harper Perennial.
Cobb, J. C. (2005). *Away Down South: A History of Southern Identity*. Oxford/New York: Oxford University Press.
Cooper, R. (2012). The European Union and the Habsburg Monarchy. *Tr@nsit Online*. http://www.iwm.at/read-listen-watch/transit-online/the-european-union-and-the-habsburg-monarchy/. Accessed 21 Mar 2020.
Cuyvers, A. (2013). *The EU as a Confederal Union of Sovereign Member Peoples: Exploring the Potential of American (Con)federalism and Popular Sovereignty for a Constitutional Theory of the EU*. Unpublished PhD dissertation, University of Leiden.
Deschouwer, K. (2006). And the Peace Goes On? Consociational Democracy and Belgian Politics in the Twenty-First Century. *West European Politics, 29*(5), 895–911.
Dimitrijević, V. (1994). The 1974 Constitution as a Factor in the Collapse of Yugoslavia or as a Sign of Decaying Totalitarianism. *EUI Working Papers. Robert Schuman Centre, 94*(9).
Dragojević Mijatović, A. (2011). Jože Mencinger: YU-sindrom hara Europom. *Novi List*, June 23. http://www.novilist.hr/Vijesti/Svijet/Joze-Mencinger-YU-sindrom-hara-Europom. Accessed 24 Mar 2020.
Dunn, W. N. (1975). Communal Federalism: Dialectics of Decentralization in Socialist Yugoslavia. *Publius: The Journal of Federalism, 5*(2), 127–143.
Economist. (2012, December 22). European Disunion Done Right.

Elazar, D. J. (2001). The United States and the European Union: Models of Their Epochs. In K. Nicolaidis & R. Howse (Eds.), *The Federal Vision. Legitimacy and Levels of Governance in the United States and the European Union* (pp. 31–53). Oxford/New York: OUP.

Eurostat. (2019). *GDP Per Capita, Consumption Per Capita and Price Level Indices.* http://ec.europa.eu/eurostat/statistics-explained/index.php/GDP_per_capita,_consumption_per_capita_and_price_level_indices#Further_Eurostat_information. Accessed 21 Mar 2020.

Fabbrini, S. (2005). Is the EU Exceptional? The EU and the US in Comparative Perspective. In S. Fabbrini (Ed.), *Democracy and Federalism in the European Union and the United States. Exploring Post-National Governance* (pp. 3–24). London/New York: Routledge, 3–24.

Fabbrini, S. (2007). *Compound Democracies: Why the United States and Europe Are Becoming Similar.* Oxford/New York: OUP.

Friedrichs, J. (2001). The Meaning of New Medievalism. *European Journal of International Relations, 7*(4), 475–501.

Gagnon, A., & Seymour, M. (Eds.). (2012). *Multinational Federalism.* Basingstoke: Palgrave.

Härter, K. (2015). Das Heilige Römische Reich deutscher Nation als mehrschichtiges Rechtssystem, 1495–1806. In S. Wendehorst (Ed.), *Die Anatomie frühneuzeitlicher Imperien: Herrschaftsmanagement jenseits von Staat und Nation* (pp. 327–347). Munich: De Gruyter-Oldenbourg.

Hartmann, P. C. (2005). *Das Heilige Römische Reich deutscher Nation in der Neuzeit 1486–1806.* Ditzingen: Reclam Philipp Jun.

Inglehart, R. F., & Woodward, M. (1967). Language Conflicts and Political Community. *Comparative Studies in Society and History, 10*(1), 27–45.

Isac, I.-N. (2007). The United States of Greater Austria: A Step Towards European Union? In I. Stanciu & S. Miloiu (Eds.), *Europe as Viewed from the Margin: An East-Central European Perspective During the Long 19th Century.* Târgoviște: Editura Cetatea de Scaun. http://www.centrulgafencu.ro/user/image/12isac.pdf

Jones, E. (2002). Consociationalism, Corporatism, and the Fate of Belgium. *Acta Politica, 37,* 86–103.

Jović, D. (2009). *Yugoslavia: A State Withered Away.* West Lafayette: Purdue University Press.

Judson, P. (2007). *Guardians of the Nation: Activists on the Language Frontiers of imperial Austria.* Cambridge, MA: Harvard University Press.

Kagan, R. (2003). *Of Paradise and Power: America and Europe in the New World Order.* New York: Alfred A. Knopf.

Kelly, T. M. (2003). Last Best Chance or Last Gasp? The Compromise of 1905 and Czech Politics in Moravia. *Austrian History Yearbook, 34,* 279–301.

Kerbler, J. (2014). Jože Mencinger: Jugoslovenski sindrom trese EU. *Večernje novosti* (Belgrade), May 3. http://www.novosti.rs/vesti/naslovna/politika/aktuelno.289.html:489913-Joze-Mencinger-Jugoslovenski-sindrom-trese-EU. Accessed 21 Mar 2020.

Khanna, P. (2009). The Next Big Thing: Neomedievalism. *Foreign Policy*, September 17. http://foreignpolicy.com/2009/09/17/the-next-big-thing-neomedievalism/. Accessed 21 Mar 2020.

Koštunica, V. (1988). The Constitution and the Federal States. In D. Rusinow (Ed.), *Yugoslavia: A Fractured Federalism*. Washington, DC: The Wilson Center Press.

Kovačević, B., & Samardžić, S. (2016). Internal Crisis of Compound Polities: Understanding the EU's Crisis in Light of the Ex-Yugoslav Federation's Failure. *Journal of Balkan and Near Eastern Studies, 18*(3), 241–262. https://doi.org/10.1080/19448953.2016.1176395.

Kumar, K. (2017). *Visions of Empire. How Five Imperial Regimes Shaped the World.* Princeton/London: Princeton University Press.

Lijphart, A. (2008). *Thinking About Democracy: Power Sharing and Majority Rule in Theory and Practice.* London/New York: Routledge.

McCulloch v. Maryland. 4 Wheat. 316 (1819).

McEvoy, J., & O'Leary, B. (Eds.). (2013). *Power Sharing in Deeply Divided Places.* Philadelphia: University of Pennsylvania Press.

McGarry, J., & O'Leary, B. (1993). Introduction: The Macro-Political Regulation of Ethnic Conflict. In J. McGarry & B. O'Leary (Eds.), *The Politics of Ethnic Conflict Regulation* (pp. 1–40). Abingdon: Routledge.

Moull, D. (2004). Lessons the EU Should Learn from the Formative Years of the US: Challenges to EU Authority in the Areas of Legitimacy and Interpretive Competence and the Implications for the Conceptualization of the EU. *Jean Monnet Working Papers in Comparative and International Politics* 51.

Neumann, V. (2002). Federalism and Nationalism in the Austro-Hungarian Monarchy: Aurel C. Popovici's Theory. *East European Politics and Societies, 16*(3), 864–897.

Pierson, P. (2004). *Politics in Time.* Princeton: Princeton University Press.

Schievelbusch, W. (2004). *The Culture of Defeat: On National Trauma, Mourning, and Recovery.* New York: Picador.

Shaw, S. J., & Shaw, E. K. (1977). *History of the Ottoman Empire and Modern Turkey, Volume II: Reform, Revolution, and Republic: The Rise of Modern Turkey, 1808–1975.* Cambridge: CUP.

Simms, B. (2013). The Ghosts of Europe Past. *New York Times*, June 10, p. A23. http://www.nytimes.com/2013/06/10/opinion/the-ghosts-of-europe-past.html. Accessed 21 Mar 2020.

Stanković, S. (1974). Yugoslavia's New Constitution Proclaimed: Some Preliminary Remarks. *Radio Free Europe Research*, February 25. http://fa.osaarchivum.org/background-reports?col=8&id=33438. Accessed 21 Mar 2020.

Stepan, A. C. (2001). *Arguing Comparative Politics*. Oxford/New York: Oxford University Press.

Stepan, A., Linz, J. J., & Yadav, Y. (2011). *Crafting State-Nations: India and Other Multinational Democracies*. Baltimore: Johns Hopkins University Press.

Stollberg-Rilinger, B. (2009). *Das Heilige Römische Reich Deutscher Nation*. Munich: C. H. Beck.

Suppan, A. (1998). *Deutsche Geschichte im Osten Europas: Zwischen Adria und Karawanken*. Berlin: Siedler Verlag.

Swenden, W., & Maarten, T. J. (2006). 'Will It Stay or Will It Go?' Federalism and the Sustainability of Belgium. *West European Politics, 29*(5), 877–894.

Taylor, A. J. P. (1976). *The Habsburg Monarchy, 1809–1918: A History of the Austrian Empire and Austria-Hungary*. Chicago: University of Chicago Press.

Taylor, C. (1994). The Politics of Recognition. In A. Gutmann (Ed.), *Multiculturalism and "the Politics of Recognition"* (pp. 25–73). Princeton: Princeton University Press.

Top Lista Nadrealista. (2015). Top Lista Nadrealista: Kako nas gleda Evropa. *Youtube*. https://www.youtube.com/watch?v=nt9cMJAAwPA. Accessed 10 Aug 2015.

Tortarolo, E. (2005). Nation and Federalism in the American Historical Experience: A Model for Europe? In S. Fabbrini (Ed.), *Democracy and Federalism in the European Union and the United States: Exploring Post-National Governance* (pp. 79–92). London/New York: Routledge.

Trost, E. (1969). *Das blieb vom Doppeladler*. Munich: DTV.

Ustav, Socijalističke Federativne Republike Jugoslavije. (1974).

Voltaire. (1877–1885). Essai sur les mœurs et l'esprit des nations. In L. Mouland (Ed.), *Oeuvres completes de Voltaire* (Vol. 11). Paris: Garnier. https://fr.wikisource.org/wiki/Essai_sur_les_m%C5%93urs. Accessed 21 Mar 2020.

Wallace, W., & Smith, J. (1995). Democracy or Technocracy? European Integration and the Problem of Popular Consent. *West European Politics, 18*(3), 137–157.

Walzer, M. (1999). *On Toleration*. New Haven: Yale University Press.

Wandruszka, A., & Urbanitsch, P. (1980). *Die Habsburgermonarchie 1848–1918, Band III: Die Völker des Reiches*. Vienna: Österreichische Akademie der Wissenschaften.

Wilson, P. H. (2016). *Heart of Europe: A History of the Holy Roman Empire*. Cambridge: Belknap Press.

Zielonka, J. (2006). *Europe as Empire*. Oxford/New York: Oxford University Press.

CHAPTER 3

# Diversity in the European Union

Following the collapse of the multinational Ottoman and Habsburg empires after World War I, the model of diversity in Europe appeared to be the creation of nation-states with some, often limited, protection of minority rights. Wilson's principle of self-determination proved hard to implement in practice as new borders were difficult to draw and millions of European became minorities, stuck on the 'wrong' side of nation-state borders. The states and the new majorities that emerged were often ill at ease with difference, and minorities that appeared as a potential threat to the state. This tension between self-perceived nation-states and large alienated minorities characterized states across the continent, in particular in Central Europe, from the Baltics to the Balkans. Minorities were instrumentalized to destabilize the new borders created in Paris in 1919, and Nazi Germany abused German minorities to justify its policy of conquest. Ironically, it was the rejection of the interwar state system by Germany and its allies that brought about its recreation after the war. At the end of World War II when peace came to Europe, gradually laying the foundations for what was to become the European Union, the continent was less diverse than it had been for many centuries. The Holocaust decimated the Jewish population, and other genocides affected other European communities, such as the Roma population, where mass murder and expulsions during and after the war brought long-established communities to an end. National socialists and fascists believed in national homogeneity and hierarchy and implemented their vision throughout the war. However, even as



F. Bieber, R. Bieber, *Negotiating Unity and Diversity in the European Union*, Palgrave Studies in European Union Politics,
https://doi.org/10.1007/978-3-030-55016-5_3

their fortunes declined, some of their opponents also adopted the notion that homogenous nation-states would provide greater stability than the heterogeneity that prevailed in many interwar states. At the same time, millions were on the move at the end of the war. Around 12 million Germans had fled Eastern Europe at the end of the war and in the subsequent years, having been expelled from Poland, Czechoslovakia, and elsewhere.

The project of European integration thus began not only after the unprecedented mass death and destruction in Europe, but also the profound undoing of communal ties and ethnic cleaning. The idea of homogeneity was not fully discredited with the end of the war, as Poles, Germans, Hungarians, and others were subsequently expelled from their homes by the millions. European integration thus occurred in a context in which diversity and difference, at least at the state level, was widely viewed as a disadvantage and a potential source of conflict. Unity on the European continent thus emerged in the context of not just the rejection of totalitarianism, but also diversity as a social reality of post-war states.

The hegemony of Nazi Germany on the European continent had also reinforced the importance of national sovereignty. Before gradual European integration began to take off, earlier attempts to promote rapid European federal or confederal integration had failed. Some were part of British or American plans for post-war Europe, earlier institutional projects including the Council of Europe and the Organization for European Economic Co-operation that were established but did not generate the integrative momentum; other plans for deeper integration failed outright, including the Pleven Plan for a European Defense Union. The integration of diverse and heterogenous states through the gradual erosion of sovereignty was not the starting point of European integration. Instead, it was the states that were considerably more homogenous than their earlier incarnations and eager to preserve their sovereignty, at least in the initial post-war environment. The states were also, as historian Timothy Snyder put it, "fragments of failed European empires" (Snyder 2019). German empire building failed through its defeat in World War II, whereas the British, French, Dutch, and Belgian colonial empires began to unravel as European integration emerged. Reduced to their metropolis, the transnational continental self-perception of European great powers receded.[1] The

[1] All founders of the European Community, with the exception of Luxembourg, had been recent colonial powers.

early period of European integration is thus closely intertwined with European late colonial history (Hansen and Jonsson 2015).

Diversity in the early stages of European integration primarily focused on the diversity *among* rather than *within* Member States. The internal diversity in terms of minorities, be they linguistic, national, or ethnic, was long neglected. The few conflicts over identity in Northern Ireland or, to a lesser degree, in South Tyrol appeared to be the exceptions to the rule. However, the rise of regionalist movements in the 1960s and 1970s across Western Europe, including the Basque region in Spain and France, Corsica, Flanders, and Scotland, highlighted that the nation-states were far less homogeneous and uncontested than conventionally thought. Finally, the enlargement to Central and Eastern Europe drew attention to large minorities in the new members, from groups with a kin state, such as Hungarians in Slovakia, to those without a kin state, such as the large Roma community in Romania. This has shifted the perception of diversity toward the differences within the Member States. Furthermore, since the European Community was founded, it also became more diverse through migration. Migrants arrived from the declining colonial empires to the European metropolises, and states recovering from the war soon sought labor forces from the Mediterranean region. In addition, a steady flow of Central and East European citizens fled communist rule, in particular from Eastern Germany, but also from Hungary after the Soviet repression of the 1956 revolution, and from Czechoslovakia after the Prague Spring was repressed by the Soviet Union in 1968. The nation-states of Europe thus did not stay or become homogenous for long. These new forms of diversity have emerged over the 60 years of European integration, including Europeans who moved within the EU for work and retirement, and labor migrants and refugees from outside the EU. Some of these processes have changed the diversity of the EU independently of European integration itself, while other forms of diversity, such as regional movements or European identity and mobility, have been profoundly stimulated and shaped by the EU itself.

Beyond the diversity of the people who constitute the inhabitants of the Union, there is the diversity of the states in the Union. One of the defining features of the European political space has been the competition among different polities. The competition is not necessarily antagonistic or conflictual. During the century following the Congress of Vienna, European powers—in particular, the Great Powers—cooperated to avoid open hostilities and sought to balance their conflicting interests. This included some limited institutional cooperation in mostly peripheral spheres, such as the post, telegraphs, and navigation. These earlier international organizations remained the exception, and cooperation took place among the European powers, with smaller states often at their mercy.

Since the emergence of sovereign states associated with the Thirty Years' War, the European state system has been based on the notion that states and their rulers are able to impose the level of diversity or homogeneity they choose, yet they have to tolerate difference in other polities. This notion is embodied in the defining formula to end the religious wars of the early modern period, 'Cuius regio, eius religio,' that is, the ruler determines the religion and with it the level of tolerable diversity. Even if this notion is only narrowly associated with the sixteenth and seventeenth centuries, it embodies the concept of unrestricted authority of the ruler over the diversity within the country. This notion has been contested with the emergence of minority and human rights, starting in the nineteenth century, but initially only at the margins.

Besides the autonomy of the polities, their competition has been a defining feature of the European political space. This competitive diversity has been both a source of conflict, when it came to projects of European domination from Napoleon, Hitler, and Stalin, and a central dynamic of colonial expansion and exploitation. It has also been an important driver of innovation and competition in terms of different political and economic policies. Several scholars attribute the decisive advantage of European powers over other more homogenous states—such as China during the early modern period—to the competition among various European kingdoms, city-states, and smaller fiefdoms. No single European ruler, even of the largest European empire, could impose a single system of laws, rules, or decisions (Kennedy 1987; Frankopan 2015). Exceptions such as Napoleon were short-lived and unable to transform wartime expansion into a permanent peace. This diversity facilitated competition and made it impossible for any single ruler to prevent innovation that defined the European state system. Once this competition became infused with the exclusionary claims of nationalism and mass politics, what might be considered a potentially benign competition resulted in two world wars and mass murder. Without further dwelling on the diversity of the European state system prior to the emergence of the European Union, the competition of European states has been central to Europe for centuries. Earlier attempts at political unity are remarkable for their exceptionalism, from the Roman Empire to Charlemagne.

As such, diversity is both the origin and the core of the European integration project. On one hand, the potentially destructive and antagonistic dimension of difference became apparent in the decades preceding European integration. On the other, the European integration project rests on the recognition and affirmation of difference, even if the diversity and institutional awareness of it has increased. This chapter thus explores the evolution of diversity in the European Union, and argues that the EU has both facilitated and been confronted with changing and growing diversity over the past decades.

## 3.1 Diversity of Diversities

Diversity is notoriously hard to grapple with. What is diversity? As stated above, a distinction is necessary between the diversity among citizens of a polity and the diversity of the political units that make up that polity. In a centralized state, there might be no difference between the regions or municipalities in how they are governed, and even in federal states, the sub-units might have considerable self-government, but do not necessarily vary unit to unit. However, in complex polities, such as the European Union, it is not just central to understand the diversity of its population, but also that of the polities.

There are two diversity paradoxes in the way the European Union is understood. Few would think of it as a union of diversity. Yet, the Union is founded on establishing communalities and shared policies, institutions, and values among states and their citizens that are inherently different. Thus, diversity is the self-evident foundation of the integration project, as the EU brings together 27 Member States and citizens of different states, so that one can best speak not just of a diverse EU, but of a polity of diverse diversities. Diversity is inherently plural, as citizens in many polities have multiple and separate markers of difference that matter for them. However, in addition, as a polity composed of a variety of political institutions, its diversity is multi-dimensional, reflected in the term 'diverse diversity' (Prügl and Thiel 2009, pp. 6–15) (see Chap. 8).

The second EU diversity paradox arises from the fact that the European Union is more aware and consciously acknowledging of its diversity than most polities around the world, although few regions of the world have experienced as many homogenizing efforts over the past two centuries as Europe.

Is the diversity of the EU more than just the sum of the diversity of its Member States? As we argued in the previous chapter, a multitude of different states, from empires to self-declared nation-states, are shaped by diversity and the political claims associated with it. Within the EU the political claims over difference are expressed and negotiated on multiple levels. The EU is a multinational polity in which no single national identity is dominant, yet it is constituted of mostly nation-states—with considerable variation in the meaning of nation-states. This tension explains why sub-state national or regional movements, such as the Scottish or the Catalan national projects, might reject the intermediate state, Britain or Spain, while embracing the larger European Union.

## 3.2 Diversity of Member States

Before turning to diversity among the citizens of the EU, the diversity of the polities in the EU matters. But what does this diversity entail? There is the diversity resulting from numbers or rather the consequences of size, as well as the diversity of the internal organization of the Member States, and finally the variation in the relationship with the EU.

The EU (and before it the EC) has existed with a diverse and growing number of members. It is often noted that the rapid growth of membership, nearly doubling within a decade from 15 in 2003 to 28 in 2013, has been a key difficulty in EU decision-making structures. In part, the challenge of functioning with a larger number of members is structural: institutional mechanisms prevent conventional decision-making by simple majorities in many domains, including de facto veto rights in key fields, such as enlargement and treaty changes. Thus, the number of actors in the Union increases the risk of blockages.

The diversity of Member States expresses itself in a multitude of ways. One prominent example is the internal degree of centralization. France represents the prototype of a centralized nation-state, but is in fact an exception. Three EU Member States are federal states, namely Germany, Austria, and Belgium. In addition, several states have a tradition of decentralization and strong regions, including the United Kingdom, especially after the 1997 devolution to Wales and Scotland, and Italy, with a number of autonomous regions and efforts to move the country toward a more federal organization. Spain has an asymmetric federal system, where some regions, most notably Catalonia, the Basque Country, and Galicia enjoy a high level of self-rule, whereas other regions lack this level of autonomy.

Even otherwise centralized states might have special arrangements for specific regions, such as Portugal for Madeira and Denmark for the Faroe Islands and Greenland. Even centralized France has granted special status to some of its overseas territories. Besides the diversity of territorial organization, there is a variety in terms of the type of democracy. Some have constitutional monarchies, while most have a president with varying powers as head of state. More significantly, the electoral systems differ, with most using a type of proportional representation, while some like the United Kingdom and France use majoritarian systems. Different electoral systems are even reflected in the election of members to the European Parliament. With a varying number of levels of legislative and administrative authority and different mechanisms of democracy, the EU is inherently required to recognize the pluralism in the organization of democracy. Consider citizenship: while a European citizenship regime (as we will discuss in Chap. 7) offers a common framework, the acquisition of citizenship varies across the Union and with it the answer to the question of who the people are. The distinction between citizenship based on descent and on territorial principle has been largely overcome in most EU Member States, as they combine both aspects. The main line of distinction is how readily citizenship is available to immigrants and the extent to which countries tolerate their citizens', in particular naturalized citizens', other citizenships (Kochenov 2019).

In effect, the third dimension includes the diversity of the relationship to the Union. The European Union does not simply provide the same set of rules for all 27 (or whatever future number) members. The degree of integration is not uniform, but varies. This is most visible when it comes to money and to the beneficiaries of (internal) free movement, the euro, and the Schengen Agreement. Some members by choice—and others for not fulfilling the legal criteria—have not been part of a key EU policies. Much less visible are the special regimes a large number of territories of EU members have. These include the outermost regions of the EU, a status given to integral parts of the EU, but which are located at some distance from the European continent. Among them are well-known and populated islands such as the Azores, Martinique, and the Canary Islands, totaling some 4.8 million inhabitants. In these territories not all EU rules apply as they do in mainland Europe and thus these outermost regions have a defined relationship with the EU, not just the country they belong to. In addition, the overseas countries and territories (OCT) are a part of an EU Member State, but are not part of the EU themselves. These include

Greenland, which changed its status from and Outermost Region to an OCT by referendum in 1985, French Polynesia, and more than a dozen small islands.

Finally, there are several regions in Europe itself that hold a special status, often based on their specific geographic position. Some, such as the Faroe Islands, the Channel Islands, and the Isle of Man, are not part of the EU, whereas others are in the EU but hold special status, such as Mount Athos in Greece, or Ceuta and Melilla, the Spanish enclaves in North Africa.

While it might be easy to dismiss these territories as irrelevant quirks of history, they effect a population greater in number than Denmark and also highlight that the relationship between the EU and the population is not only mediated through the Member State alone. Not only have some territories, like Greenland, been able to leave the EC without severing links to the Member State, others have joined the EU, such as Mayotte that became a French department in 2011 and thus became part of the EU.

Many of these territories are leftovers of much larger colonial empires. As decolonization and European integration overlapped during the 1960s and 1970s, large parts of French colonial possessions, in particular in Africa, as well as Belgian, Dutch, and Italian territories, had a special relationship with the European Community until their independence.

## 3.3 What Is Diversity?

Moving from the diversity of the Member States, the different regimes, and their relationship with the EU, there is considerable diversity among citizens. The EU is a multinational, multilingual, multi-religious, and multi-racial polity. Much of this diversity is mediated through Member States, but as later chapters will explore, they are defining features of the Union itself. Mobility within in the EU, encouraged through open borders and various programs such as Erasmus, has also made the EU a generator of diversity. While easy to evoke, both as a threat and as a positive force, diversity is hard to pin down.

One can easily list languages, national or ethnic groups, religions, or citizenships. Yet, these are lists of either self-ascribed or externally determined identities. The categories or numbers associated with them offer little insight about their political or social relevance. Identities, whether self-ascribed or imposed by others, do not indicate their depth, their divisive nature, and how they intersect with other lines of difference. For example, in Northern Ireland, just as in Germany, the ratio of Catholics to

Protestants among the population is similar. In Northern Ireland, there are approximately 40% Catholics and 41% Protestants, and in Germany 30% Catholics and 28% Protestants.[2] Yet, such numbers would give little indication of the different meaning of being Protestant or Catholic in the specific contexts. What might be simply a marker of religious affiliation, expressed mostly in private without much political meaning, can be associated with diametrically opposed political views in a different context. Thus, the depth of identity is a function of their relevance for political and social demands, enhanced by the overlap of several markers of difference, such as religion, language, national identity, and socio-economic status.

Furthermore, the number of available identities says little about their divisive potential. A society might be characterized by many relatively small groups and their high number might result in a seemingly high level of fragmentation. However, fragmentation could also reduce their political relevance, as high fragmentation can result in small groups which are unable to assert themselves without building coalitions.

The obvious difficulty deriving from the above cross-country comparison of seemingly identical markers of difference, such as religious affiliation, is that it can be meaningless, if these markers assume different meaning in different contexts.

In her study of the relationship between democracy and diversity, Pippa Norris has sought to capture fragmentation by mapping out countries according to their linguistic and religious fractionalization. Fractionalization essentially combines the number of groups and their relative size by calculating the odds of two individuals belonging to different groups. More serious than the difficulties of reliable data is the misleading assumption that religious or linguistic diversity is a good proxy for politically relevant lines of division. Thus, Norris places Yemen and Libya into the category of some of the least fractionalized countries in the world—both are overwhelmingly Arab-speaking Muslim countries, whereas some fairly peaceful societies, such as South Africa or Togo, are among the most fractionalized (Norris 2008, pp. 51–52).[3] This data-driven approach is closely associated with a quantitative approach to studying diversity, driven by economists and some political scientists. Large data sets provide for comparability, but

[2] Data from 2011 census for Northern Ireland, Church Statistics for 2015 Germany.

[3] Her list is based on the methodology of Alesina and La Ferrara (2005). See also Fearon (2003).

also contain the inherent risks of creating false comparisons (Patsiurko et al. 2012).[4]

An alternative approach to mapping identity is examining diversity based on survey data. Ferry Koster, for example, argues that the European Social Survey can help determine difference based on respondents' responses, including one's place of origin, citizenship, language, and religion (Koster 2013). However, here as well, personal markers of identity are extrapolated to be politically salient, even when they diverge in meaning. The number of residents born in other countries might be the same in Luxembourg and in Latvia, yet the political and social relevance diverges. In Latvia there is one large group of migrants (and their children) who settled in the country during the Soviet period, with a different identity pattern and relationship to the state than the more diverse migrant populations of Luxembourg, who are mostly from the EU. Comparable or even identical numbers have different meanings attached (Koster 2013, p. 584) (Chart 3.1).

Andreas Wimmer, Brian Min, and Lars-Erik Cederman have moved beyond the demographic indicators of diversity to look at politically relevant groups based on these markers of difference. Thus, it is not the mere existence of difference that matters, but rather the political claims and demands that refer to these differences (Wimmer et al. 2009).

As Rogers Brubaker and other scholars have argued, diversity and identity groups are not given and can be merely described; they are constructed and have to be constantly reconstructed by identity entrepreneurs (Brubaker 2004).

The largest entrepreneur of identity is often the state. As Wimmer et al. argue, "ethnicity matters because the nation-state itself relies on ethnonational principles of political legitimacy: the state is ruled in the name of an ethnically defined people and rulers should therefore care for 'their own people.' As a result, ethnicity and nationhood have much greater political significance in nation-states than they do in other types of polities such as empires or city-states" (Wimmer et al. 2009, p. 321).

[4] Alesina and others have also often argued that highly fragmented societies are more prone to worse economic performance and higher likelihood of violent conflict. This is confirmed in other studies. However, the emphasis has not been on diversity, but polarization or fractionalization. Thus, not diversity as such but its political salience matters according to studies in different contexts. See Campos et al. (2011), Campos and Kuzeyev (2007), Patsiurko et al. (2013), and Montalvo and Reynal-Querol (2005).

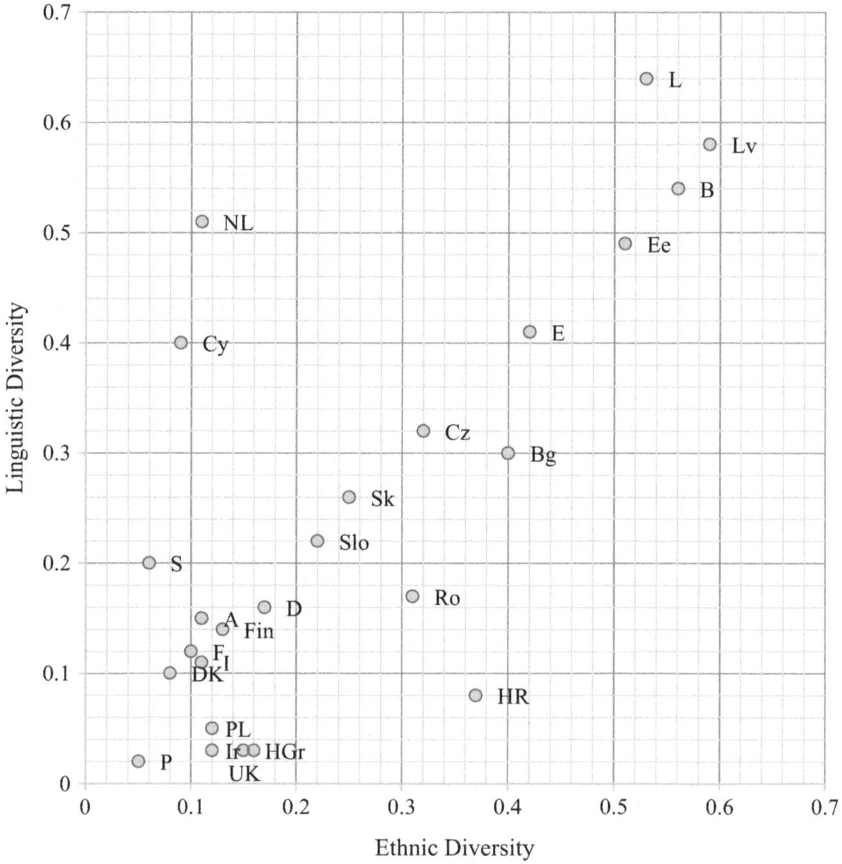


**Chart 3.1** Ethnic and Linguistic Diversity in EU members. (Note: Based on data from Koster (2013), p. 586)

To map diversity in the EU, we thus not only explore the diversity of language, national identity, and citizenship as key markers of difference, but also consider their relevance.

### *Linguistic Diversity*

While the EU with its 24 official languages is often compared (negatively) to the Tower of Babel, it is in fact not a particularly diverse place when it comes to languages. The share of global linguistic diversity stands at 1%, whereas 7.1% of the world's population lives there (Arzoz 2008, p. 4). This is no surprise. As language has been one of the markers of national identity, national movements have sought to standardize languages to promote their nation and suppress and assimilate others that do not fit in (Anderson 1991, pp. 69–84). Thus, the linguistic diversity of the EU was originally the diversity of hegemonic national languages, and the EU has (at least initially) reflected the linguistic dominance of state languages over regional variants and dialects. As a result, the multiple regional languages of France, such as Corsican and Breton, have long had no status in Europe and been marginalized in the Member States themselves. Across the EU, millions of citizens speak languages other than the official languages as their mother tongue. Some are regional languages confined to one Member State, like the ones mentioned above, or Friulian in Italy and Frisian in the Netherlands. In addition, some minority languages are spoken as transnational languages in several EU Member States, such as Basque and Catalan in Spain and France and Sami in Sweden, Finland, and Norway. The most important transnational minority language in Europe is Romani, spoken by many—but not all—Roma communities and only partly standardized.

Some state languages in one EU Member State are spoken in another, such as Swedish in Finland, German in Belgium, and Hungarian in Slovakia. Of course, the transnational minority languages also cover non-EU states, including some where the linguistic center is outside the EU, such as Russia and the Russian speakers in the Baltic states, or vice versa, where languages in the EU are spoken outside: besides English and French, there are also smaller languages such as Hungarian that are spoken in other countries, by the Hungarian minority in Ukraine, for example.

Finally, migration has also created large minority language groups. These include intra-EU migration, such as established Portuguese-speaking groups in Luxembourg, Italian speakers in France and Germany, and more recent arrivals such as Romanian and Polish speakers who moved to Western Europe after the 2004 and 2007 enlargements. Other languages include those spoken by non-European migrants in the EU, often hailing from various migratory waves (Extra and Gorter 2001).

The codification of the linguistic landscape changes both at the state and the EU level. Thus, in 1984 Luxembourgish attained the status of an official language in the country, joining French and German, yet not becoming a language of use in the EU. Irish, spoken by 5–10% of the Irish population, became an official EU language in 2007. The ascent of these languages, however, is a reflection of nation-state projects, rather than a challenge to them. In Luxembourg, the introduction of Luxembourgish was part of a nation-state building project to shore up the country's distinctiveness to its German- and French-speaking neighbors. In Ireland, Irish (or Gaelic) served to assert a distinct Irish identity over British claims, even if the language was and continues to be spoken only by a minority of the Irish population. The distinction between language and dialect is a political and not a linguistic question (Juaristi et al. 2008, p. 48). This is particularly relevant for pluricentric languages, that is, languages that are spoken in different political units. These are sometimes considered one language, such as German, with official status in four EU members—Germany, Austria, Luxembourg, and Belgium, as well as Switzerland—or English, with official status in Ireland, Malta, and, after the departure of the United Kingdom from the EU, in a total of 67 countries. Other pluricentric EU languages include French, Swedish, Portuguese, and Spanish. Serbian, Croatian, Montenegrin, and Bosnian together is another example of a pluricentric language; however, it is given different names in different states and is closely associated with national identity.

The number of citizens who speak the main state language as their mother tongue varies between 71% (Latvia) and 99% (Greece), with some exceptional cases, such as Belgium and Luxembourg which are both officially trilingual. In Belgium 93.4% of the population speaks French, Flemish, or German, whereas in Luxembourg the rate is lower, with only 70% speaking Luxembourgish, French, or German as their mother tongue. Thus, while in all EU members one language dominates with more than half of the population speaking it as a mother tongue, in eight countries that rate is below 90% (European Commission/Special Eurobarometer 2012).

The linguistic diversity of Europe is increasing, and the term 'mother tongue' or 'home language' does not fully capture this diversity. With rising numbers of multilingual families, citizens are growing up multilingual and thus have multiple languages spoken at home. Among young EU citizens (ages 15–30) surveyed in 2018, around 67% of citizens read and write in two or three languages, and only a minority of 20% consider themselves to be monolingual. This ratio is subject to great regional variation, as the United Kingdom has by far the largest share of monolingual citizens (68%), whereas in multilingual Luxembourg nearly the same share (69%) indicate that they read and write in three languages (European Commission/Flash Eurobarometer 2018).

Linguistic diversity in the EU is increasing as citizens have become more multilingual and regional languages have witnessed a revival. As the above example of pluricentric languages highlights, the relevance of language as a source of political contestation is usually the consequence of the association of language with national or regional identity, rather than the language by itself.

## 3.4 Diversity of National Identity

Linguistic diversity is closely linked to national diversity. A speaker of a minority language might identify with the larger political nation, for example a Breton speaker who considers her or himself French, or a native Bosnian speaker in Austria who views him or herself as Austrian. As national identity, unlike language knowledge, is a subjective decision, it is notoriously difficult to capture. EU members are divided on whether to ask their citizens in censuses about their ethnicity or race. In particular, countries that promote a republican understanding of the nation, such as France, do not distinguish their citizens in national or ethnic categories in official statistics. Other countries, such as Croatia, that place greater emphasis on ethnically defined nations count the national self-identification of their citizens. Thus, there is diversity in how nations are understood and defined, as well as in how they coincide with existing states. This diversity has not been central to the European Union, as the EU has not been preoccupied with this level of diversity. In part, this is a reflection of the divergence of state policies. With no transcending EU understanding of what ethnic and national diversity constitutes, formulating positions and policies would be challenging. As we will discuss in Chap. 7 about minorities, there has been a development toward recognizing minority rights in the Union over the past 30 years, but these efforts remain cautious. The diversity of Member State policies thus stands in the way of sub-national diversity.

The national diversity in the EU results from three phenomena. While the EU Member States, as noted earlier, were more homogenous at the founding of the European Communities than probably in any earlier period (or since), they were multinational states to varying degrees. These included recognized minorities such as the Danes in Germany, or the German-speaking minority in Italy's Alto Adige/South Tyrol region. In addition, new minority claims emerged among groups that were widely assumed to be assimilated into the dominant nation. In particular in

France, which has pursued a republican assimilationist national policy in which non-French speakers would be assimilated into the overarching French nation, regional nationalisms emerged. These included Bretons, Basques, and Corsicans. Often, these movements also sought to revive long-declining regional languages, as has been the case in the United Kingdom with Welsh. Where minorities are recognized and citizens can identify themselves with the regional nations and groups, it is possible to determine their size, but in France, Greece, and elsewhere where the state keeps no record of nations and other regional groups, the numbers are subject to competing claims by minority representatives who inflate numbers, and the state, which usually plays the size down. Similarly, the number of Roma, the largest transnational European minority, remains a well-informed guess. The European Commission suggests that around 6 million Roma live in the EU.[5] Not only is the recordkeeping divergent, but also the members of the community often do not publicly identify with the group. This is the consequence of state repression and social discrimination, which disincentivize self-identification as Roma. In addition, Roma are not a homogenous group—its members differ on multiple counts, so individuals might see themselves as belonging to a specific group based on historical profession, regional origin, language, and religion rather than to the larger Roma community.

Belonging to a distinct historical community does not automatically mean that its members, most or in part, claim to be distinct from the majority. There is also great variety across Europe. It is not just Roma who often consider themselves members of the majority. In some countries Jews view themselves as belonging to the dominant nation, only diverging in terms of religion. In other contexts, Jews might be recognized and see themselves as a distinct group, apart from the majority, recognized not just as a religious, but as an ethnic or national group.

Besides historical communities, new minorities have emerged, mostly after World War II through migration. These include both migrants that moved within the EU and those who entered from outside the Union. This picture is considerably more complex, as some migrants might have obtained EU citizenship in one EU country and moved to another, or moved to another country before their own country joined the EU, such as the Spaniards and Portuguese who migrated to Northern Europe well

[5] "Roma integration in the EU," https://ec.europa.eu/info/policies/justice-and-fundamental-rights/combatting-discrimination/roma-and-eu/roma-integration-eu_en

before the two countries joined in 1986. In addition, there are 'accidental' migrants who moved within one country and became migrants only due to the disintegration of the country, such as Russian speakers in Estonia and Latvia, and Yugoslav migrants in Slovenia and Croatia. Many of these migrants might identify with their new country—especially as the next generation is born in the country. However, often they have been subject to exclusionary citizenship policies. Migratory minorities are often less attached to their original national identity than historically established minorities. Both groups might overlap and mix, such as Slovenes and Croats in Austria, with some having lived in the country before the state was established, and some arriving more recently.

While this national diversity might overlap with citizenship, many attain the passports of their country of residence, but also continue to identify with their group of origin. On the other hand, the passport alone does not embody identification with the nation of origin per se. In particular, as citizenship laws are diverse across the EU, the ability to hold multiple citizenships might vary, and gives an imperfect indication of the community an individual might or might not identify with.

## 3.5 Diversity of Citizenship

Finally, the easiest marker of diversity to measure is citizenship. Holding EU citizenship, that is, the citizenship of an EU Member State, provides for a clear indication of inclusion, at least in terms of rights, obligations, and formal ability to fully participate in the politics of the given country. In essence, we can distinguish between three tiers of citizenship within the EU. The first tier includes citizens of their country of residence. They live in their country of citizenship and thus have unrestricted access to the services of the state and political participation. Of course, they might face social obstacles toward inclusion, be it due to their mother tongue, country of origin, or physical appearance. Formally, they are, however, included in the majority. EU citizens who live in a country other than the one whose citizenship they hold make up the second tier. This might include a German living in France, or a Romanian living in Spain, for example. They enjoy many of the same rights as those in the first category, but are subject to some restrictions. They are able to run and vote in local and European elections, but this right is subject to varying residence restrictions, and they are crucially not able to partake in national politics. As we will explore in greater detail in Chap. 6 on citizenship, there are other restrictions and rights that EU citizens enjoy. The third tier is made up of citizens of third countries, who are living in the EU based on varying Member State rules. Some EU rules, such as freedom of movement in the Schengen Area, also apply to them. Their legal status varies greatly—from being spouses of EU citizens or highly qualified workers to asylum seekers, the range is wide. However, none of them enjoy as many rights as EU citizens. These legal categories do not necessarily translate into social experience. A Canadian in Britain, for example, might be considered less 'foreign' by many citizens than an EU citizen from Estonia. Furthermore, within the EU, there are both legal distinctions among EU citizens, based on transitional periods after accession, and social distinctions, as EU citizens from a neighboring country might be perceived as less different than if they were from further afield.[6]

Taking the diversity of citizenship as one dimension of determining the diversity defining the EU, the variety among members is great. On one end is Luxembourg, where only 53% of the population holds the citizenship of the country, and at the other end are Bulgaria, Romania, Poland, and Lithuania, where less than 1% of the population holds any other citizenship (Chart 3.2).

Overall in the European Union, EU citizens living in a different Member State constitute only 3.1% of the population; the share of non-EU citizens stands at 4.1%. In numbers, the results are more striking, as there are just over 16 million EU citizens living in other EU countries, making them more numerous than inhabitants of Belgium (the ninth largest EU Member State); and the nine smallest EU members taken together are smaller in size than the 20.8 million non-EU citizens living in the European Union. The share of EU inhabitants born in a different country is even greater, as many are nationalized, depending on citizenship laws (Table 3.1).

Thus, the share of foreign-born population ranges from a low 1.6% in Poland to 45.2% in Luxembourg. As with the number of citizens from other countries, in most countries the number of non-EU citizens prevails over EU citizens. Exceptions are countries that are subject to extensive labor migration within the EU, such as Ireland and Luxembourg, or those with leisure migration such as Cyprus, and finally some countries in Central Europe that have a generally restrictive migration policy, little

[6] On intra-EU migration and the implications for citizenship, see McMahon (2015).

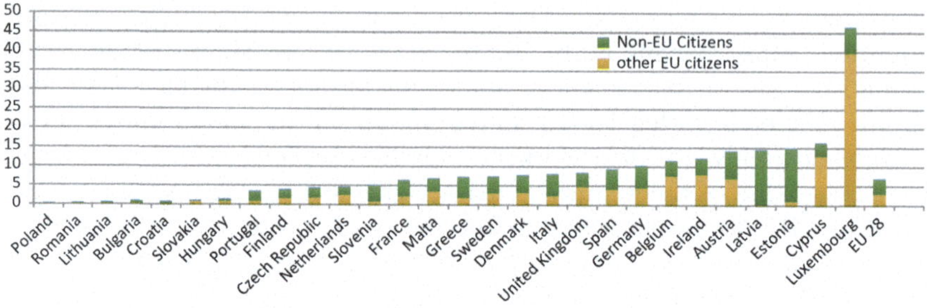


**Chart 3.2** Citizenship in EU Member States (home country, EU, and non-EU citizens) in percent. (Note: Data from national statistical agencies, between 2011 and 2016, depending on latest data available)

intra-EU labor migration, and a low foreign-born population, such as Hungary or Slovakia.

Altogether, we can identify two groups of countries in terms of non-citizens or foreign-born populations. The first group includes those with a very small size of non-citizens or foreign-born population, around 5% or less, covering seven central European countries.[7] The second group includes the bulk of EU members, namely 18,[8]with a foreign-born population greater than 10%, all (except for four) countries that joined the EU before 2004. The four Central European countries with a high rate include Estonia and Latvia, which are both still home to a large Russian-speaking community that does not hold citizenship but cannot be considered recent migrants. The other two are Slovenia and Croatia, where again intra-Yugoslav migration explains a relatively high foreign-born rate. In the middle range between 5 and 10% of foreign-born populations, only four countries can be found, with Hungary at the lower end at 5.1%, presumably due to mostly ethnic Hungarians born in Romania, Serbia, and other neighboring countries, and Italy at the upper end with 9.7%. As a result, there is a visible gap in Europe between countries with a significant share of foreign-born residents and those where either their share is small and being foreign-born does not signal ethnic diversity (Hungary), or where it is based on state dissolution (Slovenia, Croatia, Latvia, Estonia).

[7] Romania, Poland, Slovakia, Bulgaria, Croatia, Lithuania, and Hungary.

[8] Only two have a rate higher than 20%, Cyprus and Luxembourg, both of which are exceptional cases due to their small size and specific profile

**Table 3.1** Foreign-born population by country of birth, 1 January 2016 (Eurostat 2016)

| | *Total* | | *Born in another EU state* | | *Born in a non-EU state* | |
|---|---|---|---|---|---|---|
| | *In 1000s* | *In %* | *In 1000s* | *In %* | *In 1000s* | *In %* |
| Austria | 1578.2 | 18.2 | 713.6 | 8.2 | 864.6 | 9.9 |
| Belgium | 1845.6 | 16.3 | 866.8 | 7.7 | 978.8 | 8.7 |
| Bulgaria | 136.4 | 1.9 | 48.5 | 0.7 | 87.9 | 1.2 |
| Croatia | 547.9 | 13.1 | 68.6 | 1.6 | 479.4 | 11.4 |
| Cyprus | 172.8 | 20.4 | 110.4 | 13.0 | 62.4 | 7.4 |
| Czech Rep. | 433.3 | 4.1 | 171.8 | 1.5 | 261.5 | 2.5 |
| Denmark | 636.7 | 11.2 | 216.9 | 3.8 | 419.8 | 7.4 |
| Estonia | 193.8 | 14.7 | 19.2 | 1.5 | 174.6 | 13.3 |
| Finland | 329.2 | 6.0 | 118.8 | 2.2 | 210.4 | 3.8 |
| France | 7902.8 | 11.8 | 2203.8 | 3.3 | 5699.0 | 8.5 |
| Germany | 10,908.3 | 13.3 | 4351.8 | 5.3 | 6556.4 | 8.0 |
| Greece | 1220.4 | 11.3 | 350.1 | 3.2 | 870.3 | 8.1 |
| Hungary | 503.8 | 5.1 | 320.5 | 3.3 | 183.3 | 1.9 |
| Ireland | 798.6 | 16.9 | 547.6 | 11.6 | 251.0 | 5.3 |
| Italy | 5907.5 | 9.7 | 1823.8 | 3.0 | 4083.6 | 6.7 |
| Latvia | 258.9 | 13.1 | 27.6 | 1.4 | 231.3 | 11.7 |
| Lithuania | 129.7 | 4.5 | 20.8 | 0.7 | 108.9 | 3.8 |
| Luxembourg | 260.6 | 45.2 | 194.8 | 33.8 | 65.8 | 11.4 |
| Malta | 45.9 | 10.5 | 20.7 | 4.8 | 25.1 | 5.8 |
| Netherlands | 2056.5 | 12.1 | 554.9 | 3.3 | 1501.6 | 8.8 |
| Poland | 626.4 | 1.6 | 216.3 | 0.6 | 410.1 | 1.1 |
| Portugal | 872.5 | 8.4 | 232.0 | 2.2 | 640.5 | 6.2 |
| Romania | 350.8 | 1.8 | 148.4 | 0.8 | 202.3 | 1.0 |
| Slovakia | 181.6 | 3.3 | 150.5 | 2.8 | 31.1 | 0.6 |
| Slovenia | 241.2 | 11.7 | 67.0 | 3.2 | 174.2 | 8.4 |
| Spain | 5919.2 | 12.7 | 1957.0 | 4.2 | 3962.2 | 8.5 |
| Sweden | 1675.1 | 17.0 | 529.8 | 5.4 | 1145.3 | 11.6 |
| UK | 8698.2 | 13.3 | 3250.6 | 5.0 | 5447.5 | 8.3 |
| *EU total* | *54431.9* | *10.7* | *19,302.6* | *3.8* | *35,128.9* | *6.9* |

Consequently, there is a marked East—West divide in terms of this dimension of diversity. This difference played out significantly during the debates about migration in 2014–2015, but should not be taken as given. Historically, the divide in Western Europe was between North and South, with the North being longer established as a region of destination for migration, and the South more accustomed to sending migrants north than to hosting a substantial migrant population.

## 3.6 Diversity and Integration

European citizenship and the mobility of EU citizens is closely linked to the emergence of a European identity (Prügl and Thiel 2009, p. 14). While citizens of EU Member States automatically hold European citizenship, this does not always mean that these citizens understand themselves as European citizens, or participate in the European Union as the polity of their citizenship. This is closely intertwined with discussions about European constitutional patriotism and concepts of active citizenship (Prügl and Thiel 2009, p. 14).

One important measure of diversity and integration is mixed marriages. The term is problematic, as what is left unstated is who is 'mixed.' The term was originally used to discuss the question of inter-racial marriages (Lanzieri 2012a, pp. 97–98), but has been used since to denote marriage between people of distinct backgrounds, such as national identity or citizenship.[9]

In the EU context, mixed marriages based on citizenship indicate the degree to which citizens transcend citizenship-based communities. They can offer insight on the integration of migrant communities in a given state—both non-EU and EU citizens—as well as shed light on the degree to which rigid lines of division, whether language and citizenship, are eroding. Children from such marriages usually hold multiple citizenships—depending on how restrictive citizenship laws are—and often speak multiple first languages.

Of course, data on mixed marriages is only a proxy, as citizenship or place of birth is sometimes ill-suited to understanding the personal dynamics, for example whether a Hungarian with a Hungarian passport is marrying another who happens to have a Romanian passport, or a French citizen of Moroccan descent is marrying a Belgian citizen of Moroccan origin. At the same time, if a German citizen marries another, one hailing originally from Turkey, this marriage would not count as being 'mixed' (*The Economist* 2012). With this caveat in mind, the data largely reflects the differences in diversity in regard to citizenship we observed across the EU in the previous section. If the population is diverse, that is, with many inhabitants being foreign-born or holding the citizenship of another country, the odds that people meet partners of a different background increase.

[9] See, for example, the case of Yugoslavia Hodson et al. (1994).

However, beyond the simple mathematical odds, mixed marriages also indicate the integration between populations living in the same country.

In 2008–10, a total of 8.4% of the total married EU and EEA population had a partner with a different passport. The highest rates are recorded in Switzerland, Latvia, and Luxembourg at around 20%, followed by Estonia, Ireland, Germany, France, Belgium, and Austria ranging between 10% and 15.8%; the lowest rates are recorded in Bulgaria and Romania (0.4% and 0.1% respectively) (Lanzieri 2012b). Estonia and Latvia are misleading, as high rates in both countries reflect the fact that many Russian speakers do not hold Latvian or Estonian citizenship, and thus what appear as mixed marriages are in fact mostly marriages between permanent inhabitants of the two countries that might not even differ in regard to their mother tongue or background. The high rates for Luxembourg and Switzerland reflect their highly diverse populations (Gstrein et al. 2008). Many of these mixed marriages are individuals of similar linguistic and cultural backgrounds (*The Economist* 2012). In 2015, among the 13 countries reporting from the EU, the number of partners born outside the country of marriage varied between Lithuania with 6.62% and Luxembourg with 53.65%.[10]

When taken over time, there is no clear EU-wide pattern of increasing mixed marriages. Giampaolo Lanzieri noted an increase between 1990 and 2010 in Southern Europe, closely connected with an increase of foreign population, whereas in Benelux, Germany, and France, there has been a less clear change in these rates; in some countries, such as Belgium and the Netherlands, there has even been a drop (Lanzieri 2012a, pp. 81–121). Some of these fluctuations are often more effectively explained by changes in legislation in terms of migration, citizenship, and marriage (Lanzieri 2012a, pp. 100–101).

Overall, a higher level of mobility within the EU, as well as migration into the EU, has resulted in an increase of mixed marriages among citizens of EU Member States and from the outside.

## 3.7 Conclusion

The European Union is a political project that is built on diversity, which produced and facilitated new forms of diversity, and which can be best understood as being a complex polity that enables diversity.

[10] Statistics available at https://ec.europa.eu/eurostat/data/database

The EU has not unconditionally promoted diversity. For example, immigration from third states has been and remains in the remit of the Member States, and there are no policies that would particularly favor diversity at this level. To some extent, although introducing the Schengen Area facilitated the mobility of non-EU citizens within the region, it also resulted in the increase of barriers at the external borders of the Union against non-EU citizens. In addition, the rise of anti-immigrant policies across the EU, in particular since the politicization of migration following the large-scale inflow of refugees and migrants in 2014–2015, has resulted in more restrictive policies toward immigration.

Within the Union, the EU has facilitated mobility and diversity that crosses national borders and enjoys greater EU protection and support than diversity within the borders of a Member State. The beneficiaries are primarily EU citizens who cross EU boundaries. Brexit shows that this mobility can be precarious. The status of EU citizens in the United Kingdom and—to a lesser degree—British citizens in the EU has remained uncertain and fraught with considerable administrative obstacles.

Beyond the forms of diversity discussed here, there are other categories to be considered. For example, LGBTQ people have long not been recognized or accepted in Western Europe as part of diversity. Only in recent decades have LGBTQ citizens achieved legal protection and gained equality in some (but not all) EU Member States. Thus, there is both a diversity of treatment, reflecting more liberal and conservative societies, and a source of diversity that extends beyond the categories of diversity outlined above. With anti-discrimination directives, the EU has also directly intervened in preventing discrimination and thus recognizing diversity of sexual orientation (Prügl and Thiel 2009, p. 7).

The diversity of the population within the EU is real and growing. Today's EU is considerably more diverse than it was in the 1960s, in part due to migration and in part to the growth of the EU itself. Furthermore, awareness of diversity and its recognition has increased. Regional identities, languages, and sexual identities that were dismissed, criminalized, and marginalized became more accepted within the Member States and also in the EU itself. It would thus be misleading to take a snapshot of the EU and its population as a definite depiction of diversity. Instead, diversity has been evolving and will evolve. Not all of the differences among its citizens have been the concern of the EU, and much of this has come to the agenda of the Union only with the passing of time. Even if there were not much mobility within the EU or from outside, diversity exists between a

Greek EU citizen living on Crete and a Sami EU citizen living in northern Finland. This difference in language, lifestyle, habits, expectations of the role of government, social mores, and socio-economic status requires recognition within the EU. Much of this difference is mitigated and mediated by Member States, but the states are not the only actors that represent this diversity.

## References


Alesina, A., & La Ferrara, E. (2005). Ethnic Diversity and Economic Performance. *Journal of Economic Literature, 43*(3), 762–800.

Anderson, B. (1991). *Imagined Communities: Reflections on the Origins and Spread of Nationalism*. London/New York: Verso.

Arzoz, X. (2008). Introduction. In X. Arzoz (Ed.), *Respecting Linguistic Diversity in the European Union* (pp. 1–16). Amsterdam/Philadelphia: John Benjamins Publishing Company.

Brubaker, R. (2004). *Ethnicity Without Groups*. Harvard: Harvard University Press.

Campos, N. F., & Kuzeyev, V. S. (2007). On the Dynamics of Ethnic Fractionalization. *American Journal of Political Science, 51*(3), 620–639.

Campos, N. F., Saleh, A., & Kuzeyev, V. (2011). Dynamic Ethnic Fractionalization and Economic Growth. *The Journal of International Trade & Economic Development, 20*(2), 129–152.

Economist. (2012). The Mixture as Before, 6 July. https://www.economist.com/blogs/feastandfamine/2012/07/mixed-marriages. Accessed 22 Mar 2020.

European Commission. (2012). *Special Eurobarometer 386, Europeans and Their Language*. https://ec.europa.eu/commfrontoffice/publicopinion/archives/ebs/ebs_386_en.pdf. Accessed 22 Mar 2020.

European Commission. (2018). Flash Eurobarometer 466. *The European Education Area, May, 2018*, 13–14. http://data.europa.eu/euodp/en/data/dataset/S2186_466_ENG. Accessed 22 Mar 2020.

Eurostat. (2016). *Foreign-Born Population by Country of Birth, 1 January 2016*. http://ec.europa.eu/eurostat/statistics-explained/index.php/File:Foreign-born_population_by_country_of_birth,_1_January_2016_(%C2%B9).png. Accessed 22 Mar 2020.

Extra, G., & Gorter, D. (2001). Comparative Perspectives on Regional and Immigrant Minority Languages in Multicultural Europe. In G. Extra & D. Gorter (Eds.), *The Other Languages of Europe: Demographic, Sociolinguistic, and Educational Perspectives* (pp. 1–44). Clevedon: Multilingualism Matters.

Fearon, J. (2003). Ethnic and Cultural Diversity by Country. *Journal of Economic Growth, 8*, 195–222.

Frankopan, P. (2015). *The Silk Roads: A New History of the World*. London: Bloomsbury

Gstrein, M., Mateeva, L., & Schuh, U. (2008). *Mixed Marriages in the EU*. European Commission, Directorate-General "Employment, Social Affairs and Equal Opportunities", Unit E1 – Social and Demographic Analysis, Research Note, 27 p.

Hansen, P., & Jonsson, S. (2015). *Eurafrica: The Untold History of European Integration and Colonialism*. London: Bloomsbury.

Hodson, R., Sekulic, D., & Massey, G. (1994). National Tolerance in the Former Yugoslavia. *American Journal of Sociology, 99*(6), 1534–1558.

Juaristi, P., Reagan, T., & Tonkin, H. (2008). Linguistic Diversity in the European Union: An Overview. In X. Arzoz (Ed.), *Respecting Linguistic Diversity in the European Union* (pp. 47–72). Amsterdam/Philadelphia: John Benjamins Publishing Company.

Kennedy, P. (1987). *The Rise and Fall of the Great Powers: Economic Change and Military Conflict from 1500 to 2000*. New York: Random House.

Kochenov, D. (2019). *Citizenship*. Boston: MIT Press.

Koster, F. (2013). Sociality in Diverse Societies: A Regional Analysis Across European Countries. *Social Indicators Research, 111*, 579–601.

Lanzieri, G. (2012a). Mixed Marriages in Europe, 1990–2010. In D.-S. Kim (Ed.), *Cross-Border Marriage: Global Trends and Diversity* (pp. 81–121). Seoul: Korea Institute for Health and Social Affairs.

Lanzieri, G. (2012b). Merging Populations: A Look at Marriages with Foreign-Born Persons in European Countries. *Eurostat: Statistics in Focus* 29. http://ec.europa.eu/eurostat/documents/3433488/5584928/KS-SF-12-029-EN.PDF/4c0917f8-9cfa-485b-a638-960c00d66da4. Accessed 22 Mar 2020.

McMahon, S. (2015). *Immigration and Citizenship in an Enlarged European Union. The Political Dynamics of Intra-EU Mobility*. Basingstoke: Palgrave Macmillan.

Montalvo, J. G., & Reynal-Querol, M. (2005). Ethnic Diversity and Economic Development. *Journal of Development Economics, 76*(2), 293–323.

Norris, P. (2008). *Driving Democracy: Do Power-Sharing Institutions Work?* Cambridge: Cambridge University Press.

Patsiurko, N., Campbell, J. L., & Hall, J. A. (2012). Measuring Cultural Diversity: Ethnic, Linguistic and Religious Fractionalization in the OECD. *Ethnic and Racial Studies, 35*(2), 195–217.

Patsiurko, N., Campbell, J. L., & Hall, J. A. (2013). Nation-State Size, Ethnic Diversity and Economic Performance in the Advanced Capitalist Countries. *New Political Economy, 18*(6), 827–844.

Prügl, E., & Thiel, M. (2009). Understanding Diversity in the European Integration Project. In M. Thiel & E. Prügl (Eds.), *Diversity in the European Union* (pp. 3–20). Basingstoke/New York: Palgrave Macmillan.

Snyder, T. (2019). Europe's Dangerous Creation Myth. *Politico*, January 5. https://www.politico.eu/article/europe-creation-project-myth-history-nation-state/

Wimmer, A., Cederman, L. E., & Min, B. (2009). Ethnic Politics and Armed Conflict. *American Sociological Review*, *74*, 316–337.

CHAPTER 4

# Approaches to Diversity in the EU

Since 1957, the European Union has aimed for "an ever closer union among the peoples of Europe" (*Treaty establishing the European Economic Community*, 1957, preamble). This aim is reaffirmed no less than three times in the current constitutional foundations of the European Union (*Treaty on the European Union* [TEU], 2007, preamble; *Treaty on the Functioning of the European Union* [TFEU], 2007; *Charter of Fundamental Rights of the European Union* [CFR], 2000). The exact meaning of the concept has never been officially defined. In fact, union (or unity) as a goal may be conceived of as an ongoing process, which is continuously being adjusted and maintains diversity in many areas. As outlined in the previous chapter, the diversities of the EU have changed and awareness of them has also evolved. The degree of diversity may even vary among the constituent elements.

Only in 2014 did the European Council note that "the concept of ever closer union allows for different paths of integration for different countries, allowing those that want to deepen integration to move ahead, while respecting the wish of those who do not want to deepen any further."[1] Although the idea of diversity as a characteristic of the Union was rightly

[1] See European Council of 26/27 June 2014, Conclusions, No 27, Doc. EUCO 79/14 and Decision of the Heads of State or Government, meeting within the European Council, concerning a new settlement for the United Kingdom within the European Union of 18/19 February 2016, OJ C 69 I/2016, 1.



F. Bieber, R. Bieber, *Negotiating Unity and Diversity in the European Union*, Palgrave Studies in European Union Politics,
https://doi.org/10.1007/978-3-030-55016-5_4

stressed, such an interpretation hardly embraces the initial meaning of the notion of 'ever closer union.' It also adds an element that—at least at the beginning of the process of integration—was not intended, a *permanent* vertical division among Member States. The statement must be understood as a (misconceived) answer to a request by David Cameron, the Prime Minister of the United Kingdom at the time: "I want to end Britain's obligation to work towards an 'ever closer union' as set out in the Treaty… I want to do this in a formal, legally-binding and irreversible way" (Cameron/*The Telegraph* 2014, March 15; Cameron 2015, November 10). Here, diversity meant the diversity in the depth and forms of integration, rather than the diversity among its citizens and Member States, irrespective of the overall agreed level of integration. Furthermore, the statement of the European Council also focuses narrowly on diversity among the Member States and not on other types of diversity.

In 1985, Bieber, Jacqué, and Weiler offered an academic definition of union in the context of European integration:

> The term 'union' … clearly covers a multitude of structures and modalities changing over time and cannot thus … partake of a single authentic meaning. Moreover, once we direct our mind to the dualism of 'ever closer' two other basic notions come to the fore.
>
> First, if a process is to go on for 'ever' there is an implicit affirmation of a 'never': the Union is never to be consummate, final, achieved. This is not a simple semantic exegetic interpretation. It is a reflection of a basic burden and virtue of the European construct which is … rooted in a balance—not a substitution—between nation State and supranational structure: this balance is, and will remain, inherently difficult and often unstable. But that is the price for a polity the virtue of which is its truly innovative character and ability not to fall into the classical patterns of international organization or statehood.
>
> Secondly, the 'ever closer' union phraseology suggests a strong dynamic element—a process on the move. We may compare the European polity to a bicycle: essentially unstable except when in motion. The maintenance of momentum becomes thus a major concern for the European policy-maker. This characterization of Europe is clearly Sisyphean. The union will forever remain a target for which one must toil. But with many great ideals the search is as important as the ultimate goal. (Bieber et al. 1985, p. 8).

Regardless of the specific situation in a given polity, unity and diversity are not two mutually exclusive notions. Subject to the criteria chosen, any composed entity or social group may appear as—or may be conceived of as—united from one perspective and diverse from another. A discussion of unity in the European Union therefore has to identify elements of unity and elements of diversity, as well as their intrinsic driving forces. Finally, the element of time suggests that the understanding of what constitutes the two and their relationship changes. Therefore in this chapter we will explore the features of unity and diversity that the Union aims to protect, before examining the forms and procedures that render the protection operational in the subsequent chapter.

## 4.1 What Unites the Union?

### *Features of Unity*

The unity of and within the European Union is both a legal construct and a social reality linked in an ongoing evolutionary process. European unity crystallizes in a process that is grounded in and stimulated by a variety of driving forces, their intensity and relative weight being subject to change over time. Of those variables, the four most significant strands are:

- explicitly stated *promises;*
- a set of *rules* agreed upon by the participating states, giving those promises a quality beyond political rhetoric;
- *institutions* designed to render the promise real; and
- a *time factor*—its *existence* as an organization for nearly 70 years.

Unity does not require the existence of a single social group, a 'demos' or 'people.' It is perfectly conceivable—and confirmed by multiple historical and contemporary examples—to establish a union among peoples who retain separate identities, as discussed in Chap. 2. Consequently, 'homogeneity' among the peoples and states in question or their political systems is neither a precondition nor an aim of unity within the European Union.[2]

The core of an 'ever closer union' consists of a *promise* made to the peoples of Europe. This promise is, however, by definition incomplete and contradictory. It was initially made in the preamble to the *European Coal*

[2] For an opposite view see Schorkopf and Hilf (2018). The notion of 'demos' is also used to embrace all peoples of the Union. For example, the opinion of Advocate General Sharpston C – 715/17 (Commission/Poland), ECLI:EU:C:2019:917, paragraph 253.

*and Steel Community* (ECSC) Treaty in the aftermath of World War II. It offered a guarantee for the stability of the European social and economic conditions initially by way of the protection of universal values and security (at a later stage fundamental rights and safety were added) and the identification of a "general interest," conceived of as being separable from the interests of the individual states (see *TEU*, 2007, art. 17).[3] The promise was spelled out quite clearly: "to substitute for age-old rivalries the merging of their essential interests," to form "the basis for a broader and deeper community among peoples," to "create real solidarity," to "raise the standard of living and further the works of peace," and to establish "institutions which will give direction to a destiny henceforward shared" (*Treaty establishing the European Coal and Steel Community*, 1951). Although the ECSC Treaty expired in 2002, the subsequent treaties have maintained this ambitious foundation[4] of the integration process and have given it a more detailed shape. Thus, the EU Treaty of 2007 promised, among others, a common citizenship, prohibition of discrimination on grounds of nationality, an area of freedom, security, and justice without frontiers, economic and social progress, an internal market, and solidarity between the peoples of the Union (*TEU*, 2007, preamble, art. 3; *TFEU*, 2007, art. 18).

This 'set of rules' comprises international treaties that have been amended and consolidated by the 2007 Treaty of Lisbon and subsequent treaties of accession. It first took shape in the ECSC Treaty of 1951. These treaties aim to create an organization "on which the Member States have conferred competences to attain objectives they have in common" (*TEU*, 2007, art. 1). The rules were intended to unfold into a full legal system, and the rights and duties defined therein are to apply in an equal manner throughout the Union. "Equality of Member States before the Treaties" (*TEU*, 2007, art. 4[2]) is to be respected by the Union. Equality is a particularly important feature of unity in an organization with 27 Member States, the population of which varies between a few hundred thousand and over 80 million. The uniting quality of this set of rules is confirmed by the manner in which it can be changed. Under normal circumstances any amendment requires ratification prior to its entry into force by *all* Member States. The same is true of any decision on applications for membership. Only by joint action can the foundations of the Union be altered. At least

[3] "The Commission shall promote the general interest of the Union."

[4] On the "political messianism" of the European integration project, see Weiler (2011).

in legal terms, no single state or group of states can alter the foundations of the Union against the wishes of others. It is therefore misleading to describe the role of the individual states as "masters of the treaties."[5] Instead, the Member States are jointly "masters of the treaties." This does not, however, exclude situations in which one or several governments exert political or economic pressure on other governments or offer 'deals' in order to obtain changes in the structure common to all. In fact, the only action that a single Member State can take on its own entirely is that of leaving the European Union. However, even then, the departure requires a complex agreement that might not be required—as advocates of a 'hard Brexit' have argued—but prevents a potentially damaging rupture of the intricate network of links that have emerged among Member States and their citizens.

The Union has a unique, complex, and autonomous institutional structure. From the inception of the "High Authority,"[6] the institutional system was never intended to serve merely as the secretariat of an intergovernmental organization. So far it has been entrusted with the exclusive and central role of achieving the aims set out in the founding treaties (see *TEU,* 2007, art. 13[1]).[7] The first founding Treaty, the ECSC Treaty, was intended to lay down the foundations "for institutions which will give direction to a destiny henceforward shared." The interpretation of the common rules is entrusted in the last instance to the European Court of Justice (*TEU*, 2007, art. 19[1]). Thus common institutions represent a foundation for and guarantee of unity.

As with any human construct, the existence and full operation of an organization over time is marked by failure and success. The organization adopts rules and establishes precedents, and thus creates a new reality for its members, states, individuals, civil society, and sub-state entities, eventually forming a common experience, a common heritage, and a foundation for unity.

[5] German Constitutional Court decision of 30 June 2009, No 123, 267 (Lisbon Treaty), Recital 334.

[6] Proposed for the first time by the then French foreign minister Robert Schuman in his historic declaration of 9 May 1950.

[7] "The Union shall have an institutional framework which shall aim to promote its values, advance its objectives, serve its interests, those of its citizens and those of the Member States, and ensure the consistency, effectiveness and continuity of its policies and actions."

## *Limits to Unity*

In a composite organization, limits to unity may result from specific features (constitutional or otherwise) of the composing units, as well as from the conditions of existence and operation of the common entity. All European states are grounded on written and unwritten rules and practices which aim at preserving their continued existence, and as a result establish barriers against unity on a level above the state if this unity implies a loss of statehood. A transfer of traditional state functions to a new entity in all states is authorized under strict conditions only. Limits may be spelled out in the form of unalterable core provisions of national constitutions, or may result from political traditions (e.g. neutrality) or from specific economic or social factors. Contrary to many federations, those national limits are not clearly made subject to conformity with the constitutional rules of the common entity. Hence, their implementation requires a subtle balance with the requirements for the existence of the common entity.

The European Union as such is built on the prerequisite of continued statehood of its members. It is committed to respecting the inherent limits to the abrogation of statehood of its Member States insofar as those factors represent "national identities, inherent in their fundamental structures, political and constitutional" (*TEU*, 2007, art. 4[2]). In a more detailed manner, further limits to unity have been written into the founding acts of the European Union and have thus been given a particular weight, since the European Union was created by legal rules (international treaties) and its operation is grounded in the rule of law. The European Court of Justice can sanction violations of the provisions limiting its scope or intensity of action (*TFEU*, 2007, art. 263). The present wording of the EU treaties, resulting from the Treaty of Lisbon of 2007, offers an interesting example of the multiple techniques used to establish constitutional, political, economic, and social limits to (further) unity.

The most important constitutional limit is the "principal of conferral" (*TEU*, 2007, art. 5[1–2]), which authorizes an action of the Union only within the limits of the competences conferred upon it in the treaties. Moreover, the exercise of its competences is bound to respect the principles of subsidiarity and proportionality (*TEU*, 2007, art. 5[3–4]).

Other constitutional limits on the level of the Union apply to certain Member States only. They provide for temporary or permanent derogations from the applicability of specific treaty provisions or of common legislation. Examples are the various protocols annexed to the EU Treaty and the TFEU with derogations for the United Kingdom, Denmark, Ireland, and Poland, and the limits resulting from the condition to fulfill objective criteria before unity with respect to the common currency can be achieved.[8]

Other categories of limits—or at least obstacles—to unity can be found on the social level. Examples are problems of inter-group communication (e.g. different languages or different cultural traditions), perception of history, geographical situation (e.g. maritime access), and availability of natural resources. Differences in relations with third countries, notably with former colonies, may also have a considerable impact on establishing unity (e.g. on the formation of a common foreign defense and security policy, and on the common aid and development policy).

None of the aforementioned factors represent an absolute obstacle. They can change over time or their impact can be reduced. In order to bring about results, however, any striving for unity must take them into account. The Union aims at gradually reducing the obstacles that are inherently mutable while respecting the absolute limits resulting from the wording of the treaties. To this end, the most important instruments are its institutional setting, which gives voice to as many as possible actors concerned, and the decision-making process, which aims to find unity by way of compromise.[9]

## 4.2 Diversity as a Founding Principle of the European Union

### *Features of Diversity*

Diversity does not conflict with the concept of the Union. It can instead be understood as one of its intrinsic features. The most important inherent diversity of the Union consists of its number of Member States, today 27, and potentially more in years to come.

This diversity is not only grounded in the formal quality of states as legal entities, but has deeper roots in the social, cultural, and economic characteristics of the societies in question, as discussed in detail in the previous chapter. There is no historical precedent for a Union as a social and

[8] For example, *TFEU* (2007), art. 140 on the adoption of the euro.

[9] See Chap. 5.

political entity established in a free and democratic process by independent states. Prior to its founding phase in the second half of the twentieth century, any collective memory was focused on the constituent units, the states, their organization, their political substructures (i.e. political parties), and their frequently conflicting relations.

Among many other elements, diversity encompasses different perceptions of the role of the state, the democratic process, and the rule of law. For an organization like the Union, whose very existence is based on rules, their implementation, and their observance, such diversity represents a major and continuing challenge and its *raison d'être*. This challenge is met by the entrenchment of diversity in the EU Treaty and by entrusting the Union to be the guardian of diversity.

According to Article 4 (2) TEU, the Union "shall respect" the "national identities" of the Member States. Such identities are understood as "fundamental structures, political and constitutional" and comprise the essential State functions, the territorial integrity of the State, the maintenance of law and order, and the safeguarding of national security.[10] Explicitly the EU Treaty stresses that "national security remains the sole responsibility of each Member State."

Respect for national identities does not, however, imply their petrification or their immunity from being weighed against a (higher) common interest.[11]

The concept of respect for diversity, and hence for national identity, transpires from many provisions in the founding treaties. These include, for example, the possibility of unilateral withdrawal from EU membership (*TEU*, 2007, art. 50); the limitation of EU competences (*TEU*, 2007, art. 4[1]); the guarantee of respect for Member States' identity (*TEU*, 2007, art. 4[2]); the composition of the EU institutions, most of which provide for a representation of each Member State or its citizens in each institution[12]; the principle of subsidiarity as a criterion for EU legislation (*TEU*, 2007, art. 5[3]); the many possibilities for maintaining the individual positions of Member States within the common decision-making process, either as the result of the requirement of unanimity (TFEU[13]) or because of specific mechanisms providing for the protection of fundamental

[10] For a definition of the notion of "national identities" in TEU (2007), art. 4[2], see Schill and Krenn 2018 (footnote 6), notes 14–38 to article 4 TEU.

[11] See Section 4.3.

[12] For details see Chap. 5.

[13] For example, *TFEU* (2007), art. 113, 352.

interests[14]; the clauses which authorize Member States to deviate from common rules for reasons of higher national interest which are listed in the TFEU[15]; the specific procedural rules protecting individual Member States' interests in matters of judicial cooperation (*TFEU*, 2007, art. 81[3], 82[3], 83[3]); the legislative instrument of the directive, which leaves transposition into national law to the Member States (*TFEU*, 2007, art. 288), and a presumption in favor of national competence for the implementation of EU law according to national rules (*TFEU*, 2007, art. 291[1]); and in certain areas a restriction of EU legislative powers to adopt minimum standards or minimum harmonization rules only, thus leaving discretion regarding the introduction of supplementing legislation with the Member States.[16]

Moreover, diversity is preserved by transitional clauses, applicable after accession, by permanent or temporary derogations from the application of treaty provisions,[17] and the various forms of special (closer) cooperation among a certain number of Member States (e.g. *TEU*, 2007, art. 20, art. 46, art. 82[2–3]). While in most cases of the said 'closer cooperation' the resulting rules fall under the law of the Union and therefore entail an element of unity, cooperation in accordance with Article 136 (3) TFEU (euro area) allows for the conclusion of agreements outside the scope of Union law and is therefore characterized by a greater potential for diversity.[18]

Overall, the EU in its legal system provides for considerable recognition of the diversity reflected by the Member States and allows for states to safeguard this identity, both individually and jointly, through additional cooperation. This recognition is, however, counter-balanced by the need to allow for unity.

### *Limits to Diversity*

Since most of the features of diversity within the European Union mentioned above are anchored in the EU treaties, the limitations to their protection also result from the treaties, as well as from their political, social,

[14] For example, *TEU* (2007), art. 31(1–2), 42(2); *TFEU* (2007), art. 82(3), 83(3), 87(3).

[15] For example, *TFEU* (2007), art. 36 (public morality, public security, protection of health, life, national treasures), 45 (3), 52, 65.

[16] For example, *TFEU* (2007), art. 153(2)(b) (minimum requirements in the field of social policy).

[17] For example, Protocol Nos 19, 20, 21 to the EU Treaty on judicial cooperation and on the application of the "Schengen rules" on border controls and so on.

[18] See ECJ, Case C-370/12 *Pringle*, ECLI:EU:C:2012:756.

and economic context. The most important limit enshrined in the treaties is the obligation of Member States to respect the fundamental rights, guaranteed in the Charter of Fundamental Rights of the European Union, when they are implementing Union law (*CFR*, 2000, art. 51[1]).[19] An example of a treaty-based limit to diversity is the prohibition of discrimination on grounds of nationality (*TFEU*, 2007, art. 18).

In general terms, restrictions on Member States' autonomy stem from the duty of sincere cooperation with the institutions of the Union and between each other ("principle of loyalty").[20] This duty implies, for example, prior consultation with the European Commission when the exercise of a national competence is likely to affect other Member States or the Union. That duty of genuine cooperation does not depend on whether the Union competence concerned is exclusive, or on any right of the Member States to autonomously adopt legislation or to enter into obligations toward non-member countries.[21]

Specifically, Member States have "to take any appropriate measure … to ensure fulfilment of the obligations arising out of the Treaties or resulting from the acts of the institutions of the Union" (*TEU*, 2007, art. 4[3]). Moreover, Member States are to "refrain from any measure which could jeopardize the attainment of the Union's objectives" (*TEU*, 2007, art. 4[3]). Unless explicitly authorized by the Treaty, a Member State may not, in order to refuse to implement EU law, invoke a "national interest."[22] This rule applies not only to the sphere of EU competences, but reaches beyond into the sphere of Member States' competences, whenever the proper functioning of the Union is at stake.[23]

Diversity is also restricted each time the Union makes use of its legislative powers or its powers to enter into international agreements. Here, Member States' competence to act in the area covered by the legislation or international agreement in question is pre-empted, either because the

[19] On the scope of implementation see ECJ, Case C-617/10 *Akerberg Fransson*, ECLI:EU:C:2013:105, paragraphs 18–29.

[20] See Klamert (2014).

[21] ECJ, Case C-266/03 *Commission* v *Luxembourg*, ECLI:EU:C:2005:341, paragraphs 58–66.

[22] ECJ, Case 39/72 *Commission* v *Italy*, ECLI:EU:C:1973:13, paragraph 20: "it cannot be accepted that a Member State should apply in an incomplete or selective manner provisions of a Community Regulation so as to render abortive certain aspects of Community legislation which it has opposed or which it considers contrary to its national interests."

[23] ECJ, Case 208/80 *Lord Bruce of Donington*, ECLI:EU:C:1981:194, paragraph 14.

Union acted on the basis of a "shared" competence (*TFEU*, 2007, art. 2[2]), or because of the effects of the supremacy of EU law.[24]

Limits to diversity may also stem from overarching political factors. Traditionally, national political parties prepare political decisions at the national level. The most important actors in the European Parliament are, however, political groups, which by definition have to be composed of representatives from several Member States.[25] This requirement has led to the formation of transnational political parties, which have received formal recognition by the EU Treaty (*TEU*, 2007, art. 10[4]).[26] National parties remain, for the time being, the most important actors within the European parties. This does not, however, preclude national political programs from being increasingly influenced by common platforms agreed upon by the European party in question. Conflicting programs of the same political orientation at national and European level would diminish their credibility. It is therefore likely that diversity between political parties with a similar orientation in the different Member States is structurally reduced (Sigalas and Pollak 2012). Solidarity, whether pragmatic or ideological, is strong within party families, as could be seen in the reluctance of the European People's Party to exclude the Hungarian member party FIDESZ over serious abuses of rule of law and anti-EU campaigns, and similarly in the position of the Party of European Socialists toward its member party in Romania (see Scheppele 2019, March 28).

## 4.3 Unity and Diversity as Constituent Features of the Union's Identity

### *Unity, Diversity, and Identity*

Discussing unity and diversity in the context of the European Union leads to a fundamental issue rather than just an interesting paradox: the very existence of the Union, its foundation, and its aim presuppose the continuing presence of both strands, the relationship of which is grounded in the continuing voluntary contribution of diverse actors to the common

[24] ECJ, Case 106/77 *Simmenthal II*, ECLI:EU:C:1978:49, paragraphs 17 and 18 and Opinion 2/2013, ECLI:EU:C:2014:2:54, paragraphs 157 and 166.

[25] See EP Rules of Procedure, Article 3.

[26] "Political parties at European level contribute to forming European political awareness and to expressing the will of citizens of the Union." See also *TFEU* (2007), art. 224.

project. In comparison to federations or international organizations, it is unique in the way it balances and acknowledges the two strands. In combination with other factors (e.g. history, culture, and evolution) the specific relationship between unity and diversity marks the Union's *identity*. This uniqueness is amplified further by a combination of several factors: first, its identity differs from that of any association (e.g. a golf club) by its scope and by the intensity of its task of exercising jurisdiction in a given territory and in a large range of policies; second, because the claim to jurisdiction reaches much further than any comparable claim based on a voluntary decision by those affected; and third, because this identity by definition is subject to a qualitative change by opening up accession to new members, who are only vaguely restricted.

Uniqueness has a price, especially when it is not rooted in a subjective collective (positive) memory. In order to fulfill its tasks and to endure, it needs a substantially higher legitimacy than conventional polities, which may result from the credibility of their promises, from their output, or from input legitimacy based on the participation of those concerned in the decision-making process. Such an identity is more fragile and more easily exposed to questioning of its *raison d'être*.

The identity of any social group or individual results from its conception and self-perception and from its perception by others. Conception and perception are subject to change, owing in particular to their interactive effects.

Group identity especially is not a static phenomenon. It changes according to time, substance, and membership. Moreover, the identity of the European Union does not exist in isolation but is influenced by communication with other identities within and outside its territory. However, the strongest potential for change—which may even lead to the loss of its specific identity—results from the fact that unity and diversity are antagonistic concepts that constantly pull the polity in opposing directions, either toward a centralized polity (which implies loss of diversity) or toward fragmentation, which would mean abandoning unity. If, for example, European citizens perceive the Union over a long period of time predominantly as a 'Brussels bureaucracy' to which they do not feel any allegiance, the conceived identity risks losing its significance.

Before we turn to a discussion of the relationship between national and European identities, we briefly present three different forms of European identity (Checkel and Katzenstein 2009; Jones 2012).

### *Different Forms of Identity of the European Union*

The identity of a group has four different facets. It can be objective (a); it can be self-proclaimed (b); it can be the identity perceived by others (c); and it can be situational, depending on the context where it is evoked or held (d). All four may differ from each other and vary over time. The less these facets correspond to each other, the weaker their unifying effect.

*Objective Identity*

The objective identity of the Union comprises elements of unity and diversity that either appear separate or stem from a single compact. An example of the latter consists in the founding Treaties and the Charter of Fundamental Rights. Since the common currency has not been introduced in all Member States, it also encapsulates simultaneously unity and diversity. The same is true of European citizenship because of its mandatory connection to national citizenship.[27]

The most visible elements of unity consist of the Union's material appearance: its representatives, manifestations in the public and the media, buildings, symbols,[28] and events of symbolic meaning (e.g. European capital of culture [European Parliament and Council-Decision 445/2014, 2014). Other tangible elements of unity are the political rights of European citizens. Elements of identity that are only indirectly visible comprise the suppression of internal borders and the prohibition of discrimination on grounds of nationality.

Elements of diversity (and of unity) as parts of the Union's identity are present in the institutions and procedures of its operation.[29] Diversity is served by substantive provisions of the founding treaties, which are mentioned above in Section 2 a).

*The Self-Proclaimed Identity of the Union*

The self-declared identity of the European Union is enshrined in the Preambles to the EU Treaty and Charter of Fundamental Rights and Articles 2 and 3 of the EU Treaty. In those provisions, the aims and foundations of the Union are circumscribed.[30] As early as 1973 the heads of

[27] See Chap. 7.
[28] See Chap. 6.
[29] See Chap. 5.
[30] See Section B.1a).

state and government of the then nine Member States adopted a solemn declaration "On the European Identity," which stated

> The Nine wish to ensure that the cherished values of their legal, political and moral order are respected, and to preserve the rich variety of their national cultures. Sharing as they do the same attitudes to life, based on a determination to build a society which measures up to the needs of the individual, they are determined to defend the principles of representative democracy, of the rule of law, of social justice—which is the ultimate goal of economic progress—and of respect for human rights.
>
> All of these are fundamental elements of the European Identity. (*EC Bulletin* 12, 1973, p. 131).

The elements mentioned in both this declaration and Articles 2 and 3 TEU represent the core of what we have described as "factors of unity."[31] The formal acknowledgement of the Union's identity was, however, made only reluctantly. This becomes obvious when comparing the status of "European identity" and "national identity" in the TEU. Following the Treaty of Maastricht (preamble, recital 9) the EU Treaty of 2007 mentions both a "European identity" (to be reinforced) and "national identities" of the Member States (to be respected). However, the affirmation of the two identities lacks an equal legal quality. While the former is mentioned in the preamble and refers to the common foreign and security policy only, the latter has been worded as a general obligation to be respected by the Union under the control of the ECJ.

Since the values listed in Article 2 TEU are common to the EU and its Member States and the elements of national identity which the Treaty requires the Union to respect (fundamental political and constitutional structures) are qualities of the Union as well, a stronger affirmation of the Union's identity would appear appropriate, although the Union cannot of course be considered to be a nation or a state. Such an affirmation would facilitate a structured co-existence of both identities.[32]

These self-proclaimed elements of identity result from values and principles common to the Member States, and accordingly, national and European identities condition each other. National identity is, however,

[31] Section B.1.a).

[32] On the confrontation of national and European identity see the Opinion of Advocate General *Cruz Villalón*, ECJ Case C-62/14 *Gauweiler and Others*, ECLI:EU:C:2015:7, paragraphs 58–61.

subject to its compatibility with the identity of the Union insofar as the Union can impose a sanction for breaches by a Member State of the values marking the Union's identity (Article 7 TEU).

Finally, on the level of individual EU citizens, a significant number identify either primarily or also as Europeans, giving the self-identification a dimension transcending the Union and its institutions. Similarly, Member States identify themselves with varying degrees of strength and symbolic investment as members.

*Identity Perceived from the Outside*

By its very existence, any polity creates an image set against the backdrop of its environment. Considerable differences may exist between this image, reality, and the self-perception of the polity. Both the image held by external actors and the differences between how the various images interact may become factors that influence political decisions.

The case of the European Union is even more complex, for two reasons. First, its citizens perceive the Union as an actor existing outside their traditional understanding of belonging and as a polity of immediate concern to them. The Union is not really perceived as 'us.' Second, the governments of the Member States hardly ever assume responsibility for their activities as central actors in the Union system. They tend to present the Union as an organization that acts outside their sphere of responsibility ('Brussels bureaucracy'). According to the prevailing national narrative, it is 'Brussels' that either imposes rules described as unnecessary (or even unjustified) or does not intervene in situations—usually in other Member States—that are regarded as unfair or illegal. The doublespeak of national governments is reflected clearly in the national media. Neither political parties at European level nor the few outlets of transnational media present the Union's reality from a common perspective—or when they do so they are directed at a narrow audience.

This introduces an unintended element of substantive diversity (although this behavior on the part of the national political class is common to nearly all Member States), obscuring and therefore threatening the genuine value of the careful constitutional balance of diversity and unity.

*Situational Identity*
If a relation between an individual and his or her environment is defined as (situational) identity, we note two features concerning individuals living in the European Union.

First, nationality continues to be a prevailing marker of political identity. Yet, it co-exists with a simultaneous albeit weaker identity, which can be labeled 'European.' The former clearly refers to a specific state of which an individual is a citizen. The latter is less clearly defined. It is true that EU citizenship provides a formal attachment comparable to national citizenship. Any perceived 'European' identity is, however, more characterized by its transnational quality than by its bond with a given political entity like the European Union. Moreover, different from most national citizenships, the legal construct of "European citizenship"[33] by definition acknowledges the possibility of the simultaneous holding of several identities. It thus represents an intrinsic quality of its own.

Hence, in the European Union we can observe multiple situational identities, both horizontal among the different states and vertical between the states and the Union.

In a similar manner, group identities within (e.g. French or Italian) are substantially stronger than the perceived 'European' identity.

## 4.4 Plurality of Identities

The simultaneous presence of several identities, of unity, and of diversity in the same actors within the European Union raises questions concerning the implications of this co-existence for the identities of individuals and their organized groups. Four of these questions will briefly be addressed here.

- Can identity and plurality durably co-exist within one single political system?
- Does such a system possess a single identity, several identities, or both?
- What conditions have to be fulfilled for preserving multiple identities?
- What are the implications of the answers to the previous questions for the European Union, its citizens, and the EU Member States?

[33] See Chap. 7 on citizenship

The answer to the *first question* depends on whether or not identity can be conceived of as 'shared' or 'multiple,' or whether it implies exclusivity by definition. In a political context, any identity is a social construct.[34] As such, it is by definition subject to creation, evolution, change, and disappearance, and it can never be all-encompassing. Human beings have individual identities and multiple allegiances, which may bring about additional and overlapping group identities of various kinds (e.g. gender-related, political, cultural, or religious). European history is marked by the relativity of group identities that result from the interaction on the same continent between a multitude of different cultures and other identities and overarching ideas, values, and structures. Early examples are the dualism between church and empire, between private and public law, and between local autonomy and territorial government, some of which we discussed in Chap. 2. If, as we argue, individual and group identities always comprise a multiplicity of allegiances, identity by definition does not imply, let alone require, exclusivity (see Jones 2012; Sen 2006, pp. 18ff.). Thus, a plurality of identities can very well exist within the same territory. Federations and other complex states offer practical examples of such co-existence. Whereas nation-states have at times sought to claim exclusivity over identity and demand from their citizens stronger identification with the nation than with other group identities—whether they are at a lower, higher, or transnational level—such claims always rest uneasily with social reality and require enforcement.

Once we accept the possibility of multiple identities within a given frame or society, the answer to the *second question* concerning the description of a system which comprises several identities and claims an identity for itself becomes obvious: it is perfectly possible to conceive of a political system that has an identity of its own while at the same time comprising a multitude of other identities. The manner in which these identities co-exist depends on the constitutional construct in question. The less hierarchically it is organized, the more it brings about the ideals of democracy, the possibility of self-determination, and the political representation of these different identities.

On the *third question* (about necessary conditions): in order to offer a certain stability of social conditions, a system which consists of multiple

[34] The constructed nature of the EU identity is quite apparent in the introduction of the Declaration on the European identity (see Section 2.b): "They have decided to *define* the European Identity with the dynamic nature of the Community in mind" (authors' emphasis).

identities requires first and foremost the mutual acceptance of and respect for all identities involved. To this end, it is indispensable to have a binding framework that enables each identity to enjoy maximum autonomy and self-confirmation and to have a voice in every structure of which it is a part. In an ideal situation, this binding framework is not self-contained but provides simultaneously for change and stability by establishing institutions and procedures that promote common solutions based on broad public support and allow for conflict resolution mechanisms that are regarded as legitimate. Principles such as "loyal cooperation" (*TEU*, 2007, art. 4[3]) and their observance are pivotal for the continued existence of such a system. In the case of the EU, it is the task of the ECJ to protect the respect of national identity against interference from the institutions of the European Union and vice versa.[35]

On the *fourth question*, concerning the consequences of unity and diversity for the identity of the European Union, its citizens, and its Member States, the most important and at the same time obvious answer consists of the acknowledgement that all these identities can perfectly well continue to exist without presenting a threat to each other. In fact, the Union was founded on the premise that overarching identity is necessary for the preservation and full exercise of the constituent identities. The Union does not represent an identity that simply adds to the previously existing ones. Its existence alters, by definition, the quality of the participating identities, since the acts of accession to the Union replace (at least in certain areas) the power previously exercised autonomously with a common system of governance: national sovereignty thus becomes shared sovereignty. This does not, however, exclude conflicts between the various identities.

The traditional technique for reconciling antagonistic concepts consists of compromise based on elements of both, or by the establishment of a hierarchy between the two. With regard to European unity and diversity, a different answer that optimizes unity and diversity seems possible if unity and diversity are not conceptualized as isolated phenomena. The binary approach of 'us' versus 'them' would have to give way to the acceptance of diversity as the unifying element, as the common value, and as part of the European identity. Not only individuals but also organizations can in

[35] See ECJ Case C-208/09 (Sayn Wittgenstein), ECLI:EU:C:2010:806; Loic Azoulai (2013); Bogdany and Schill (2011).

fact develop a genuine identity by assembling different identities, without rendering them exclusive or absorbing them.

The capacity for rational and peaceful settlement by institutions and procedures—based on democratic choices that are accepted by the people, even when taken by a majority composed of other peoples of the Union—marks a decisive element of the Union's identity.

The Union's genetic code embraces the protection of the identities of its citizens, of its Member States, and of peoples within the scope of the application of its law.

If the Union is to fulfill its tasks while respecting its inherent diversity, the capacity "to decide in case of conflict, on the relative importance of the different identities for the particular decision in question" matters particularly (Sen 2006, p. 29). Thus, it is less important to be able to rely on coercion or on a written compact that lays down an exact demarcation of competences. Instead, the key tool is a process whereby the various national actors agree to apply the law of the Union as a voluntary act. Joseph Weiler forcefully described this particular quality of the European Union as "constitutional tolerance" (Weiler 2001). However, tolerance remains a guideline for behavior and does not by itself answer questions about the applicable rule where there are several possibilities. Therefore, accommodating several identities within one polity still implies their structured coordination in a constitutional arrangement. That is where federalism comes into focus.

## 4.5 Federation or Confederation: or Something New?

From its very beginning, the process of European integration was influenced by two preconceived concepts in which complex polities can be organized—federation and confederation. Both stem from earlier experiences of governing diverse polities. The problem with both was—and still is—threefold. First, the identification of statehood and sovereignty and the claim that sovereignty is indivisible. This concept implies categorizing all forms of governance under the notion of the (sovereign) state, while considering all other forms of governance to be "non-states" (Oeter 2011). Hence a federation has to be a state, while a group of states that have not merged into a new state necessarily remain a group of states, described as an international organization or confederation. This one-dimensional analysis influenced, for example, the German Constitutional Court's decision on the Maastricht Treaty.[36] The obvious weak point of this line of argument is the incapacity to imagine, let alone acknowledge, the existence of other forms of political organization which match neither of the two accepted alternatives and which, for example, would provide for the exercise of parts of or all (sovereign) power jointly or in a shared manner (Moravcsik 2001; Nicolaidis 2001). A second problem with the terms 'federal' and 'confederal' consists of their multitude of definitions, usually based on a mix of abstraction from specific constitutions and purely theoretical considerations. One illustration is the official name of Switzerland ('Swiss Confederation'), although the country is considered (and considers itself) to be a federal state. The two types are merely ideal types on a continuum of political systems of varying degrees of decentralization. Yet in practice, each polity that is structured by either has a set of specific features that place it along this continuum. Finally, the notions are frequently used to serve political ends and are distorted for that purpose. This binary approach to the organization of shared power was chosen once in an official text of European integration. Article 38 of the (never ratified) Treaty establishing the European Defence Community of 1952 provided for a choice between the two concepts for the future organization of Europe (*Treaty Constituting the European Defence Community*, 1952, art. 38).[37]

In the preparatory phase of the Treaty of Maastricht on 18 June 1991, the government of Luxembourg presented a draft treaty which, in its introductory provisions, provided for an article "A" which read: "This Treaty marks a new stage in a process leading gradually to a Union with a *federal goal*" (Agence Europe 1991; Laursen 2011, p. 14). This proposal was not accepted, nor have the labels 'federal' and 'confederal' been officially attached to any of the existing Treaties or any other legal text within the European Union.

In light of the very different perceptions of these notions in the Member States, this was wise self-restraint. Moreover, from its beginning until the present, any legal formula concerning European integration has sought to

[36] For a detailed critique see Weiler (1995), p. 651.

[37] "...the Assembly shall study: (a) ..., (b)..., (c).... The definitive organization which will take the place of the present transitional organization should be conceived as to be capable of constituting one of the elements of an *ultimate Federal or confederal structure*, based upon the principle of the separation of powers and including, particularly, a bicameral representative system" (authors' italics).

avoid using politico-judicial terms derived from notions that have a distinct meaning in any given national constitutional system.

Yet, in its most general definition, the term ‘federal’ encapsulates the very idea of a permanent search for a balanced combination of unity and diversity within a given polity: “federalism is a political and legal philosophy which adapts itself to all political contexts… wherever and whenever two basic prerequisites are fulfilled: the search for unity, combined with genuine respect for the autonomy and legitimate interests of the participant entities” (Pescatore 1982).

The most important conclusion on federalism concerns its limits: it is not the only blueprint for the organization of a complex polity. It is, however, a concept of the acknowledgement of multiple allegiances and multiple identities for the purpose of governance in common. As such, it is a powerful source of legitimacy for any level in the exercise of power. A multitude of levels of governance implies a permanent search for the most appropriate level of decision and requires permanent reconciling of various individual and common interests. Such a construct is simultaneously fragile (it cannot offer the promise of permanent stability) and strong (it can acquire a broader source of legitimacy and can react more easily to new internal or external challenges), as long as its fundamental premise is accepted: the refusal of any petrification of a political system as a system of governance for the sake of a continuing need and willingness to “search for the appropriate scale of (the) collective endeavour” (Nicolaidis 2001, p. 444).

The closest constitutional articulation of this concept that can be found in the EU Treaty is the principle of “sincere cooperation” between the Union and the Member States, and among the Member States (*TEU*, 2007, art. 4[3]). It is aimed at achieving common goals while respecting the plurality of actors, their interests, and their identity. This concept encapsulates both an acceptance (if need be) of a hierarchy, as between the legal orders and recourse, and mutually agreed solutions wherever possible. In other words, hierarchy in the Union’s legal order is not the rule but the exception. This view comes close to Maduros’ definition of “constitutional pluralism” (Maduro 2012). It is, however, different from that of other proponents of this concept who eliminate hierarchy within the constitutional order of the Union and its Member States altogether.[38] Hierarchy is, however, intrinsic to the law of the Union insofar as breaches

[38] For a presentation of the various concepts see Jaklic (2014).

of the hierarchy by individuals and Member States are measured against the yardstick of the common legal order, and sanctions can be imposed. The subtlety of the system resides in the fact that sanctions against Member States cannot be implemented without the consent of the Member State in question: compliance is expected as part of the principle of sincere cooperation, which implies assistance by the Union to foster the ability of a State to comply. The real burden in that respect has to be borne by the governments of the Member States, which have to explain to their citizens the reasons for compliance. To date, Member States often do not comply with this duty of internal communication. Hence, 'sincere cooperation' requires continuing efforts to strive for unity by way of compromise among the representatives of diversity.

## References


Agence Europe. (1991), Europe Documents No 1722, July 5.

Azoulai, L. (2013). The European Court of Justice and the Duty to Respect Sensitive National Interests. In B. de Witte, E. Muir, & M. Dawson (Eds.), *Judicial Activism of the European Court of Justice* (pp. 167–187). Cheltenham: Edward Elgar.

Bieber, R., Jacqué, J. P., & Weiler, J. H. H. (1985). Introduction. In R. Bieber, J. P. Jacqué, & J. H. H. Weiler (Eds.), *An Ever Closer Union* (pp. 7–14). Luxembourg: Office for Official Publications of the European Communities.

Bogdandy, A. v., & Schill, S. (2011). Overcoming Absolute Primacy: Respect for National Identity Under the Lisbon Treaty. *Common Market Law Review, 48*(5), 1417–1453.

Cameron, D. (2014). David Cameron: The EU Is Not Working and We Will Change It. *The Telegraph*, March 15. https://www.telegraph.co.uk/news/newstopics/eureferendum/10700644/David-Cameron-the-EU-is-not-working-and-we-will-change-it.html. Accessed 23 Apr 2020.

Cameron, D. (2015). *Letter to the European Council*, November 10. https://www.gov.uk/government/uploads/system/uploads/attachment_data/file/475679/Donald_Tusk_letter.pdf. Accessed 26 Mar 2020.

Checkel, J. T., & Katzenstein, P. J. (Eds.). (2009). *European Identity*. Cambridge: CUP.

Jaklic, K. (2014). *Constitutional Pluralism in the EU*. Oxford: OUP.

Jones, E. (2012). Identity and Solidarity. In E. Jones, A. Menon, & S. Weatherill (Eds.), *The Oxford Handbook of the European Union* (pp. 690–702). Oxford: OUP.

Klamert, M. (2014). *The principle of loyalty in EU law*. Oxford: OUP.

Laursen, F. (2011). *The EU and Federalism*. London: Ashgate.

Maduro, M. P. (2012). Three Claims of Constitutional Pluralism. In M. Avbelj & J. Komárek (Eds.), *Constitutional Pluralism in the European Union and Beyond* (pp. 67–84). Oxford: OUP.

Moravcsik, A. (2001). European Federalism. In K. Nicolaidis & R. Howse (Eds.), *The Federal Vision* (pp. 161–187). Oxford: OUP.

Nicolaidis, K. (2001). Conclusion: The Federal Vision Beyond the Federal State. In K. Nicolaidis & R. Howse (Eds.), *The Federal Vision* (pp. 439–481). Oxford: OUP.

Oeter, S. (2011). Federalism and Democracy. In A. v. Bogdandy & J. Bast (Eds.), *Principles of European Constitutional Law* (pp. 51–81). Oxford/Munich: Hart/C.H. Beck.

Pescatore, P. (1982). Foreword. In T. Sandalow, & E. Stein (Eds), *Courts and Free Markets* Vol. I (pp. IX–X). Oxford: OUP.

Scheppele, K. L. (2019). Europe's Largest Party Suspends Its Resident Autocrat – for Now. *Foreign Affairs*, March 2. https://www.foreignaffairs.com/articles/hungary/2019-03-28/europes-largest-party-suspends-its-resident-autocrat-now. Accessed 26 Mar 2020.

Schill, C., & Krenn, S. (2018). Artikel 4 EUV – Prinzipien der föderativen Grundstruktur. In E. Grabitz, M. Hilf, & M. Nettesheim (Eds.), *Das Recht der Europäischen Union* (Kommentar, Vol. I). München: C.H. Beck.

Schorkopf, F., & Hilf, M. (2018). Art. 2 EUV – Grundlegende Werte. In E. Grabitz, M. Hilf, & M. Nettesheim (Eds.), *Das Recht der Europäischen Union* (Kommentar, Vol. I). München: C.H. Beck.

Sen, A. (2006). *Identity and Violence*. London: Penguin.

Sigalas, E., & Pollak, J. (2012). Political Parties at the European Level: Do They Satisfy the Condition of Programmatic Convergence? In S. Kröger & D. Friedrich (Eds.), *The Challenge of Democratic Representation in the European Union* (pp. 23–40). London: Palgrave Macmillan.

Weiler, J. H. H. (1995). The State "über alles": Demos, telos and the German Maastricht decision. In O. Due et al. (Eds.), *Festschrift für Ulrich Everling* (Vol. I). Baden-Baden: Nomos.

Weiler, J. H. H. (2001). Federalism Without Constitutionalism: Europe's *Sonderweg*. In K. Nicolaidis & R. Howse (Eds.), *The Federal Vision* (pp. 54–70). Oxford: OUP.

Weiler, J. H. H. (2011). The Political and Legal Culture of European Integration: An Exploratory Essay. *International Journal of Constitutional Law, 9*, 678–694.

CHAPTER 5

# Unity and Diversity Through the EU Institutions and Procedures

Any polity based on democratic governance, and hence on the self-determination of the individual, oscillates between freedom and structure, both of which represent unity and diversity. Constitutions provide the tools of articulating and channeling both, thus ensuring compromises for a given period of time. The compromises reached in the institutional setting of the European Union offer a singular example of the possibilities and limitations of such compromise in a multinational political system.

The institutional and procedural design for framing unity and diversity raises complex questions, which include the capacity to voice common interests and achieve common goals, the appropriate articulation of identities, the balancing of equality with the protection of minorities, and the relationship between the institutions of the same polity and with institutions representing sub-entities.

Institutions and procedures are prerequisites for establishing a balance between unity and diversity. Much of the literature on multinational states in recent decades has focused on institutions. One of the key questions of the debate has been the balance between the cohesive aspects of the institutions—what we could call the institutional mechanism of unity—and those that ensure representation and inclusion of the identity groups, that is, diversity. Proponents of consociationalism have argued that institutions need to provide mechanisms not just to represent different groups through various guarantees of proportional representation (or even



F. Bieber, R. Bieber, *Negotiating Unity and Diversity in the European Union*, Palgrave Studies in European Union Politics,
https://doi.org/10.1007/978-3-030-55016-5_5

over-representation), but also to ensure not being outvoted, including veto rights.[1] Critics have found that these institutions too often reinforce identities and their antagonistic relationship. Thus, arguing for additional instruments that promote representation and decision-making crosses the salient identity divides (Bogaards 2019). There is no perfect institutional mix; instead, each polity has adopted a (often imperfect) set of institutions and procedures based on the nature of the divide, the institutional legacy, and the varying opportunities to deliberately design institutions.

Due to its dynamic quality, the balance does not just result from a given constitutional arrangement of institutions and procedures. It is achieved in the political process—the interplay of the various actors at a given moment—and thus will change over time. It is therefore misleading, if not blatantly wrong, for the ECJ to systematically (but without any definition) derive legal consequences from a supposedly existing "principle of institutional balance, characteristic of the institutional structure of the European Union."[2] Instead, the EU is profoundly a "process-oriented polity" that derives its balance from continuous processes of recalibration.

When the basic institutional structure of the European Union was conceived in 1950, it did not reflect a coherent theoretical concept of managing diversity and unity. The founders were not interested in building institutions in order to enhance the identity of the Union or to articulate diversity. Their primary concern was—and remains—the achievement of material aims. This primary intention is confirmed by the declaration in the preamble of the TEU of 2007: "Desiring to enhance further the democratic and efficient functioning of the institutions so as to enable them better to carry out, within a single institutional framework, the tasks entrusted to them" (*Treaty on the European Union* [TEU], 2007, preamble, ind. 7). Hence the achievement of a balance between unity and diversity was not only the result of the behavior of the institutions once established, but has been inherent to their structure. The drafters of the original institutions took into account the diverging national traditions of governance that were based on democracy and the rule of law, the goal of securing maximum national influence over the activities of the new organization, and the political compromises between differing views among

[1] For a recent review of the field, see Bogaards et al. (2019); McCulloch and McGarry (2005); Bieber (2020); Rothchild and Roeder (2005).

[2] For example, ECJ, Case C-409/13 (Council/Commission), ECLI:EU:C:2015:217, paragraph 64.

governments as to its future.[3] Other sources of inspiration were existing international organizations, such as the United Nations and the Council of Europe. They provided the model for the equal representation of States and for the distribution of seats in the Common (Parliamentary) Assembly.[4] It is, however, worth remembering that the original institutional setup of the ECSC was genuinely inventive and novel: an independent supranational body invested with the power to adopt decisions binding on the Member States (see Schuman 1950).[5] The sole other institution, mentioned only indirectly in the initial proposal, was a "means of appeal," an embryonic form of the Court of Justice.

The institutional system provided for in the ECSC Treaty (i.e. the High Authority, Council of Ministers, Common Assembly, and Court of Justice) was transmuted into the present system of the Union in several steps, the most recent being the Treaty of Lisbon of 2007 and its implementing decisions.[6] The original institutions had in fact been conceived of as a provisional structure that would be adapted in light of future experience. Subsequent amendments were driven by opposing forces. On the one hand, the governments of the Member States wished to maintain their individual influence over the activities of the Union and small States did not want to give up privileges in terms of representation and voting rights. On the other hand, the demand for increased legitimacy and greater efficiency of the institutions entailed changes in the composition of the European Parliament and its powers, in the composition of the Commission, and in the voting procedures in Council.

[3] On the negotiations concerning the institutions, see Küsters (1988).

[4] See Statute of the Council of Europe, Articles 25 and 26.

[5] (extract, authors' italics) "By pooling basic production and by instituting *a new High Authority, whose decisions will bind France, Germany and other member countries*, this proposal will lead to the realization of the first concrete foundation of a European federation indispensable to the preservation of peace. … The common High Authority entrusted with the management of the scheme will be composed of independent persons appointed by the governments, *giving equal representation*. A chairman will be chosen by common agreement between the governments. The Authority's *decisions will be enforceable in France, Germany and other member countries*. Appropriate measures will be provided for *means of appeal against the decisions of the Authority*" (Schuman 1950).

[6] One of them is the European Council Decision 2013/272/EU concerning the number of members of the European Commission (2013). *Official Journal* L165, 18 June, p. 98, derogating from the wording of Article 17 (5) TEU and providing for the representation of all Member States in the European Commission.

Institutional and procedural reforms were severely hampered by the inertia of the system, caused by the high hurdles for the necessary Treaty amendment (under normal circumstances, the unanimity of all 27 Member States). Therefore, in order to be met with approval, changes do not only, or even primarily, need to be 'reasonable.' Approval depends on the acceptance of compromises that offer some advantage for each Member State, even if the results are far from some institutional ideal.

As long as the common institutions—the European Parliament and European Commission—have no decisive role in changes to the institutional setup, diversity and unity have to rely on the common agreement of Member States' governments, parliament, and at times citizens directly. At first glance, this secures smaller states a voice greater than their number of inhabitants might justify and goes beyond minority protection. However, this effect is canceled out by the substantially higher bargaining power which the big Member States can mobilize for economic and political reasons.

A specific feature of balancing unity and diversity in the European Union consists of the relative autonomy of the institutions and their interlocking and overlapping relationship with the institutions of the Member States. In some EU institutions (i.e. the European Council, Council, and ECB Council), members of national institutions directly participate, whereas in other cases (i.e. the Commission, Court of Justice, Court of Auditors, Executive Board of the ECB, Economic and Social Committee, and Committee of the Regions) they exert direct influence on the choice and appointment. The overlap and linkage between national and European institutions serves several purposes. It renders the transfer of competences to the Union easier for Member States because the transfer does not necessarily imply a loss of control. In addition, the possibility of making use of national institutions and their experience increases the efficiency of Union governance. National institutions participate in decision-making,[7] implementation, and control of Union policies and laws.[8] Moreover, there is no strict separation of legislative, judicial, and administrative competences between the Union and the Member States.

[7] On the role of national Parliaments, see Article 12 TEU and Protocol No 1 to the TEU on the role of National Parliaments in the European Union.

[8] On judicial control, see Article 19 (1) TEU; on financial control, see Article 287 (3) TFEU.

In respect to the *legislation*, the Union enjoys exclusive competence only in a few specifically enumerated areas (*TEU*, 2007, art. 3), while competences are shared in other areas (*Treaty on the Functioning of the European Union* [TFEU], 2007, art. 2).[9] In *judicial matters* the respective competences are neatly divided between national courts and the European Court by attributing to the ECJ an exceptional competence in enumerated cases only (*TEU*, 2007, art. 19[1], [3])[10] but the two systems are connected by the preliminary ruling procedure (*TFEU*, 2007, art. 267). As far as *administration* is concerned, the Treaty favors national competences over the Union, but authorizes direct implementation by the Union "where uniform conditions for [implementation] are needed" (*TFEU*, 2007, art. 291[2]).

Hence, the basic concept for the balancing of unity and diversity that transpires from the interplay between the institutions of the Member States and of the Union is pluralistic and does not rely first and foremost on hierarchy. Its operation does, however, provide for hierarchy when certain predetermined criteria are met, for example the exclusive competence of the Union in matters of economic policy, which precludes Member States that have introduced the euro from any action in this field, or the exercise of a shared competence by the Union, which precludes Member States from legislative action insofar as the specific subject matter is concerned.

The existence and the function of a polity that exercises public authority and that is founded, like the European Union, on values such as human dignity, freedom, and democracy (*TEU*, 2007, art. 2) requires legitimacy, meaning the acceptance and loyalty of those from whom its authority derives. In such a system, self-determination of the individual is the ultimate source of public authority. In a representative democracy, elections to the legislative bodies certainly are the focal point of legitimacy. However, in addition to elections, a stable democratic polity needs the guarantee and effective protection of fundamental rights and respect for the rule of law at all levels of the polity, effective decision-making institutions, and a functioning system of communication. It furthermore needs instruments that enable citizens to participate actively and directly in decisions affecting

[9] On the different forms of competences, see Azoulai (2014).

[10] The most important ones being decisions on disputes between the Union and its Member States and preliminary rulings on questions submitted by national courts on the interpretation of Union law or the validity of acts adopted by the EU institutions.

them— in short, a participatory democracy. Hence, the legitimacy of any organization results from a web of sources, which may be universal to an entire organization or may consist of bits and pieces. The fragmentation of sources of legitimacy does not necessarily imply their weakening. It may even be a source of strength of its own.[11]

One constant feature of the EU's institutional design is it reliance on *multiple sources of legitimacy*, based on their different origins and different natures. The strongest initial source of input legitimacy is the ratification of the founding treaties, treaties providing for their amendment, and the accession treaties by national parliaments and/or referenda. These are complemented by ongoing participation or other forms of involvement by national governments in the EU institutions. Although missing from Robert Schuman's declaration of 9 May 1950 and initially entrusted with only very limited powers, the European Parliament represents a genuine form of transnational legitimacy, which did not derive from the Member States' governments but from their parliaments until 1979, and from direct elections thereafter.

A different source of legitimacy stems from the support which institutions receive for their capacity to articulate and fulfill expectations, that is, their output legitimacy. The strength of this source is, however, subject to variation and contains an element of ambivalence. For example, the suppression of border controls as a consequence of the principle of free movement of persons generates public support because of its inherent increase in individual freedom while at the same time meeting opposition because of fear over the perceived loss of security—possibly by the very same people who also appreciate its advantages.

Legitimacy depends on information and communication, whether objective, subjective, or distorted. Either way, communication has a unifying effect (see Canel and Luoma-Aho 2019, pp. 139–157; Risse 2015). To this end the most obvious vehicle is language. At the same time, communication divides those who communicate with each other from those who are not able to participate in the exchange. Therefore, language is not just the link among some, it is also the most prominent obstacle to communication with others.

There is no single language for all European citizens: more than 20 languages are used in the European Union, as discussed in more detail in

[11] For example, the fragmentation of the European Parliament's legitimacy resulting from the electoral system, see below, Section 5.1.

Chap. 3. Language may have a dividing effect in a multilingual group of people. However, neither is the use of the same language capable of generating unity on its own, nor does the absence of a single language preclude the existence of a shared polity. Thus, a single language is not a necessary prerequisite for the unity of any given entity. What matters, however, for parts of it and for individual members, is being able to make oneself heard, to have "voice" (Hirschman 1970). Voice is understood here as any form of expression on the part of individuals or groups that has implications for unity or diversity in the context of the operation of the Union. This refers namely to direct or representative participation and consultation, but includes other forms of expression of opinion as well.

The experience of many states proves that difficulties of communication resulting from multiple languages can be compensated or resolved, including EU Member States such as Belgium, or multinational Federations such as Canada, Switzerland, and India. The European Union has committed itself "to respect its rich cultural and linguistic diversity" (TEU, 2007, art. 3[3]; *Charter of Fundamental Rights of the European Union*, 2010, art. 22). This means not only that the Union is striving to overcome the practical problems resulting from the many languages, but that its identity specifically comprises a multitude of languages. Consequently, multilingualism and the absence of a mono-lingual space for communication are defining features of the Union. The ensuing implications and challenges are discussed in section 5.2 of this chapter.

Another challenge to legitimacy is the principle of 'equality' among members of a given entity. Equality is not, however, an independent principle. Its purpose consists of the protection of individuals and groups against any arbitrary use of power, and the protection of weaker members of a group against abuses of power by the stronger. Where implementation of formal criteria for equal treatment does not bring about a protective result, it has to be assessed against other values, notably the protection of minorities. Deviation from strict equal treatment by those who have to confront 'unequal' treatment aimed at giving voice to minorities may be perceived as threats to the legitimacy of the system. Balancing such threats against the gain in legitimacy arising from justified means of minority protection is best achieved by compensating mechanisms and a policy of transparent discussion of the values at stake. The distribution of seats in the European Parliament provides an illustration of the resulting problems.[12]

[12] See Section 5.1. below and Chap. 7 (Citizenship), Section 3.

In this chapter we do not present a blueprint for an ideal system of institutions and procedures in a polity that aims at balancing unity and diversity. Such an ideal would not live up to the test of practical politics. Furthermore, institutions do not grow from imagined ideals, but develop from or in contrast to previous experiences. Thus, institutions are the product of diversity and those who negotiate them, rather than something designed in a vacuum. The EU in particular is evidence of the evolving dynamics of institutions to accommodate diversity. We therefore ask instead whether and to what extent the institutions of the European Union are up to the task of giving effect to unity and diversity in a balanced, efficient, and legitimate manner. A *balanced* institutional system results from an appropriate burden being assigned on one hand to the representation of interests, of individuals, of civil society, and of external political authorities (i.e. states and intra-state authorities) (*TEU*, 2007, art. 10[2]; *TFEU*, 2007, art. 300[2–3]) and on the other hand to the protection of its values and of the "general interest of the Union" (*TEU*, 2007, art. 17[1]). Such a balance is certainly a matter of controversy and will vary over time. A possible yardstick for measuring the stability of the balance is the statement of reasons on which decisions are based, in particular the degree to which they respond to the claims of protection of diversity or unity (*TEU*, 2007, art. 5[3]).[13]

Assessing the *efficiency* of the Union in respect to unity and diversity has to be based on a comparison between the aims and the means used for their achievement (i.e. the proportionality test, cf. *TEU*, 2007, art. 5[4]). Efficiency also requires that consideration be given to the sustainability of acts, to the possibility of their adaptation and evolution, and to the acceptance by those concerned.

In order for actions by the Union to be *legitimate*, they need to be consistent with and respectful of its values (*TEU*, 2007, art. 2, 3[1]), be issued following the appropriate procedures for their adoption, and meet the tacit or explicit acceptance by national parliaments[14] and by those directly concerned.

In order to embrace the interplay of the various actors which characterizes a pluralist polity, we must go beyond the "institutional framework" (*TEU*, 2007, art. 13) of the European Union and include those national

[13] 'Subsidiarity test.'

[14] On the role of national parliaments see *TEU* (2007), art. 12 in conjunction with Protocols No 1 and 2, annexed to the TEU and the TFEU.

actors that may have a direct impact on the functioning of the EU system. From a similar perspective, national procedures need to be taken into account as well. The term *procedures* not only refers to the manner in which laws are made and interpreted and conflicts settled, but also includes the preparation and implementation of rules.

## 5.1 Institutions

With regard to unity and diversity, the institutions of the European Union have to fulfill potentially conflicting roles. They must, for example, simultaneously serve the interests of the Union, of its citizens, and of the Member States (*TEU*, 2007, art. 13[1]). In order to ascertain the contribution of the institutions to unity and diversity, we will discuss their relationship with citizens, civil society, sub-entities, and national institutions (1); their size and composition (2); their mode of designation (3); and their functions (4).

### *Relationship with Citizens, Civil Society, Sub-entities, and National Institutions*

*Citizens and Civil Society*

As a general rule, unity is served by the right of EU citizens "to participate in the democratic life of the Union" (*TEU*, 2007, art. 10[3]). To that end, the institutions should maintain an open, transparent, and regular dialogue with representative associations and civil society (*TEU*, 2007, art. 11 [2]). Moreover, citizens "of a significant number of Member States" may invite the Commission to submit legislative proposals (*TEU*, 2007, art. 11[4]).[15] This type of citizens' initiative has existed only since the 2007 Treaty of Lisbon. It was inspired by proposals submitted to the inter-governmental conference that prepared the Treaty of Amsterdam (1996) and by the Council Decision of January 2004, which established a program on the promotion of an "active European citizenship."[16]

[15] Minimum thresholds: 1 million citizens from one quarter of the Member States. For details, see European Parliament and Council Regulation 788/2019 on the European citizens' initiative (2019). *Official Journal* L130, 17 May, p. 55–81.

[16] European Parliament and Council Decision 100/2004 establishing a Community action program to promote active European citizenship (2004). *Official Journal* L30, 4 February, p. 6–14.

In order to ensure similar conditions across Member States for the support of a citizens' initiative, a minimum number of signatures had to be obtained within a Member State, based on the number of its inhabitants. The minimum number of signatories required in each Member State corresponds to the number of Members of the European Parliament elected from that state, multiplied by the total number of Members of the European Parliament (European Union Regulation 788/2019, 2019, art. 3[1] and annex I).

Not having been fixed by the Treaty, the latter provision on the required number of signatures offers an interesting example of recent efforts to balance unity and diversity by way of legislation: the composition of the European Parliament is also fixed in an adjusted reverse proportion to the number of inhabitants ("degressively proportional," *TEU*, 2007, art. 14[2]). In addition, it provides for a minimum threshold of six EP members per State. As a result, the votes of citizens from larger Member States have a relatively lower weight in the European Parliament than votes of citizens from smaller states. This result is intended to give voice to the political forces of small Member States. By contrast, taking the number of seats in the European Parliament as a reference for the calculation of the minimum number of signatures required in each State for the citizens' initiative gives a relative advantage to the larger Member States. At first glance, this threshold might seem like a compensation for disadvantageous representation in the European Parliament. However, the two issues are not connected by constitutional logic. They do, however, highlight the concern of balancing the protection of minorities—meaning diversity—with the equality principle.[17]

Citizens are, moreover, entitled to address the institutions and advisory bodies of the Union in any of the Treaty languages and to obtain a reply in the same language; they have the right to petition the European Parliament and to apply to the European Ombudsman (*TFEU*, 2007, art. 20[2][d]), together with the right of access to documents of the Union's institutions (*TFEU,* 2007, art. 15[3]); and the institutions are under an obligation of transparency in their activity, in particular in relation to their proceedings (*TFEU*, art. 15[1], [3]). These rights are confirmed in Articles 41–44 of the Charter of Fundamental Rights. Citizens and other persons may also institute proceedings before the EU General Court against acts

[17] See the next section on *Size and composition of institutions.*

of the institutions that are of direct and individual concern to them (*TFEU*, 2007, art. 263).[18]

Direct communication between the EU institutions, civil society, and interest groups is part of the democratic process that is organized at the level of the Union in two ways, both of which may be regarded as institutionalized forms of balancing diversity and unity.

First, Articles 11 (1) and (2) TEU stress the importance of an "open, transparent, and regular dialogue." In practice, the dialogue is held between the institutions, namely the European Parliament and the Commission, and interest groups, which are organized at the level of the Union but often consist of an extension of national groups onto the level of the Union.[19]

Second, an advisory body, the Economic and Social Committee, "shall consist of representatives of organizations of employers, of the employed, and of other parties representative of civil society, notably in socio-economic, civic, professional, and cultural areas" (*TFEU*, 2007, art. 300[2]). Although the members are chosen by the EU Council from lists drawn up by Member States, they are completely independent and perform their duties "in the Union's general interest" (*TFEU*, 2007, art. 300[4], 302).[20] Accordingly, they represent all citizens of the Union in accordance with the different criteria for which they are included, such as belonging to a specific group of interest or professional organization.

*Relations with Sub-entities and National Institutions*

Besides the direct participation of representatives of Member States and/or national governments in the European Council and the EU Council and national central banks in the Governing Council of the European Central Bank,[21] three national institutions and sub-entities enjoy structured relationships with the institutions of the Union: national parliaments, courts, and regions and local bodies—via direct participation in the decision-making process of the Union, or in the implementation of EU

[18] On the detailed conditions, see ECJ, Case C-50/00 P (Union de Pequenos Agricultures v Council), ECLI:EU:C:2002:462, paragraphs 34–45.

[19] See the contributions in Shotton and Nixon (2015). On the implementation see European Commission (2018).

[20] On a definition of the notion of 'civil society,' see Economic and Social Committee (1999), p. 30. See also European Commission (2006).

[21] See Articles 1 and 14, Protocol No 4 to the TEU on the Statute of the European System of Central Banks and of the European Central Bank.

acts by national parliaments[22] and national administrations (*TFEU*, 2007, art. 197, 291[1]), the performance of advisory functions of representatives of regional and local bodies via the Committee of the Regions (*TFEU*, 2007, art. 300[3], 307), or via specific cooperation between national courts and the ECJ for the purpose of interpretation and judicial control of EU acts via the preliminary ruling procedure (*TFEU*, 2007, art. 267).

These relationships are intended to give privileged voice to diversity or to ensure uniform application of EU law among the various actors. They do not, however, imply any tradeoff between unity and diversity, because the autonomy of the common institutions remains intact. The efficient interplay among the various actors that represent diversity and those that participate in the expression of the common interest is safeguarded by the constitutionally guaranteed autonomy of the EU institutions and by procedures that have constantly been adjusted for the optimal performance of this function.[23]

### *Size and Composition of Institutions*

The balance between unity and diversity is also reflected in the size and composition of the institutions. Although there is no generally applicable formula for the size of institutions in democratic political systems, certain aspects are generally valid. Hence, the capacity for rapid decision-making is a decisive element for any body that performs executive functions. Institutions with legislative functions must first be able to fulfill their task of representing the citizens and/or sub-entities, and second, to reach decisions within a reasonable period of time. For consultative bodies, the capacity to represent the groups in question determines their size. Institutions that perform supervisory functions have to be composed of a sufficiently large number of members to ensure that the likely amount of work can be done within a reasonable period of time. In essence, the balance here is between efficiency (output legitimacy) and representation (input legitimacy).

The need for compromise between the different criteria becomes obvious when combined with efforts to strike a balance between unity and

[22] See Article 12 TEU and the Protocols No 1 and 2 annexed to the Treaties.

[23] Example: The co–decision procedure (*TFEU*, 2007, art. 294) introduced by the Treaty of Lisbon, which gives equal weight to the European Parliament and the Council.

diversity. The prevailing criterion for the composition of the institutions remains, however, the diversity resulting from their members' nationality.

The most striking example of the enduring impact of nationality is provided by the Commission. From a purely functional point of view, its predominantly executive functions, which must be performed within a short period of time and wholly independently of the Member States, would suggest a small size, comparable to the size of national governments. Based on the average size of European governments, 20 members would be an appropriate figure. In fact, the TEU provides for a size of "two thirds of the number of Member States" (*TEU*, 2007, art. 17[5]). With the current number of 27 Member States, the Commission would comprise 18 members. The consequence of the implementation of this provision would have been that not all Member States would be represented among the members of the Commission. From a purely functional perspective, this would be perfectly appropriate. The Commission's task is not to 'represent' the Member States. It promotes the general interest of the Union, which can be clearly identified irrespective of any citizenship. However, the aim to respect diversity has led the European Council to make use of the derogation clause in Article 17 (5) TEU to maintain the previous system, wherein each Member State is represented, producing an oversized institution and reduced efficiency. In this case, diversity has been given priority over unity, and thus the efficient functioning of the institution. This example highlights that the give-and-take between unity and diversity in the institutions of the EU is not always based on functional allocation of institutions to preserve diversity, such as the European Parliament, or unity, such as the Commission, but that it is a balancing act across all institutions and thus might not establish an ideal equilibrium between the two. In fact, Member State governments are also not only based on the ideal size, taking into account the number of portfolios available, but are a consequence of coalition-building that considers the interests of the political parties participating in government.

On the other hand, the composition of the other executive institution, the Executive Board of the European Central Bank, has been determined strictly in accordance with criteria of efficiency (six members, irrespective of the number of Member States, see *TFEU*, 2007, art. 283[2]). The difference in the composition of the Commission can be explained by the priority granted by the Treaty to technical expertise in the functioning of the Executive Board of the Central Bank,[24] while Commission membership (and its task) reflects a broader political mandate.[25]

The composition of the two legislative institutions is strongly anchored in the Member States, because they are composed of members elected within the frame of Member States or representing governments of Member States. Yet they more closely represent a balance between unity and diversity, inasmuch as that balance does not lead to a significant reduction of efficiency. The Council's function of representing the Member States' governments in the legislative process can easily be performed by 27 members who are members of their respective national governments. At first glance, the equal representation of the Member States in the Council (one member irrespective of the size of the state) seems to reduce diversity by evening out differences in size, number of inhabitants, economic weight, and so on among the Member States. On the other hand, this composition ensures that small states have a greater voice relative to their size; this protects diversity. Moreover, formal equality in the composition is compensated for by the majority requirements in the decision-making procedure, which combines the majority of states with a majority (65%) of the population (*TEU*, 2007, art. 16[4]).[26]

The other legislative institution is at the other end of the spectrum in terms of size. The European Parliament with a maximum number of 751 (in 2020, 705) members (*TEU*, 2007, art. 14[2])[27] is large by national standards. For an institution that has the task of representing 445 million citizens living in 27 states and who are organized in more than 100 political parties, this number represents a workable compromise between the efficiency of parliamentary work and representation of the most important political forces in all Member States. Its size exceeds that of any lower-chamber parliament in a democracy (i.e. the House of Representatives in the United States with 435, India with 543, the House of Commons in

[24] According to Article 283(2) TFEU, the Governing Board has to be chosen "from among persons of recognised standing and professional experience in monetary or banking matters."

[25] "The members of the Commission shall be chosen on the ground of their general competence and European commitment from persons whose independence is beyond doubt" (*TEU*, 2007, art. 17[2]).

[26] See Section 5.2.

[27] See also European Council Decision 937/2018 establishing the composition of the European Parliament (2018). *Official Journal* L165I, 2 July, pp. 1–3.

the United Kingdom with 650), except the German Bundestag (with 709 MPs), even if not necessarily by proportionality to population.

More problematic (and controversial) is the distribution of the seats among the Member States. The TEU provides for an adapted proportional representation of citizens with a minimum threshold of six members per Member State and a maximum of 96 seats. The limitation of the total number of members required either sacrifices to diversity (i.e. the representation of minorities) or leads to restrictions in equality of representation. The authors of the Treaty gave priority to diversity over the unitary principle of equality. It should be remembered as well that citizens of larger Member States obtain a form of compensation in the requirements for the citizens' initiative, as noted above.[28]

Hence the composition of the European Parliament results in it reflecting a genuine balance between diversity and unity. Furthermore, classic federal states often have a two-chamber system that includes one chamber based on proportional representation and one representing the constituent units. The prime example is the United States, with a Senate that grants equal representation to Wyoming—similar in size to Luxembourg in the EU—with a population of around 600,000, and California, with nearly 40 million. Not being a two-chamber parliament, the European Parliament combines the defining features of both chambers in conventional federal systems. We will return to the representation of the citizens from different Member States in Chap. 6, where we will examine the implications for citizenship.

The size of the supervisory institutions, the Court and the Court of Auditors, results from the equal representation of nationals (one) of each Member State, which brings together diversity and unity. Although 'representation' of Member States is not necessary for the performance of their tasks, this representation corresponds to their functional needs and increases their acceptance, and hence their legitimacy.

The Economic and Social Committee and the Committee of the Regions are identical in size, with the Treaty only fixing a maximum number of 350 members. According to the Treaty of Lisbon, the distribution of seats has been left to a (unanimous) decision of the Council, thus potentially facilitating the fine-tuning necessary to take diversity into account.

[28] See Section 5.1. above.

The distribution between Member States is based approximately according to their respective number of inhabitants. At first glance, the system is less elaborate than the distribution of seats in the European Parliament, insofar as differences in the numbers of Member States' inhabitants are reflected in 13 categories of seats in the European Parliament, while for the composition of the Committees only 8 categories have been established.[29] The TFEU, in Article 300 (2) and (3), provides, however, for both Committees' rules on their internal composition, which substantially increase their capacity to represent the interests specifically mentioned. At the same time, those interests are not framed according to Member State. Hence, the representative function of both bodies derives first and foremost from the diversity of different interest groups.

EU law does not impose a specific citizenship requirement for members of the Council, the European Parliament, the Court, the Economic and Social Committee, or the Committee of the Regions, while members of the Commission, the Board of Directors of the ECB, and the Court of Auditors have to be citizens of Member States (*TEU*, 2007, art. 17[5]; *TFEU*, 2007, art. 283[3], 285).

### *Mode of Appointment and Status of Members*

The mode of appointment of the members of EU institutions provides a further example of the continuous effort to balance unity and diversity that is intrinsic to the Union. On the one hand, the mode of appointment is aimed at providing institutional autonomy and efficiency in order to serve the "general interest of the Union" (*TEU*, 2007, art. 17[1]), and on the other hand, following the traditional method of composing the institutions of an international organization, it aims to ensure a maximum influence for national interests in the institutional system via the direct intervention of national governments. The latter is achieved most obviously in the coupling of membership of the European Council[30] and the Council with Heads of State or Government or membership in national government respectively.

[29] Concerning the composition of the Committee of the Regions, see Council of the European Union Decision 2019/852 determining the composition of the Committee of the Regions (2019). *Official Journal* L139, 27 May, p. 13–14.

[30] Exception: the President of the European Council and President of the Commission neither of whom hold a national office.

Moreover, Member States' governments exercise a central role in the choice and appointment of the members of the Commission, the Court, the Court of Auditors, and the Executive Board of the ECB. A similar influence is exercised with regard to the Economic and Social Committee and the Committee of the Regions. It should, however, be noted that following their appointment, members of these institutions enjoy a status that guarantees their full independence from any national influence. The Treaty mentions explicitly that members of the Commission, the Court of Auditors, the Economic and Social Committee, and the Committee of the Regions perform their duties in the Union's general interest. In fact, in the hearings of candidates nominated for the Commission in the European Parliament, their independence from the national governments that nominated them is an important theme. Hence, diversity is achieved by way of the designation procedure, while unity is achieved through the definition of the duties to be performed through full-time exercise of office for a defined period of time (Commission, ECJ, Executive Board of the ECB, and the Court of Auditors) and through the guarantees of members' independence from any national influence. It should, however, be noted that the members of the two consultative institutions—the Economic and Social Committee and the Committee of the Regions—are chosen on the basis of certain criteria, the fulfillment of which is determined at national level, so that the institution in question can speak for these constituencies at the level of the Union. It follows that members of those two institutions act in the Union's general interest when they contribute to translating the positions they represent into the common positions of the common institution in question.

Completely separate from national institutions, the members of the European Parliament are designated in direct elections (since 1979). In most Member States, however, candidates for elections have to be put forward by political parties, which in practice are organized at national level. At least in theory, a European political party is also able to put forward candidates in some or all Member States.[31] The electoral procedure is settled by a combination of common and national provisions.[32] Members

[31] Example: para. 8, electoral law ("Europawahlgesetz") of Germany (1994, last amendment in 2018).

[32] Article 223 TFEU and Direct Elections Act of 20 September 1976, last amendment by EU Council decision 2018/994, OJ 2018 L 178, p. 1.

of the European Parliament enjoy an independent status as well (Direct Elections Act, 1976, art. 6).[33]

### *Functions of the Institutions*

First and foremost, EU institutions should serve the interests of the Union and its citizens (*TEU*, 2007, art. 13[1]). While this may be the most obvious criterion for the performance of the institutions, their role is not limited to this single function. In fact, Article 13 TEU explicitly assigns to the institutions the task of serving the interests of the Member States as well. This is normally fulfilled through weighing national interests against Union interests in the legislative process (e.g. when examining conditions for subsidiarity), thus balancing unity and diversity.

The European Parliament has the specific task of serving as a forum for public debate on any issue considered relevant to the European Union. This 'forum function' serves both the expression of diversity and the expression of unity. Because of its strong legitimacy as a directly elected institution, this function leads—at least in ideal circumstances—to an ideal balance of unity and diversity. It gives voice to diversity by, for example, enabling local interests to be articulated by individual members while at the same time bundling opinions through the adoption (by majority) of 'Resolutions.'

In addition, in an effort to promote cohesion and solidarity among Member States, the Treaty invites the institutions to address the specific problems of individual states or regions, with the aim of reducing economic and social diversity in favor of greater unity (*TEU*, 2007, art. 3[3]). For example, in the establishment of the internal market, the Commission is mandated to take into account differences in the economic development of certain Member States and may to that end propose limited derogations from Treaty obligations (*TFEU*, 2007, art. 27). Moreover, in order to strengthen cohesion within the Union, the institutions may pursue appropriate actions (*TFEU*, 2007, art. 174). On the basis of this provision, the Union has established a Cohesion Fund, which contributes inter alia to transport infrastructure projects of European added value.[34] In

[33] They may, however, exercise other professional activities parallel to their mandate, exception: Incompatibilities listed in Article 7 of the Direct Elections Act.

[34] European Parliament and Council Regulation 1300/2013 on the Cohesion Fund and repealing Council Regulation (EC) No 1084/2006 (2013). *Official Journal* L347, 20 December, pp. 281–288.

exceptional cases, the Union may grant financial or other assistance to individual Member States that are in particular difficulties (*TFEU*, 2007, art. 122).[35]

The Member States may by separate instruments confer on the institutions the task of performing functions outside the Treaties. In this latter case, the separate instrument guides the conduct of the institutions.[36] This may lead to interference with the performance of the ordinary (and primary) functions of the institution and may therefore deviate from the common interest. Therefore, the ECJ has established a limit to such instruments that they do not alter the identity of the institutions or the essential character of the powers conferred on them by the EU and FEU Treaties.[37]

The contribution of the institutional system to the balance of unity and diversity does not only flow from the specific features of each institution, but results as well from their interplay—from their procedures as laid down in the constitutional document and resulting from constitutional practice.

## 5.2 Procedures

In the European Union, procedures for adopting binding acts (legislation), for amending the basic texts (Constitution or founding Treaty), and for the conclusion of international agreements do not differ fundamentally from other polities with law-making functions. They are, however, marked by a strong concern for consideration of diversity, leading to a high degree of complexity in the decision-making system. An obvious example is linguistic diversity,[38] which among other things has led the European

[35] Such grants were authorized for Portugal in 2011 (OJ 2011 L 159, p. 88); Ireland in 2011 (OJ 2011 L 30, p. 34) and Greece in 2016 (OJ 2016 L 91, p. 22).

[36] Example: *Treaty establishing the European Stability Mechanism* (ESM Treaty, 2012), preamble, recital 10.

[37] ECJ, Case C-370/12 (Pringle), ECLI:EU:C:2012:756, para. 158 (on the ESM Treaty, supra, note 36).

[38] See Article 3 (3) TEU and Article 1 of Council Regulation No 1 of 15 April 1958 determining the languages to be used by the European Economic Community (OJ 2013 L 158, p. 71): "The official languages and the working languages of the institutions of the Union shall be Bulgarian, Croatian, Czech, Danish, Dutch, English, Estonian, Finnish, French, German, Greek, Hungarian, Irish, Italian, Latvian, Lithuanian, Maltese, Polish, Portuguese, Romanian, Slovak, Slovenian, Spanish, and Swedish."

Parliament to stipulate: "All Members shall have the right to speak in Parliament in the official language of their choice. Speeches delivered in one of the official languages shall be simultaneously interpreted into the other official languages and into any other language the Bureau may consider necessary" (*TFEU*, 2007, art. 167[2]; EP-Rules of Procedure 2019).

Like the priorities that led to the specific institutional setup, the procedures for the performance of their tasks are determined by the striving for a balance between giving voice to diversity and enabling efficient decision-making in the interest of unity. The means for achieving balance in procedures have evolved over time. They provide an example of the provisional setup of the Union's mechanism, which is gradually transmuted in light of experience into an ever-more sophisticated and differentiated institutional system.

In contrast with most national systems, the revision and amendment of the founding treaties, or the 'constitutional procedure,' is conceived of as entirely separate from legislative procedures. While legislation is decided upon exclusively by the EU institutions (with national parliaments being heard), constitutional procedures under normal circumstances[39] require cooperation between national and European institutions, inasmuch as amendments to the founding Treaties cannot come into effect without the assent of all Member States. Accordingly, the search for the appropriate balance between unity and diversity is entrusted to the complex interplay between the European Parliament, the Commission, the European Council, and the Council on the one hand, and, on the other, to each national government and parliament acting individually. As a result, the constitutional procedure is heavily biased in favor of diversity: each single Member State can prevent changes to the constitutional foundations, even if they are supported by the combined authority of the common institutions and by the 26 other Member States. This bias is amplified further by the possibility open to Member States of unilaterally deciding to leave the Union, while the Union does not possess the corollary, a right of expulsion.

The following discussion of constitutional procedures will examine (1), legislative procedures (2), procedures governing the implementation of legislation and the adoption of delegated acts (3), the procedures for the

[39] In exceptional cases, which are listed in the Treaties, the European Council, acting unanimously, may decide amendments alone (e.g. changes in the number of members of the Commission, *TEU*, 2007, art. 17[5]).

adoption of international agreements (4) and finally how the balance between unity and diversity is achieved.

### *Constitutional Procedures*

Constitutional procedures aimed at amending the Treaties (*TEU*, 2007, art. 48) are characterized by a right of initiative vested in the governments of the Member States, the Commission, or the European Parliament, and by the requirement of approval by all Member States. After consulting the European Parliament and the Commission (the ECB has to be consulted if changes to monetary matters have been proposed), the European Council decides, by simple majority, whether or not to examine the proposal and to convene a Convention composed of representatives of the national Parliaments, of the Heads of State or Government of the Member States, of the European Parliament, and of the Commission. The Convention examines the proposal and recommends the convening of a conference of representatives of the governments of the Member States which is, by common accord, to determine the amendments to be made to the Treaties. Subsequently, the amendments are submitted to Member States for ratification.

Although the TEU, in Article 48 (6, 7), provides for two simplified revision procedures that are applicable in specific matters only and which do not require the convening of a convention, the procedure remains extremely cumbersome, giving the last word to the parliaments and governments of each Member State acting individually. This procedure represents the culminating point of respect for diversity within the Union, at the price of reducing the efficiency of the Union's decision-making and of neglecting the combined legitimacy of the institutions and a majority of Member States, in some of which referenda have to be held or higher majority requirements in parliaments may have to be fulfilled.

Special procedures exist for certain issues, for example the admission of new Member States (*TEU*, 2007, art. 49). They are simplified in comparison to the ordinary procedure, but still require the formal consent of all Member States.[40]

[40] See, however, the procedure of withdrawal from the Union (*TEU*, 2007, art. 50), according to which an agreement on the arrangement for withdrawal can be adopted by the Council (deciding by a qualified majority) and the European Parliament (simple majority) without intervention of national institutions.

### *Legislative and Budgetary Procedures*

Since the Treaty of Lisbon, EU legislation has been adopted either according to the "ordinary legislative procedure" (*TFEU*, 2007, art. 294) or according to special legislative procedures, the latter to be followed in accordance with certain specific provisions of the Treaties. Save for a few exceptional cases in which the Council may decide alone (e.g. *TFEU*, 2007, art. 342), the common feature of all procedures is the involvement of the Commission, Parliament, and Council in the decision-making process. Especially since the reform, this "institutional triangle" acts on an equal footing, the Commission enjoying the monopoly of initiative[41] and the Parliament and the Council acting as co-legislators, the latter two not being able to substitute for each other. Moreover, the procedure implies in most cases a right of consultation of the Economic and Social Committee and/or of the Committee of the Regions.

The procedure combines the three strands of the Union's legitimacy, the representation of national governments (within the Council), the representation of the citizens by the directly elected Parliament, and the representation of the general interest by the Commission.

The resulting structural balance of diversity and unity is further enhanced by two requirements aimed at emphasizing the rationality of the decision-making procedure: the institutions are obliged to practice "mutual sincere cooperation" (*TEU*, 2007, art. 13[2]; *TFEU*, 2007, art. 295) and to state the reasons on which legal acts are based (*TFEU*, 2007, art. 296). The statement of reasons for an EU measure must show clearly and unequivocally the reasoning of the author of the measure in question, so as to enable the persons concerned to ascertain the reasons for the measure and to enable the Court to exercise its power of review. It is not, however, required to go into every relevant point of fact and law.[42]

Although in a few cases the Council has to decide by unanimity,[43] in normal circumstances each institution can decide by a majority decision.[44] However, minority interests, represented by the governments of the Member States, enjoy particular protection. To that end, majorities in

[41] Exception: *TFEU* (2007), art. 76 (Area of freedom, security and justice, where the right of initiative is shared with a quarter of the Member States).

[42] ECJ, Case C-62/14 (Gauweiler et al.), ECLI:EU:C:2015:400, paragraph 70.

[43] For example, harmonization of tax legislation, *TFEU* (2007), art. 113.

[44] Council: *TEU*, 2007, art. 16(4); European Parliament: *TFEU*, 2007, art. 231; Commission: *TFEU*, 2007, art. 250.

Council have to be 'qualified,' that is, 55% of the Members of the Council, comprising at least 15 members, and representing Member States comprising at least 65% of the population of the Union. A specific feature for protecting minorities in the Council's votes is the 'blocking minority' of at least four Council members, representing more than 35% of the participating states plus one member, which can block decisions that need to be adopted by qualified majority. Moreover, in practice, negotiations in the Council aim to find a consensus among members, so that formal votes that might show a majority/minority situation are often avoided. In addition, in the area of cooperation in civil and criminal matters, specific provisions protect national interests in the decision-making procedure (*TFEU*, 2007, art. 81[2], 82[3], 83[3]).

In theory, such a combined legitimacy allows for a maximum of diversity, while allowing for efficient decision-making in the interests of unity. It should, however, be kept in mind that various political considerations attenuate the strict application of the procedural provisions.[45]

Some decision-making practices in the Council bring about paradoxical results. For example, the aim of taking into account as many interests as possible, by means, among other methods, of 'package deals,' whereby specific advantages, not necessarily related to the topic in question, are offered to certain Member States in order to obtain their approval for a given legislative project, appears to be grounded in the widest legitimacy among the Member States' governments. Yet, the rationality of the act in question is blurred ('no alternative') and the agreement resembles an opaque 'backroom deal.' As a consequence, it is more difficult for citizens to identify with the common legislation, and this allows for governments to distance themselves from particular decisions regarding their electorate.

In addition, the procedural requirement of unanimity brings about ambiguous results when the necessary unanimity for the adoption of an act has been found once but cannot be mustered for later amendments ('unanimity trap'). An example of this problem is the decision on own resources of the European Union, which has to be adopted at regular intervals by unanimity (*TFEU*, 2007, art. 311, par. 3), the last dating from 2014. In 1984, the United Kingdom, under very specific economic conditions, obtained a special "correction" of its share in the own resources.[46]

[45] For example, the speeding up of the ordinary legislative procedure by 'trilogues' between Council, Commission, and Parliament. See Curtin and Leino (2017).

[46] Now: Article 4 of the own resources decision of 2014.

Over the 30 years since then, despite several attempts, it has not proved possible to obtain the necessary unanimity for the abolition of the correction, although it had been understood that the 'correction' would cease under changing economic conditions.[47]

### *Administrative Procedures*

A special procedure that is situated between legislation and implementation has been introduced by Article 290 TFEU, which authorizes a delegation of power to the Commission to "supplement or amend certain non-essential elements of legislative acts." This power is exercised under the control of the European Parliament and the Council (*TFEU*, 2007, art. 290[2]), thus enabling these two institutions to revoke the delegation or to block the entry into force of a given delegated act.

The implementation of EU law is dominated by considerations of diversity, inasmuch as it is principally left by the TFEU to the Member States, who act with institutional and procedural autonomy (*TFEU*, 2007, art. 291[1]).[48] Yet, where uniform conditions for implementation are needed, the EU legislature may empower the Commission to carry out implementation at the level of the Union. The decision on whether such a need exists is left to the EU legislature, thus favoring the common element of the procedure. Yet in this case, the Member States are able to control the Commission's exercise of these powers (*TFEU*, 2007, art. 291[2]). To that end, rules have been laid down that provide for the creation of committees composed of the representatives of the Member States and chaired by the Commission. Certain categories of implementing acts cannot be adopted by the Commission if they are not in accordance with the opinion of the committee, while in other (less important) matters the committees have an advisory function only.[49] In practice, an intensive cooperation between the European and the national administrations has developed that can be described as an "administrative network" (see Hoffmann and Türk 2006), thus giving shape to an additional layer of unity and diversity.

[47] European Council meeting of 25/26 June 1984, Conclusions of the Presidency, No 1.4: "The Council will re-examine the question as a whole and will take the appropriate decisions ex novo."

[48] For limits and details see Becker (2007).

[49] European Parliament and Council Regulation 182/2011 laying down the rules and general principles concerning mechanisms for control by Member States of the Commission's exercise of implementing powers (2011). *Official Journal* L55, 28 February, pp. 13–18.

### *Procedures in International Relations*

In external relations two subject areas have to be distinguished. In matters falling specifically within the scope of the Common Foreign and Security Policy, the European Council and the Council make decisions acting unanimously, unless otherwise provided (*TEU*, 2007, art. 31[1]). Other acts related to foreign policy are adopted according to the ordinary legislative procedure. Like the legislative procedure, the procedure for the conclusion of international agreements by the Union is left to the institutions of the Union acting jointly (*TEU*, 2007, art. 207, 218).

Special procedures provide for, among other things, the conclusion of agreements that relate principally to the common foreign and security policy, to the agreement on accession of the Union to the European Convention of Human Rights (*TFEU*, 2007, art. 218[3], [8]), and to monetary affairs (*TFEU*, 2007, art. 219). The special procedures provide for unanimity in the Council and (in the case of monetary affairs) for the participation of the ECB.

For agreements that only partly cover matters for which the Union is competent, the practice has developed of using the instrument of 'mixed agreements.' Their approval needs both ratification by the Member States according to their internal constitutional requirements, and the adoption by the institutions of the Union in accordance with the procedure provided for in Article 218 TFEU. In the field of international relations, consistent action of the European Union for reasons of efficiency would require the sole intervention of the unitary actors, notably as far as the conclusion of international agreements is concerned.[50] Yet, the individual external representation is of primary concern to most Member States. Therefore, the aim to find the appropriate balance between diversity and unity is a particularly dynamic venture that frequently has to be settled by the European Court of Justice (see Cremona 2014).

[50] ECJ case 467/98 (Commission /Denmark) ECLI:EU:C:2002:625, paragraph 77 ("open sky cases"): "each time the Community, with a view to implementing a common policy envisaged by the Treaty, adopts provisions laying down common rules, whatever form these may take, the Member States no longer have the right, acting individually or even collectively, to undertake obligations towards non-member countries which affect those rules or distort their scope; and that, as and when such common rules come into being, the Community alone is in a position to assume and carry out contractual obligations towards non-member countries affecting the whole sphere of application of the Community legal system."

In the European Union, the institutional system and the various procedures for its operation reflect the challenge of ensuring the representation of diversity and unity. Both are potentially able to accumulate input and output legitimacy. Despite its resulting complexity, the system is capable of efficient decision-making, and over time an evolution of the institutions and procedures to reflect the growing commitment to greater cooperation as well. Whether the results at any given moment may be regarded as optimal cannot be determined according to objective criteria. When measured against the aims sought, we can observe both successes and failures. Common policies (e.g. in the field of agriculture and transport) have been introduced and the internal market has been established. On the other hand, the institutional setup has not so far been able to bring about economic, social, and territorial cohesion and solidarity among Member States (e.g. reduction of economic disparities or a common policy on asylum and immigration). If compared with the goals and achievements within Member States alone, the shortcomings at the level of the Union appear less dramatic.

More problematic is, however, the perception of the institutional system by EU citizens. Despite its high degree of transparency, the institutional output is scarcely perceived as such, and is frequently viewed in a distorted manner. The main cause of this lies with the national actors in the system. The members of national governments in particular do not acknowledge responsibility for their activity within the EU Council, the co-legislator. Frequently, legislation or other measures are ascribed to 'them' rather than 'us.' In doing so, national governments can distance themselves from EU legislation rather than explaining its rationale. Measures of the EU institutions, when adopted in the form of Directives (which have to be transposed into national law), are communicated to citizens as national acts, although the political choices which they represent have been made in the EU institutional system. As a result, EU decisions are either invisible or, if convenient to national actors, portrayed as impositions by outsiders, often subsumed in the term 'Brussels.'

In the same way as the shortcomings in practice, the conceptualization of the European Union's complex framework of checks and balances—and of unity and diversity—still needs refinement. Although the theory of constitutional pluralism offers a valuable tool for its understanding, it was conceived in the context of and is still discussed mostly with regard to relations between the European and national judiciary.[51] The interplay between parliaments, administrations, and governmental institutions needs to be explored in this context in order to grasp, for example, the aforementioned dysfunctionalities.

## References


Avbelj, M., & Komárek, J. (Eds.). (2012). *Constitutional Pluralism in the European Union and Beyond*. Oxford: Hart.

Azoulai, L. (Ed.). (2014). *The Question of Competence in the European Union*. Oxford: OUP.

Becker, F. (2007). Application of Community Law by Member States' Public Authorities: Between Autonomy and Effectiveness. *Common Market Law Review, 44*(4), 1035–1056.

Bieber, F. (2020). Moving the Power-Sharing Debate Forward. *Ethnopolitics, 19*(1), 96–99.

Bogaards, M. (2019). Consociationalism and Centripetalism: Friends or Foes? *Swiss Political Science Review, 25*(4), 519–537.

Bogaards, M., Helms, L., & Lijphart, A. (2019). The Importance of Consociationalism for Twenty-First Century Politics and Political Science. *Swiss Political Science Review, 25*(4), 341–356.

Canel, M.-J., & Luoma-Aho, V. (2019). *Public Sector Communication*. Hoboken: Wiley Blackwell.

*Charter of Fundamental Rights of the European Union* (2010). *Official Journal* C83, March 30, pp. 389–406.

Cremona, M. (2014). EU External Relations: Unity and Conferral of Powers. In L. Azoulai (Ed.), *The Question of Competence in the European Union* (pp. 65–85). Oxford: OUP.

Curtin, D., & Leino, P. (2017). In Search of Transparency for EU Law – Making: Trilogues on the Cusp of Dawn. *Common Market Law Review, 54*(6), 1673–1712.

Economic and Social Committee (1999). *Opinion on "The Role and contribution of civil society organisations in the building of Europe."* Official Journal C329, 17 November, pp. 30–38.

EP Rules of Procedure. (2019). *Official Journal* L 302, November 22, pp. 1–128.

European Commission. (2006). Green Paper: European Transparency Initiative. *COM* 194.


[51] See Avbelj and Komárek (eds.) (2012), in particular the contribution of Poiares Maduro; on the institutional lacuna of the theory, see the contribution by Jan Komárek.

European Commission (Ed.) (2018). Report on the Mid-Term Evaluation of the Implementation of the Europe for Citizens Programme 2014–2020. *COM* 17, April 6.

Hirschman, A. O. (1970). *Exit, Voice, and Loyalty*. Cambridge/London: Harvard University Press.

Hoffmann, H. C. H., & Türk, A. H. (2006). Introduction. In H. C. H. Hofmann & A. H. Türk (Eds.), *EU Administrative Governance* (pp. 1–10). Cheltenham: Edward Elgar.

Komárek, J. (2012). Institutional Dimension of Constitutional Pluralism. In M. Avbelj & J. Komárek (Eds.), *Constitutional Pluralism in the European Union and Beyond* (pp. 231–247). Oxford: Hart Publishing.

Küsters, H. J. (1988). Die Verhandlungen über das institutionelle System zur Gründung der Europäischen Gemeinschaft für Kohle und Stahl. In K. Schwabe (Ed.), *The beginnings of the Schuman plan/Die Anfänge des Schuman – Plans 1950/51* (pp. 73–102). Baden-Baden: Nomos.

Maduro, P. (2012). Three Claims of Constitutional Pluralism. In M. Avbelj & J. Komárek (Eds.), *Constitutional Pluralism in the European Union and Beyond* (pp. 67–84). Oxford: Hart.

McCulloch, A., & McGarry, J. (2005). *Power-Sharing: Empirical and Normative Challenges*. London: Routledge.

Risse, T. (Ed.). (2015). *European Public Spheres*. Cambridge: Cambridge University Press.

Rothchild, D., & Roeder, P. G. (2005). Dilemmas of State-Building in Divided Societies. In P. G. Roeder & D. Rothchild (Eds.), *Sustainable Peace: Power and Democracy After Civil Wars* (pp. 1–26). Ithaca: Cornell University Press.

Schuman, R. (1950). The Schuman-Declaration of 9 May 1950. https://europa.eu/european-union/about-eu/symbols/europe-day/schuman-declaration_en. Accessed 29 Mar 2020.

Shotton, P. A., & Nixon, P. G. (Eds.). (2015). *Lobbying the European Union*. Farnham: Ashgate.

CHAPTER 6

# 'Europe' as a Symbol: Symbols of Europe

'Europe' is simultaneously a symbol and a reality. While the symbolic power of the term 'Europe' offers significant potential for the European Union, it also constitutes a challenge: the notion of Europe does not have clearly and indisputably defined substance, nor do the imagined or real symbols of Europe transmit clear messages that stimulate identification with it. The aims and symbols of the European Union do not match—and indeed even contradict—each other, thus weakening their potential for identification. Moreover, the complexity of multi-layered governance ('integration') renders symbolization more difficult than the symbolization of a coherent entity. The European Union motto—which is not universally endorsed—of 'unity and diversity' attempts to encompass the unprecedented process of transformation of the traditional European nation-states and to bridge the gap between traditional identities and new, evolving ones. There is furthermore an inherent ambiguity in the term 'Europe' itself. Not only is Europe broader than the EU, but when both are used synonymously, there is an exclusionary dimension toward the countries that are in Europe but not in the EU, that is, the United Kingdom and Russia. In addition, the term 'Europe' carries baggage in the global context, as it was European power that constituted colonial empires and dominated most of the globe. As a consequence, Europe is also burdened by the legacy of colonialism and the associated racism.

In parallel with the evolution of the European Union, a number of symbols with either a positive or negative connotation have emerged or



F. Bieber, R. Bieber, *Negotiating Unity and Diversity in the European Union*, Palgrave Studies in European Union Politics,
https://doi.org/10.1007/978-3-030-55016-5_6

been formally introduced. They raise questions concerning their relationship with the object or concept they aim to represent and with the existing symbols of individual Member States.

Symbols represent ideas, values, institutions, and objects that are external to them. For psychologists, cultural symbols are "important constituents of our mental make-up and vital forces in the building up of human society; and they cannot be eradicated without serious loss" (Jung 1946, p. 93). Symbols, by definition, differ from the idea or object represented. However, between symbols and a given reality there exists a reciprocal relationship. In fact, an idea, an institution, or an object may take on the quality of a symbol.

The intrinsic value of symbols lies in their potential to represent and to aggregate phenomena that do not have a material existence: they can articulate identity (see Delsol 2010, p. 4; Lindahl 1997). At the same time this indicates a potential weakness. Without the existence of the object represented, a symbol remains an empty shell, while abstract values acquire their authority only with the help of symbols. The degree of abstraction that distinguishes the symbol from its material foundation renders it multifunctional, entailing an increased risk of abuse.

Symbols may have a negative or a positive connotation or may be perceived as neutral. This quality may occur simultaneously, so that a symbol may be perceived by some as representing something desirable, while for others it entails a negative message. Symbols may also change their meaning over time. Especially when a symbol represents belonging to a particular group, it can be perceived as a positive signal to group members, and at the same time evoke hostile reactions among some who do not belong to this group (either by choice or exclusion).[1] The substance represented by symbols may change over time, and symbols may alter their meaning accordingly. It is, however, also possible that symbols do not reflect changes in the substance represented, thus helping to obscure the changes.

Symbols may evolve over time, but they can also be created, dismantled, and restructured (Hobsbawm 2013, p. 13). Symbols of political power are particularly susceptible to the risk of confusion between reality and fiction, as they may serve as "the emperor's new clothes" (Andersen 1837), or "the cap on the pole" (Schiller 1804), as in the story of Wilhelm Tell, where the local overlord appointed by the Habsburgs required his subjects to greet a pole with his hat on it.

[1] For example, the flags and other souvenirs of football clubs.

Aniconism, the prohibition of the material representation of the natural or supranational world, in particular of god in certain religions, can be seen as an attempt to preserve the authenticity and uniqueness that gets lost in representation and symbolization.

The term 'symbol' encapsulates a broad range of meanings: from specific objects like flags, to ideas such as certain social values. Symbols may be used to evoke positive identification, rejection, or just acknowledgement; they may represent stability or change. Moreover, we can draw a distinction between 'official' symbols, which have been adopted or recognized by the authorities of a given entity and which are intended to represent that entity, and other symbols used in a society for the purpose of shorthand communication in order to refer to objects or events ('genuine' symbols).[2]

Symbols have been used for millennia due to their ability to be depicted as markers of collectives. These include the cross or the eagle (single- or later double-headed) as symbols of empires. Symbols have gained a ubiquitous meaning in the era of the nation-state, including the formal markers that all states are expected to possess, such as a flag and an anthem, as well as symbols that are based on shared myths that might be communicated and promoted within a nation or a state. In addition, other collective groups, such as parties or football clubs, use symbols to distinguish themselves, often using the same type of symbol that states do (flags and anthems). The use of these symbols might be legally defined or just a feature of collective agreement; as they mark group membership, they are inherently exclusionary. In some instances, this exclusion might be based on choice; in others, exclusion might be violent and imposed.

Complex polities struggle with symbols in particular, as they have to account for the symbols and the identities their constituent units embody. One path is that of the Union Flag of the United Kingdom that combines the flags of England (St George's Cross) and Scotland (St Andrew's Cross). Such a synthesis of symbols is rare, and even here the red dragon of Wales is not incorporated. Another symbolic choice is to disregard the established symbols of groups and regions as they might create greater antagonism. This is striking in post-war multinational polities, such as Cyprus, Bosnia and Herzegovina, and Kosovo, which all adopted generic symbols that evoke the shape of the country (Cyprus and Kosovo) or

[2] For example, the use of the name of the capital of a country in order to designate its government.

European integration (Kosovo and Bosnia and Herzegovina). Beyond the state flags, there is also a wider question in terms of the toleration and use of symbols that embody both unity and diversity. Beyond balancing the shared polity and the recognition of the constituent identities, there is also the question of how symbols can generate a shared identification with a polity. As such, symbols are not empty vessels. Symbols, like myths, can be misinterpreted and new meaning can be ascribed to them—consider how the swastika became a symbol of racism and national socialism in the twentieth century although it had very different connotations earlier. They are also able to embody inclusion or exclusion. Of course, a racist or ethnonationalist symbol might exclude others a priori, but the dynamics of symbolism can be subtler. For example, the new state of Bosnia and Herzegovina in 1992 adopted the medieval *fleur-de-lis* as its flag. The symbol evoked the medieval Kotromanić dynasty predating modern nations and referenced a French aristocratic symbol. Yet the war and the opposition to the state by Croat and Serb nationalist insurgents meant that the flag, although neutral in form, became associated with the Muslim/Bosniak majority (Kolstø 2006). Thus, when exploring the symbols associated with the European Union—and Europe—and the challenge of embodying the Union and its diversity at once through symbols, we will need to move beyond just the 12 yellow stars on a blue background.

## 6.1 Symbols and European Integration

### *The Paradox of Symbolization of the European Union*

Europe's origin is itself a myth and symbol. The Phoenician princess *Europa* is the mythological origin of the name of the European semicontinent. However, the European Union is not the mythical land that Zeus, in the shape of a bull, reached with the princess on his back. What constitutes Europe has moved over the centuries from the Southeast to the West, reflecting shifts in power, both political and economic, and the absence in the West of another term to describe the region. With the collapse of the Roman Empire in the West, Europe became the substitute that merged Roman legacies with those of the barbarian invaders. In the East, where 'Europe' as a term originated, the Byzantine Empire described its realm as the Roman Empire or Realm and the inhabitants as Romans, a term later adopted in the Ottoman period that described its European possessions as Rumelia.

Instead of fulfilling Greek legends, the European Union (and its predecessors) has been future-oriented and has embodied a new approach toward common governance for this part of the world.

The symbolization of these new goals within a new system of governance occurred in a slow and partly hidden process, which has not as yet fully matured. It is a paradox, insofar as symbols are meant to represent an entity and therefore must be visible. The symbols of the European Union are to a large degree invisible, partly because the institutions of the EU have shied away from openly emphasizing the symbolic quality of principles and objects, and partly because some Member States have hesitated and at times rejected the symbols of an entity to which they belong, but which transcends the nation-state.

A step with lasting symbolic purpose and effect was taken in 1960 by the Parliamentary Assembly of the (then) European Communities with the adoption of the name 'European Parliament.'[3] This move was only recognized 27 years later, in 1987, in the founding treaties (Single European Act, 1986, p. 1, art. 3, title II). The ECJ established another (discreet) layer of symbols: the case law on the guiding principles of EU law and its relationship with the legal orders of the Member States (direct effect, supremacy, concurrent and exclusive competences, protection of fundamental rights, etc.[4]). In doing so it shaped the substance of a constitutional order, which symbolized the (voluntary) submission of the Member States to a common polity. For any polity the principles circumscribing the essence of its being—its identity—and namely its constitution (or, as it was called by the Court for the first time in 1986, "the Constitutional Charter") is of major symbolic significance.[5]

These gradual steps of the Parliament and the Court could be seen as part of the emergence of discreet symbols of European integration. While they might not have been widely received or instrumental in shaping the identification of citizens with the European Union, they helped shape the self-understanding of the EU and emancipate it from an institutional system fully shaped and determined by its Members. Nevertheless, the European Union and its Member States were late in becoming aware of

[3] *Official Journal* 1962 No 31, p. 1045.

[4] For a summary and appraisal of the most important cases see Poiares Maduro and Azoulai (2010). An early analysis of the significance of those decisions beyond the purely legal sphere had been put forward by Weiler (1981). An updated version is published in Weiler (1999).

[5] On this point see Walker (2010).

the importance of creating symbols representing the integration process. Awareness of the problems associated with this process was even less present among the EU and its Members.

The notion of a "Constitution for Europe" in a *Treaty establishing a Constitution for Europe* (2004) appeared quite appropriate to describe the evolving new legal order, but it remained highly controversial and ultimately failed in 2005 in referenda in France and the Netherlands and could not therefore come into force. While the failure of the Constitution in the two referenda probably owes more to reasons external to the Constitution and the European Union, there can be little doubt that the terms Constitution and Europe constituted a symbolic reach that was strongly contested.

In this Treaty an attempt was made to consolidate the formal symbols of the European Union. Article I-8 ("The symbols of the Union") of this Treaty reads:

> *The flag of the Union shall be a circle of twelve golden stars on a blue background.*
>
> *The anthem of the Union shall be based on the 'Ode to Joy' from the Ninth Symphony by Ludwig van Beethoven.*
>
> *The motto of the Union shall be: 'United in diversity'.*
>
> *The currency of the Union shall be the euro.*
>
> *Europe day shall be celebrated on 9 May throughout the Union.*

Except for the motto, this provision did not contain anything new and the text was not particularly controversial. Some Member States did not, however, wish to constitutionally 'upgrade' the status of the EU symbols. As the ratification of the Treaty failed, the provision did not come into force.[6]

The leap between acknowledging the fact of the existence of a new polity and the acceptance of symbols which had hitherto been the prerogative of states was apparently too great. The follow-up 'Lisbon Treaty' reverted to more conventional forms of change in the EU and carefully avoided any reference either to the term 'constitution' or to notions associated with constitutions. Therefore, no provision on the symbols of the Union appears in this most recent founding text of the European Union.

This did not, however, mark the end of these symbols, which, after all, had been in use for decades. In a Declaration annexed to the Lisbon

[6] For a critical assessment see Haltern (2003), p. 4.

Treaty, 16 Member States declared that "the flag with a circle of twelve golden stars on a blue background, the anthem based on the 'Ode to Joy' from the Ninth Symphony by Ludwig van Beethoven, the motto 'United in diversity', the euro as the currency of the European Union and Europe Day on 9 May will for them continue as symbols to express the sense of community of the people in the European Union and their allegiance to it."[7]

As a result, the proposed motto 'united in diversity' was not formally enacted, but was put into practice as Member States granted different status to the symbols of the joint project.

### *The History of the Official EU Symbols*

The history of the EU symbols is itself an illustration of the gap between their de facto acceptance over time based on their gradual introduction and the rejection of their formal and symbolic recognition, embodied by the failure of the 2005 'Constitution for Europe.' Thus, the emergence of these symbols is a suitable illustration of the difficulties the EU faces in symbolizing itself.

In 1984, more than 25 years after the enactment of the Treaty of Rome, and following a Resolution of the European Parliament in 1983 on the adoption of a flag for the European Community,[8] the European Council, uniting the Heads of State and Government of the Member States, considered it to be

> …essential that the Community should respond to the expectations of the people of Europe by adopting measures to strengthen and promote its identity and its image both for its citizens and for the rest of the world. An ad hoc committee will be set up to prepare and coordinate this action. It will be composed of representatives of the Heads of State or Government of the Member States. The Committee will examine inter alia the following

[7] Declaration No 52, Official Journal 2008 C 115, p. 355. Among the states which did not sign the Declaration were Ireland, Poland, and the United Kingdom. France approved the declaration in 2018.

[8] European Parliament, Minutes of Proceedings of the sitting of 11 April 1983. *Official Journal* 1983, C128, p. 18.

> suggestions:*symbols of the Community's existence, such as a flag and an anthem.*[9]

A subsequent report of an 'ad hoc Committee,' composed of personal representatives of the then Heads of State or Government,[10] submitted in June 1985, gave detailed consideration of this first mention of the notion of 'symbols' in the European context:

> There is clearly a need, for both practical and symbolic reasons, for a flag and an emblem to be used at national and international events, exhibitions and other occasions where the existence of the Community needs to be brought to public attention. A decision on this matter is required in order to avoid misunderstanding and confusion. The Committee agrees with the European Parliament's idea that a design which could be used for both a Community emblem and a flag should be basically that chosen by the Council of Europe. However, bearing in mind the independence and the different nature of the two organizations, the Committee proposes to the European Council that the European Community emblem and flag should be a blue rectangle with, in the centre, a circle of 12 five-pointed gold stars which do not touch, surrounding a gold letter E, of the design already used by the Commission.
>
> The European Council should express the hope that the emblem and flag will be used at appropriate places and on suitable occasions, without of course affecting the use of national flags, and asks the institutions to agree to regulate the use of flag and emblem.
>
> The music of the 'Ode to Joy' from the fourth movement of Beethoven's ninth symphony is in fact used at European events. This anthem has also been recognized by the Council of Europe as being representative of the European idea.
>
> The Committee recommends to the European Council that this anthem be played at appropriate events and ceremonies.[11]

Accordingly, the Foreign Affairs Council, at its meeting on 21 and 22 April 1986, acknowledged a declaration of its president according to which the Council would use the flag and the anthem of the Community

[9] European Council Fontainebleau, 25 and 26 June 1984, Conclusions, Bulletin of the European Communities, supplement 7/1985, p. 5 (authors' emphasis).

[10] Chairman Pietro Adonnino, representative of the Italian Prime Minister and Member of the European Parliament.

[11] "A People's Europe" Report from the ad hoc Committee, Bulletin of the European Communities, Supplement 7/1985, p 29, No 9.1, 9.2.

as proposed by the report of the ad hoc Committee (*Bulletin of the European Communities,* 1986, p. 54). On the same occasion the Commission made a similar declaration (*Bulletin of the European Communities,* 1986, p. 57). On 29 May 1986 the presidents of the three EU institutions (Commission, Parliament, and Council), in the presence of the Secretary-General of the Council of Europe, officially inaugurated the flag.[12]

The European Parliament, for its part, introduced a specific provision ("The symbols of the Union") in its Rules of Procedure:

> Parliament shall recognise and espouse the following symbols of the Union:
> -the flag showing a circle of twelve golden stars on a blue background,
> -the anthem based on the 'Ode to Joy' from the Ninth Symphony by Ludwig van Beethoven,
> -the motto 'United in diversity'.[13]

In practice, the institutions have used the symbols since these decisions were made, as if they were enacted by a formal Treaty provision.[14] What has been lacking, however, is the symbolic 'blessing' of the symbols at the level of the Union.

### *'Genuine' Symbols in the European Union*

In parallel with the introduction of formal symbols, the European Union has strengthened its identity, and hence the substance of potential and often less tangible symbols. This process resulted from the implementation of the treaties on which the Union was founded by the EU legislature and the Court. It was accentuated by the sharpening of the Union's profile, that is, by the spelling out of the common values, common inheritance, and fundamental principles such as liberty, democracy, and respect for human rights and fundamental freedoms and for the rule of law (*Treaty Establishing the European Union* [TEU], 2007, preamble). Moreover, rights for citizens that had both a practical and a symbolic dimension were inserted into the treaties. These include EU citizenship and the right of

[12] The event is described in Lager (1995), p. 56–57.

[13] Rule 238(1), *Official Journal* 2019 L302, p. 1.

[14] Several Member States, for example Austria and Germany, have legally introduced the symbols in their legislation.

free movement within the Union.[15] Other instruments that increased the visibility of the Union, and hence are of a symbolic quality, include the European passport,[16] the common form of driving license,[17] the common currency (*TEU*, 2007, art. 3[4]), and specific advantages for EU citizens crossing internal and external borders.[18]

The formation of 'practical' symbols does not render formal symbols superfluous. The Union's still fragile identity can in fact crystallize around both traditional formal symbols like a flag and more 'practical' representations. Even the designation "Union" has only gradually become such a crystallizing factor since it replaced the term "European Community" or "European Communities" (*TEU*, 2007, art. 1).[19]

Instruments that combine practical advantage and visibility provide for potentially strong symbolic effects. At the same time, these 'symbols of practical use' reflect our central theme of 'united in diversity.' In the case of passports, coins, or driving licenses, besides common features of shape, format, color, and text, they all contain references to the issuing Member State. This is particularly obvious on the coins of the common currency, which have a common 'European' side and a national side that the Member States are free to fill.[20] The resulting differences between French and German passports or euro coins issued in those countries do not affect their legal equality within the Union, yet they also clearly identify the shared symbols (flag) and substance (currency, citizenship).

Coins and the 'common' currency in general reflect, however, a further paradox of EU symbols: in 2020 only 19 of the 27 Member States have adopted the common currency. It follows that the euro simultaneously serves as a symbol of the Union and its common currency (for the 19) and as a symbol of difference vis-à-vis those Member States which do not wish,

[15] European Parliament and Council Regulation 399/2016 on a Union Code on the rules governing the movement of persons across borders (Schengen Border Code). *Official Journal* L77, 23 March 2016, p.1. See also Chap. 7.

[16] Resolution of the Representatives of the Governments of the Member States of the European Communities, meeting within the Council of 23 June 1981, OJ 1981 C 241, p. 1, as confirmed and amended by several subsequent Resolutions.

[17] European Parliament and Council Directive 2006/126/EC on driving licenses. *Official Journal* 2006, L403, 30 December, p. 18.

[18] European Parliament and Council Regulation 399/2016, 2016, art. 8[2], 22.

[19] On the previous situation see Constantinesco (1997).

[20] When filling 'their' space, Member States must, however, respect certain common criteria, European Council Regulation 729/2014 on denominations and technical specifications of euro coins intended for circulation. *Official Journal* L194, 2 July 2014, p.1, Articles 4–8.

or have not qualified, to introduce the common currency. Thus, the currency is unable to function as a symbol that is shared among all members.

In addition, from the point of view of their value as symbols, euro bills are problematic for another reason. Their common feature, the quality of unity,' remains highly abstract and nearly invisible. The images on the bank notes show abstractions of various historic bridges or arches. They are thus abstract and link to neither unity—symbols that signify the common project of the European Union—nor diversity, by not clearly identifying the difference as a value. Abstraction is thus an escape from the dilemma of diversity and unity in the case of the currency.

Other measures pursuing the same objective are the designation of 'European Capitals of Culture' and the award of a 'European Heritage Label' by the Union, which will be discussed in more detail below.[21]

### *Another Paradox: The Easy Way to European Symbols in the Council of Europe*

The Council of Europe has been the source of the choice of symbols for European unity, as the ad hoc Committee, as noted above, acknowledged in its report.[22] Indeed, as early as 1950 the Parliamentary Assembly of the Council of Europe discussed the topic (Göldner 1988, p. 37ff.). The Council of Europe's aim, "to achieve a greater unity between its members for the purpose of safeguarding and realizing the ideals and principles which are their common heritage and facilitating their economic and social progress" (*Statute of the Council of Europe*, 1949, art. 1[a]), is not fundamentally different from the aims of the European Union. Nevertheless, the topic of symbols for this organization was never as sensitive as in the European Union. This difference can be understood by the structure of each organization, rather than the symbols: the Council of Europe remains within the realm of traditional international organizations, which does not permit direct intervention in the legal order of its Member States; accordingly, Member States do not perceive the organization and its symbols as a potential competitor to their identity and their national symbols. However, in the European Union the borders between the organization and statehood are blurred, and the Union continues to evolve "towards an

[21] European Parliament and Council Decision 1194/2011 establishing a European Union action for the European Heritage Label. *Official Journal* L303, 22 November 2011, pp. 1–9.

[22] "A People's Europe" Report from the ad hoc Committee 1985.

unknown destination" (Shonfield 1973). Membership of the European Union implies an opening up of national identity toward an osmotic relationship between the Union and its Member States as well as among Member States. The more the Union becomes 'visible,' the more this change in the traditional quality of the state has to be acknowledged. Symbols of the European Union reflect this challenge to the traditional message of exclusivity inherent in national symbols. It is therefore not surprising that some Member States have struggled in openly acknowledging this transformation of their identity.

The Parliamentary[23] Assembly of the Council of Europe focused at first on the flag and discussed criteria for its choice. This new flag was to represent the idea of a community of states, be simple, understandable, harmonious, and agreeable, and have a recognized heraldic appearance. On the basis of Recommendation 88 of 25 October 1955 of the (then) Consultative Assembly, the Committee of Ministers, on 9 December 1955, decided "to adopt for the Council of Europe the following emblem: on a field azure a circle of twelve mullets with their points not touching." The following "symbolical description" was assigned to it:

"Against the blue sky of the Western world, the stars symbolize the peoples of Europe in the form of a circle, the sign of union. The stars are twelve in number and are invariable, the figure twelve being the symbol of perfection and entirety."[24]

The flag was not supposed to remain a symbol of the Council of Europe only. In fact, the Parliamentary Assembly, in its resolution of 25 October 1955, recommended that it should "enter into negotiations with the other European institutions to ensure that the emblems adopted by them shall resemble that adopted by the Council of Europe."[25] Thus, at its inception, the symbol was intended to evoke European integration more broadly than just of the Council of Europe.

More than 30 years were to elapse before the European Union formally reacted to this proposal—and it initially responded unexpectedly. When its institutions began discussions on the topic, the Council of Europe had declined in significance as compared with the European Union, and the

[23] Initially the official name was "*Consultative* Assembly".

[24] Council of Europe, Document CM (55) 161. Most likely the symbolic meanings of the circle and the number twelve have been confused in this text. According to its Latin origin, 'rotundus,' the circle stands for 'round' and 'perfection,' while the number twelve stands for togetherness and unity. See Göldner (1988), p. 83.

[25] Consultative Assembly of the Council of Europe, 17th Session, Doc. 443.

purpose of adopting the flag was motivated less by the intention of coming under the umbrella of the Council of Europe (at least symbolically), and more by the desire to strengthen the Union's identity, and the symbols of the Council of Europe provided for a readymade solution.

## 6.2 The Difficult Co-existence of Symbols in the European Union

The inconsistent development and application of the symbols of the European Union reflect to a large extent the complex relationship between the Union and its Member States. Symbols relating to governance aim at rendering *visible* the abstract phenomenon of power. To this end their intrinsic value lies in their capacity to reduce the complexity of the political systems and their interdependence. Traditionally, emphasizing differences in comparison with neighboring systems can reduce complexity. Territory, language, and history are easy markers to distinguish one system of power from another. The EU, however, cannot be separated from the political systems of its Member States. Therefore its existence precludes the Member States from relying on their traditional narrative of exclusivity. National symbols lose their quality and exclusivity as representations of the political system by which individual citizens are governed.

An organization that has emerged through the process of vertical power-sharing has to find its genuine expression in symbols that represent the plurality of authorities. In this respect the European Union and its Member States are still in search of adequate symbolization of this complex relationship.

So far this co-existence is represented by the parallel use of the flags of the European Union and of its Member States. In many Member States on official occasions, the flag of the European Union is displayed alongside the flag of the Member State in question.[26] It is ironic that the United Kingdom prior to its departure from the EU was the Member State in which the EU flag was displayed the least, since it was also a Member State very familiar with multiple flags in use to signify different communities within the state, including the Scottish, English, and Welsh flags. In respect to the currency, the common symbol on one side of the coins co-exists easily with the different national symbols on the other. Certain sym-

[26] See, for example, Germany, Erlass der Bundesregierung über die Beflaggung der Dienstgebäude des Bundes 22 March 2005.

bols do not, however, co-exist so easily. A prerequisite of their use is a hierarchy between national and European symbols to determine questions such as which anthem should be played first at official ceremonies.

In a more general sense, the European Union itself became a symbol of the desire of the peoples of Europe for a peaceful, safe, and secure existence, economic and social progress, and the rule of law. The continued demands to join the EU illustrate the strength of this symbol despite the fact that within the Union those aims are frequently taken for granted and are not necessarily attributed to the Union.

One can, on the other hand, observe within the Union a tendency to render the Union responsible for all sorts of problems that either have their origin at the global level or result from situations for which national authorities are responsible. The symbol for this presumed negative quality of the European Union is the label 'Brussels bureaucracy' or simply 'Brussels.' Also at the national level it is not uncommon to refer to national institutions, in particular the government, using notions of geography or locality (e.g. 'Washington,' 'Berlin,' 'Downing Street,' or 'Elysée'). However, while those notions/symbols are used with a neutral meaning, the public discourse referring to the European Union uses the symbol 'Brussels' with a clearly negative connotation.

## 6.3 Symbols and the Identity of a Polity

Politics needs symbols, since symbols provide for identity and assurance. Only with the help of symbols can a group identify as such and legitimize institutions. Symbols establish a bridge between citizens and government. The unifying effect of political symbols may result from symbols with a purely aesthetic substance (e.g. flags) but also from historic events, from buildings, sites, or common rules, and shared principles, which reflect identity and create unity beyond their immediate purpose (e.g. fundamental rights, civic rights, or constitutional principles).

Symbols are group-making mechanisms that define the (supposed) substance of group membership and also its borders, defining the limits in respect to those who do not belong to the group in question. Hence symbols are frequently a sign of exclusiveness and—although not necessarily—of exclusion.

Symbols may consolidate their specific quality over a long period of time. They can, however, also acquire this quality in one brief moment. That is notably the case of pictures, which are quickly disseminated electronically (e.g. the attacks on the World Trade Centre and the Pentagon, for which even the date '9/11' has become a symbol).

The relationship between a symbol and the object or idea represented may change over time. Symbols may convey a meaning that is different from the initial message. But in order to fulfill their purpose, they have to be easily and generally recognizable. Therefore, the prevailing nature of symbols is their permanence, recognizability, and clarity.

Changes in the nature of symbols may result either from transformations of the object/idea represented or from modification of the symbol itself. An example of the latter is the introduction of a new flag for a country. An example of a transformation of the object represented without a corresponding modification of the symbol is the European Union: at the time of introduction of its symbols in 1986, the European Union consisted of 12 Member States as opposed to 27 in 2020. Furthermore, its legal foundation in the EEC Treaty has since then been considerably altered by means of several Treaty amendments, the latest being the Treaty of Lisbon (2009).

The symbols of the European Union do not reflect either this specific evolution or in a more general sense the dynamic nature of 'an ever closer union' of a polity that subsequently has to be brought into being (*TEU*, 2007, art. 3[3–4]).[27] Quite the contrary; the only definition of the flag, given in 1955, emphasized "unity," and "perfection and entirety,"[28] criteria which refer to a static meaning.

The discrepancy between the static symbol and the dynamic quality of the entity represented renders the perception of the nature of the Union more difficult and therefore weakens the symbolizing quality of the flag. This is not to argue that the symbols should change with the changes of the Union, as this would undermine the constituent features of symbols.

The difficulty is aggravated by the unprecedented nature of the European Union. A union of states resulting from a voluntary decision (or rather many such decisions over six decades) and achieved through a democratic process has never before been attempted. Therefore, this experiment lacks previous experience or clear-cut comparison. Thus the reference to the past is only possible through references to general European history, such as ancient Greek mythology or the empire of Charlemagne, or

[27] "The Union *shall establish* an internal market"/"The Union *shall establish* an economic and monetary union whose currency is the euro" (authors' italics).

[28] See footnote 24.

by negative examples, such as World War II. The EU is both intrinsically future-oriented and based on the idea of rationality, rather than an emotional evocation of the past. Thus, the future is not the promise of a return to a golden era, as nationalist mythology often argues, but rather a 'voyage to an unknown destination.' Yet trust in the future has to be grounded on a promise. In this context symbols can have a strong effect. They can stand for the promise–or the dream.

The myth and symbol of Europa on the bull might stand for such a dream. The current symbols of the European Union, at least its flag, do not evoke dreams or hope (although this may be different in states which aspire to become members of the Union). The issue is further complicated by the fact that the Union is not the only polity on the territory concerned. Its identity exists alongside the continuing identities of the Member States. Such co-existence is not unfamiliar to the citizens of federal states or other complex states. However, the identity of federations can in most cases rely on deep historic roots, although even then strong tensions can be observed between the center and the constituent entities. Furthermore, conventional international organizations, such as the United Nations or NATO, use their symbols in parallel with state symbols. Traditional international organizations do not exercise activities that cast doubt on the exclusive identity of states, and their symbols are used only in narrowly circumscribed contexts. Thus, the NATO or UN flag is not commonly used by municipalities of its Member States or even by their governments unless there is a particular occasion, such as a specific day or event.

The European Union's identity is ambiguous: it is distinct from its Member States and yet it cannot exist without them. Moreover, its identity is distinct from its international environment. Yet, as a consequence of accession or departure its identity in relation to its international environment is subject to change. This ambiguity is echoed on the level of symbols. On the one hand, the Union is itself a symbol of the desire of the peoples of Europe for a peaceful and secure co-existence in economic prosperity and social welfare beyond the nation-state. On the other hand, its component states continue to exist and in comparison to them the Union is a more distant reality. In order to be perceived by and to obtain the approval of its citizens, it needs to have symbols that represent identity and openness as the specific features of European integration. However, symbols can only have such an effect when the polity that they aim to represent has achieved a certain degree of consolidation.

The symbols of the European Union do not only need to grow and justify the existence of the EU. Their very existence creates a challenge to existing national symbols and they must thus find their place alongside traditional national symbols. This raises the broader problems of shared sovereignty and the connected question of the multiple loyalties of citizens. In this context the parallel use of flags does not represent a problem; however, national anthems cannot be played simultaneously. They have to be brought into a hierarchy, which in turn questions the specific value of European integration as a non-centralized venture. While the European Union makes no claim of exclusivity, nation-state projects have historically often made such claims, which explains why they have struggled more with the explicit and implicit multiple levels of loyalty the European Union's symbolism evokes.

## 6.4 Pluralism and Symbols ('Unity and Diversity')

The Union not only has an unprecedented history and shape, it also pursues an exceptional aim that is encapsulated in its motto 'united in diversity.' Many provisions of the Treaties are meant to protect diversity (cultural, linguistic [*Charter of Fundamental Rights of the European Union,* 2000, art. 22], national identity [*TEU*, 2007, art. 4[2]], and qualified national interests[*TEU*, 2007, art. 31[2]; *Treaty on the Functioning of the European Union* [TFEU], 2007, art. 82[3], 83[3]), while others provide for mechanisms to introduce measures, policies, or acts, most of which are of a binding nature and apply to most if not all Member States and their citizens, thus gradually building unity.

Conventional polities—like most states—are organized in a hierarchical manner: the degree of diversity within that state is settled by the Constitution and in most cases decided at the top level of the hierarchy, which could be a supreme court, a central parliament, or a referendum of the citizens of the state. The relationship between the European Union, its Member States, and its citizens is not, however, characterized by hierarchy. Its founding principles are voluntary membership, voluntary compliance, and "sincere cooperation" (*TEU*, 2007, art. 4[3]).

Such a system has obvious virtues and shortcomings.

On the one hand, nation-states offer an easily understandable and—at first glance—efficient framework for democratic governance. However, States are no longer capable of fully answering the expectations and needs of their citizens. Neither are they capable of representing their multiple identities, allegiances, and loyalties. Furthermore, the ability to govern smaller states is increasingly limited. Individuals can achieve an optimum of autonomy only with a system of governance that is large, transnational, and founded on a plurality of actors, where no single actor claims the ultimate authority and multiple layers of belonging and co-existence are protected. A political system of this kind is inevitably complex, difficult to frame, and does not produce quick and easily predicted answers. Moreover, if we call this system in the real world 'the European Union,' it consists of nation-states, which for a multitude of reasons are eager to maintain their identity. The motto of the Union ('united in diversity') stands in contrast to the motto of the United States of America, 'e pluribus unum' ('out of many, one').

Unity *and* diversity in the European Union can only be achieved simultaneously when perceived as components of an inherently dynamic system. Since they are antagonistic notions, they cannot be achieved in isolation from each other. Any policy in this system has to strive for equilibrium between both strands. In order to achieve this equilibrium, democratic legitimacy in respect to *both* aims is indispensable. At present the European Union still strives for acceptance of its identity. The strand of acceptance of difference in particular is still weak. In order to bring about the unique principle of respect for diversity as a fundamental value of the identity of the European Union, the instruments and symbols regarding respect of 'otherness' still need to be strengthened, rather than just emphasizing difference at its core.

Symbolizing a pluralist and evolutionary system is a unique and highly demanding exercise. If the core values of a humane society which is grounded in self-determination and justice (human rights, democracy, rule of law, etc.) are already protected within the framework of the national system in question (although at times with serious imperfections as one can observe in the erosion of these norms in recent years in Hungary, for example), the added value of additional protection by the Union is not immediately perceptible.[29]

On the other hand, some citizens of the Member States might expect direct intervention by the Union in the case of serious shortcomings, for example with regard to the implementation of 'good governance' or the rule of law. However, the Union has only very limited means at its disposal to sanction Member States in case of non-compliance with European law,

[29] See, however, the operation of the European Convention on Human Rights.

and Member State governments often evoke national narratives to reject and oppose intervention by the Union.[30] In such situations 'diversity' as one foundation of the Union becomes an obstacle to maintaining the unity of the common values.

It is therefore not surprising that the symbols of the European Union used at present are not yet capable of providing an attractive and powerful message, expressing the value of striving for unity *and* diversity.

## 6.5 The Co-creation of the European Union's Symbolic Landscape

Much of the symbolic construction of Europe has occurred less through the formal and top-level symbols, such as the flag, anthem, or motto, and more through a rich symbolic infrastructure that has been advanced by multiple European actors. Through European Cities of Culture and the European Heritage Label, to name just two examples, the EU has encouraged a bottom-up creation of symbols that embody the need to incorporate diversity into the process of the definition of symbols. Furthermore, symbolic narratives have also been important to the EU and have been co-shaped by Member States. The original narrative of European integration has centered on defining the project as an answer to World War II, namely the rejection of extreme nationalism and war and favoring of transnational cooperation. A narrative of free association of European states in the aftermath of World War II provided for a powerful founding myth of European integration. Thus, economic integration and cooperation was symbolically underpinned by its ultimate goal, the prevention of renewed war in the EU among its Member States. This peace narrative was reaffirmed when the EU received the Nobel Peace Prize in 2012 (Manners and Murray 2015). In the aftermath of the Nobel Peace Price the European Parliament and the Commission sought to formulate "A New Narrative for Europe" in 2013–2014 (Kaiser 2015) to account for the crisis of the peace narrative. However, this top-down effort was unable to create a new encompassing story, and the experience showed the limitation of creating such a narrative through a top-down process.

The peace narrative began to reach its limitations after the 2004–2007 enlargement with the inclusion of ten countries of Central and Eastern Europe that had been under Soviet domination or part of Yugoslavia.

[30] For example respect for national identities, see chapter 4.2.

Their experience was very different from the prevailing founding myth of the EU. As they could not participate in the earlier decades of EU integration, the main narrative tool employed here was the concept of the 'return to Europe,' that is, the notion that socialism and Soviet rule or Yugoslavia prevented the self-determination of the countries in joining the European integration process and the values embodied by it earlier. This notion is partially true, yet also problematic. In the case of Yugoslavia, the countries that joined the EU, Slovenia and Croatia, were not forcibly dominated by the Yugoslav state, but instead it was a joint (authoritarian) state that based its rule on the legitimacy of anti-fascism and rejection of the Cold War blocs. For the other countries, Soviet dominance was indeed the prime reason for communist rule and authoritarian control. At the same time, the European alternative was highly hypothetical. Considering the struggle for democracy in Southern Europe (Portugal, Spain, Greece), and their relatively late accession to the Union, democracy and European integration was not the only alternative in Europe during the decades after World War II. The narrative of the return to Europe also gave rise to the effort of equating fascism and communism. What had been a highly contested and inconclusive debate in the German *Historikerstreit* during the 1980s was easily incorporated into European narratives two decades later.

The larger narrative that the Union has been shaping about its past has been described as the EU memory framework by Milošević and Touquet (2018). This framework includes a number of declarations and documents produced by the European Parliament and the Commission that outline a European interpretation of important commemorative events and guides to the past, and provides a way to make sense of this in a European framework. This includes a number of declarations on the Holocaust and other instances of mass violence and genocide, such as Srebrenica and the Armenian genocide. For the larger narrative, three documents are particularly relevant, namely the establishment of a "European Day of Remembrance for the Victims of Stalinism and Nazism" (August 23) by an overwhelming vote in the European Parliament and the declaration on "European conscience and totalitarianism," in 2009 and in the following year the European Commission report on "The memory of the crimes committed by totalitarian regimes in Europe" (European Commission 2010). The Declaration on "European conscience and totalitarianism" links European integration and a shared memory by noting "Europe will be united only when it is capable to reach a common point of view on its history, recognize communism, Nazism and fascism as collective legacy and lead an honest and thorough debate on all totalitarian crimes of the last century."[31]

As a result, the founding myth of the EU has evolved from the centrality of peace, the European commemoration of the Holocaust, and the rejection of National Socialism to incorporate communism under the larger umbrella of totalitarianism. This reinterpretation is highly problematic for equating the four decades of communist rule, which included both early totalitarian phases during the Stalinist era and late communism that was considerably less oppressive than fascism and national socialism.

Although it is ironic that this narrative would appear more befitting of the Cold War, it gained relevance after the accession of new members from Central and Eastern Europe to the EU. This shift can be understood as a way to reflect the prevailing experience of new members in the Union and thus the EU as constituting its defining myth based on the experiences of old and new members. However, there is another symbolic level. The countries of Central Europe entered the EU from a position of weakness, both in terms of economic development and pronounced stereotypes toward Europe's East (Subotić 2019). This view was best represented by Jacques Chirac, French president from 1995 to 2007, who in a statement in 2003 called the countries of Central and Eastern Europe irresponsible and "pas très bien élevé", that is, not very well brought up (Levieux and Levieux/*New York Times* 2003, February 23). The re-shaping of the European narrative and its founding myth has thus been introduced as a bottom-up process, that is, by the Member States to both be able to anchor their national narratives better in the European framework and also to overcome what Jelena Subotić has described as the ontological insecurity of countries in Central and Southeastern Europe.[32]

The way in which Europe is symbolically defined can also be found in other processes that are more deliberate, based both on the definition of sites of symbolism by the EU and their bottom-up accrual of content. An example of this is the European Capital of Culture, a program initiated by

[31] European conscience and totalitarianism European Parliament resolution of 2 April 2009 on European conscience and totalitarianism, Official Journal C 137E, 27 May 2010, p. 25–27.

[32] The term has gained widespread use in International Relations and Political Science and here described the uncertainty on the position of the country and the narratives about itself in the aftermath of the end of Communist rule, when previous narratives collapsed. Subotić (2019), pp. 27–29.

Melina Mercouri and Jack Lang, the Greek and French Ministers of Culture in 1985. The cities and regions that have held the title since have been able to fill the title with meaning. These often emphasis local specificities, but also draw on symbols that represent notions of both diversity and unity, as well as Europeanness. As has been noted in regard to the visual representation of applicant cities, "in the European Capital of Culture scheme Europeanness is stylized and performatively reinscribed for a cross-cultural audience through the repetition of generic cultural details or identity markers" (Aiello and Thurlow 2006, p. 160). Often, the label is mostly about the branding of cities rather than promoting a shared European idea (Immler and Sakkers 2014). The idea of the Cultural Capital was conceived to promote the European concept, but also to highlight through its annual 'migration' and frequent granting of the title to cities that are not Member State capitals that there is no singular European capital in terms of culture. This explicitly highlights the diversity of European culture and does not presuppose a center or the intent to establish one.[33] The focus on cities bypasses Member States and highlights how "the unity in diversity has gained strength and how the idea of a 'multipolar' Europe with a diverse heritage has been promoted and adopted" (Palonen 2010, p. 104). As cities seek to make their tenure as Cultural Capital a success, they symbolically co-define European culture and with it the symbols that mark the EU. Particularly since the early 2000s, Cultural Capitals have often sought to demonstrate their own experiences of diversity, global and European connections, and formative and traumatic European historical experiences, such as the Holocaust and World War II. Another site in which the EU has been shaping symbols has been through the European Heritage Label. The notion of heritage has a long history of being appropriated by both national myths and transnational narratives, such as the UNESCO World Heritage Centre (Lähdesmäki 2014, pp. 401–402). As such, physical and immaterial remains of the past are open to be interpreted in a number of ways for the present. Conceptualizing heritage as European does not challenge the national or state claims to the heritage but adds an additional layer and allows for the specific site or tradition to be associated with 'Europe,' offering a wide scope of heritage.

[33] European Parliament and Council Decision 445/2014 establishing a Union action for the European Capitals of Culture for the years 2020 to 2033 and repealing Decision No 1622/2006/EC (2014). *Official Journal* L132, 3 May 2014, pp. 1–12.

On one hand, the European label could be interpreted as overcoming a nation-centric view of cultural heritage. Thus, key sites are not just associated with a particular nation, but with Europe more widely. On the other, the symbolic notion of European heritage also reaffirms the nation's framework, as nominating sites to be recognized as European heritage requires the sites to be proposed through a Member State selection process. Although transnational sites are possible, the site is national. With Member States as gatekeepers, Europeanness is mediated through the Member States.

Thus, Member States are also able to promote their national concepts through the label and other transnational tools, offering them recognition for a national interpretation of heritage. The European Heritage list thus appears to offer no coherent view of what constitutes heritage for Europe, but as of 2020 includes 38 sites, from places of broad historical relevance such as ancient Athens to places of relevance for the history of European integration, such as Robert Schuman's House and the village of Schengen, and places of European conflict, such as cemeteries of World War I and a former concentration camp.[34] However, the list appears rather random, as it includes some peripheral places to European heritage, such as Fort Cadine, Austro-Hungarian fortifications in today's Trento, and omits central places, such as the Auschwitz concentration camp.

The European Heritage Label and the European Cultural Capitals show how the EU has provided spaces for bottom-up processes to symbolically define Europe and its relationship with particular sites and cities. This emphasis on diversity reflects the inability and unwillingness of the EU to impose a unified understanding of European culture or the symbols to mark it. The experience highlights the difficulty in generating shared symbols, as in some cases Europe becomes a label rather than an idea with which cities or places engage. In other cases, such as the debates about the historical legacies that precede European integration, Member States and nations seek to inject their understanding into the wider European historical understanding and create a position to link national narratives with larger European narratives of the past. As such, the symbolic practices are highlighted not just symbolically by unity and diversity, but also in practice, where the European symbols are not just adopted and used, but shaped. Thus, Europeanization captures both the manner in which

[34] https://ec.europa.eu/programmes/creative-europe/actions/heritage-label_en

national and local culture is framed in European and transnational terms, and also how the notion of European symbols is shaped and re-shaped by the national and sub-national actors within the Union.

## 6.6 Conclusions

Historically, the Phoenician princess on the bull symbolized Europe. The bull was none other than the Greek god Zeus, who transformed into a bull to abduct Europa and take her to Crete. If the myth comes too close to reality, it lays itself open to ridicule, like the efforts to symbolize Europe with the help of sculptures in front of the EU buildings in Brussels and Strasbourg. The enigma of the myth remains, however, intact. Does it represent a political project, an adventure, something radically new on the European semi-continent, or does it stand only for the dreams of increased individual freedom?

Either way, the starting point is characterized by the antagonism between two quite different actors: a god who seduces and a princess who is seduced and abducted to become queen of Crete. At first glance, the European Union does not share that antagonism. According to the official interpretation, its symbol—the circle of stars—reflects togetherness, perfection, and unity, resulting from a voluntary union. Moreover, it does not stress the differences, or even contradictions, between its component units; in any case there is no intention to acknowledge these differences in the common symbols. Quite the contrary: the Union is based on non-discrimination and equality under the law. It also aims to speak with one voice to the outside world and to create an area without internal frontiers.

The difference between the Greek myth and the modern symbolization of the European Union could explain why the symbolic bull with the princess finds such a faint echo in the modern symbols of Europe. The apparent difference hides, however, an intrinsic connection: at its core the Union is also founded on an ambiguous concept. Its motto, 'unity in diversity,' encapsulates two strands of European integration. On the one hand, the Union aims to preserve its origins—the multitude of states, peoples, and cultures.[35] On the other, the Treaty on the European Union "marks a new stage in the process of creating an ever closer union among

[35] For example, *TEU* (2007), art. 4(2): "The Union shall respect the equality of Member States before the Treaties as well as the national identities, inherent in their fundamental structures, political and constitutional, inclusive of regional and local self- government" and

the peoples of Europe" (*TEU*, 2007, preamble, art. 1). The Union aims, among other things, to "promote economic, social, and territorial cohesion and solidarity among Member States" (*TEU*, 2007, art. 3[3]). To that end, "common action to eliminate the barriers which divide Europe" (*TFEU*, 2007, preamble) is the aim.

When implementing these goals, tension between the two strands is inevitable. Under ideal conditions that tension should stimulate a permanent search for the most appropriate balance. It may, however, also lead to paralysis or even self-destruction. The risks can be limited if the balance is conceived as an ongoing process that maintains a dynamic of its own. In that respect the Union can be compared to the bull riding across the Mediterranean Sea. If the bull had stopped on its journey, it could only have been saved from drowning by revealing its true identity—the ancient Greek god Zeus—and as such nothing else but the product of human imagination.

Like this particular bull, the European Union does not possess an unquestionably solid substance. It consists of states that jealously guard their identity and their symbols.

An identity resulting from antagonistic strands is particularly difficult to crystalize in symbols. It cannot (yet) rely on the genuine and solid loyalty of its citizens. Its representation needs simple truths and simple symbols. The subtle and ambitious project of uniting at least 27 peoples on a voluntary basis for a "journey to an unknown destination" requires, however, complex symbols that have not yet been found.

## References

Aiello, G., & Thurlow, C. (2006). Symbolic Capitals: Visual Discourse and Intercultural Exchange in the European Capital of Culture Scheme. *Language and Intercultural Communication, 6*(2), 148–162.

Andersen, H. C. (1837). *The Emperor's New Clothes*. Copenhagen.

Constantinesco, V. (1997). Les Noms de l'Europe. In J.-F. Flauss & P. Wachsmann (Eds.), *Études à la mémoire de Jacques Schwob* (pp. 309–330). Brussels: Bruylant.

Delsol, C. (2010). Introduction. In C. Delsol & J.-F. Mattéi (Eds.), *L'identité de l'Europe* (pp. 1–7). Paris: PUF.

Article 22, Charter of Fundamental Rights of the European Union: "The Union shall respect cultural, religious and linguistic diversity" (cf. *TEU*, 2007, art. 3[3]).

European Commission. (2010). Report from the Commission to the European Parliament and to the Council, The Memory of the Crimes Committed by totalitarian regimes in Europe, Brussels, 22.12., *COM*(2010) 783 final.

Göldner, M. (1988). *Politische Symbole der europäischen Integration*. Frankfurt/ Main & Berne: Lang.

Haltern, U. (2003). Pathos and Patina. The Failure and Promise of Constitutionalism in European Integration. *European Law Journal, 9*(1), 14–44.

Hobsbawm, E. (2013). Introduction. In E. Hobsbawm & T. Ranger (Eds.), *The Invention of Tradition* (pp. 1–14). Cambridge: CUP.

Immler, N. L., & Sakkers, H. (2014). (Re)Programming Europe: European Capitals of Culture: Rethinking the Role of Culture. *Journal of European Studies, 44*(1), 3–29.

Jung, C. G. (1946). *Man and His Symbols*. London: Arkana.

Kaiser, W. (2015). Clash of Cultures: Two Milieus in the European Union's 'A New Narrative for Europe' Project. *Journal of Contemporary European Studies, 23*(3), 364–377.

Kolstø, P. (2006). National Symbols as Signs of Unity and Division. *Ethnic and Racial Studies, 29*(4), 676–701.

Lager, C. (1995). *L'Europe en quête de ses symboles*. Berlin & Frankfurt/Main: Berne.

Lähdesmäki, T. (2014). The EU's Explicit and Implicit Heritage Politics. *European Societies, 16*(3), 401–421.

Levieux, E., & Levieux, M. (2003, February 23). The World; No, Chirac Didn't Say "Shut Up". *New York Times*. https://www.nytimes.com/2003/02/23/weekinreview/the-world-no-chirac-didn-t-say-shut-up.html. Accessed 31 Mar 2020.

Lindahl, H. (1997). Sovereignty and Symbolization. *Rechtstheorie, 28*, 347–371.

Manners, I., & Murray, P. (2015). The end of a Noble Narrative? European Integration Narratives After the Nobel Peace Prize. *JCMS, 54*(1), 185–202.

Milošević, A., & Touquet, H. (2018). Unintended Consequences: The EU memory Framework and the Politics of Memory in Serbia and Croatia. *Southeast European and Black Sea Studies, 18*(3), 381–399.

Palonen, E. (2010). Multi-Level Cultural Policy and Politics of European Capitals of Culture. *Nordisk Kulturpolitisk Tidskrift, 13*(1), 87–108.

Poiares Maduro, M., & Azoulai, L. (Eds.). (2010). *The Past and Future of EU Law*. Oxford/Portland: Hart.

Schiller, F. (1804). *William Tell*.

Shonfield, A. (1973). *Europe: Journey to an Unknown Destination*. London: Penguin.

Subotić, J. (2019). *Yellow Star, Red Star: Holocaust Remembrance After Communism*. Ithaca: Cornell University Press.

Walker, N. (2010). Opening or Closure? The Constitutional Intimations of the ECJ. In M. Poiares Maduro & L. Azoulai (Eds.), *The Past and Future of EU Law* (pp. 333–342). Oxford/Portland: Hart.
Weiler, J. H. H. (1981). The Community System: The Dual Character of Supranationalism. *Yearbook of European Law, 1*(1), 267–306.
Weiler, J. H. H. (1999). *The Constitution of Europe*. Cambridge: CUP.

CHAPTER 7

# Exclusion and Belonging: The Ambiguities of European Citizenship

Citizenship is neither a comprehensive nor an exclusive category for members of a polity. Instead, citizenship is a legal construct for identifying individuals who share certain qualities for that purpose.[1] It exists alongside other objective or subjective qualities such as residence, ethnic belonging, religion, and sex, and may in principle be held together with other citizenships. Although formulated in legal terms, citizenship is a factual element and, as such, a symbol of belonging to a particular political community. The substance and protection of the rights of an individual depend upon the variables applicable within the polity in question. Citizenship may symbolize allegiance to a polity and solidarity with fellow citizens. Yet neither effect is logically inherent or exclusive to the quality of citizenship. Allegiances and solidarity may well—as is increasingly the case—be connected to residence without the simultaneous holding of citizenship. Furthermore, citizens might live far from the country that gave them citizenship and hold but few connections with it. Yossi Harpaz recently noted that citizenship can best be understood as holding four dimensions: offering status, rights, and identity, and serving as global sorter. The status takes on multiple dimensions (political, economic, social, and territorial) that offer a citizen accession that others lack (Harpaz 2019, pp. 3–8). Closely linked are rights, as citizenship serves to bestow certain rights and duties. To this end it establishes equality in law among its holders. As a

[1] On citizenship in general, see Beiner (1995) and Heater (1999).



F. Bieber, R. Bieber, *Negotiating Unity and Diversity in the European Union*, Palgrave Studies in European Union Politics,
https://doi.org/10.1007/978-3-030-55016-5_7

consequence of such equal rights and its quality as a vehicle for identification with the group in question, citizenship generates unity. At the same time, it marks difference and diversity, insofar as it distinguishes between individuals who belong to a given group and others who do not. Any polity grants preferential treatment to holders of its citizenship compared to non-citizens and will discriminate against foreigners. Discrimination—or, in more neutral terms, different treatment (generally less favorable)—can be flexible in regard to the foreigners discriminated against and the subject wherein discrimination applies. As such, citizenship also reinforces identities, as it privileges one identity over others. If citizenship and national identity coincide, citizenship strengthens the centrality of the nation-state. As a result, citizenship can have a unifying effect and thereby stresses diversity, as it provides equality among citizens, irrespective of other dimensions of diversity. Thus, citizenship can unite citizens who might otherwise speak different languages and hail from different ethnic or religious backgrounds. In many polities this effect is amplified by the exclusive nature of citizenship where parallel citizenships are not tolerated. However, because of its quality as a legal construct, citizenship is not a necessary precondition for the holding of rights, nor do such rights have to be exclusive in the sense that they are necessarily granted to a particular group of persons only. This effect can be reduced by means of various mechanisms that may be implemented cumulatively or individually (Benhabib 2002; Bauböck and Guirodon 2009; Joppke 2007; Kymlicka 1995).

One mechanism consists of decoupling rights from citizenship altogether and establishing certain rights, which are not bound to a specific polity and which all participating communities respect. This model has been chosen by the authors of the European Convention on Human Rights. Rights deriving from the Convention are guaranteed to 'everyone' within the jurisdiction of a contracting state. In a similar manner the EU Charter of Fundamental Rights distinguishes between 'everyone' and 'citizens' and reserves only a small number of rights for European citizens, the majority of those rights being guaranteed to 'everyone.'

Another approach consists of authorizing multiple citizenships generally or individually, thus attenuating the exclusionary effect of the single citizenship concept. In fact, citizenship is not necessarily exclusive; a person may simultaneously hold several. Yet, in the absence of rules on coordination, it may be difficult and sometimes impossible for one person to hold several citizenships. Moreover, the ability to acquire and hold several citizenships individually does not eliminate the cleavage between citizenships as markers of different parallel groups. Citizenships are also not equal. Not only are holders of citizenship of a state treated differently from others, but also citizenships hold different worth, as they offer different access to travel and migration globally.[2] Arguably, the global hierarchy of citizenship has reinforced the European citizenship, as it offers a set of rights and status that the individual Member State citizenship by itself does not hold. The result has been the popularity of acquiring European citizenship as a compensatory citizenship, which supplements weaker citizenship. Access to European citizenship is then gained through a number of channels available to third-country citizens, such as on the basis of descent, ethnicity, strategic birth, or acquisition through investments (Harpaz 2019, pp. 11–12).

The early stages of the evolution of federations from previously separate entities provide an example of the merging of different citizenships (Schönberger 2005, 2007, p. 61). Such osmosis can begin with a prohibition of discrimination on grounds of nationality among the participating entities and may gradually lead to the establishment of a proper status for those who are regarded as citizens of the overarching polity. It may result in multi-layered citizenship, consisting of an overarching citizenship, or at least a certain number of rules and rights that would apply to citizens of all participating polities while different citizenships are maintained. This is the path chosen by the European Union.[3]

The initial integration project from which the European Union emanated did not question the traditional mode of various national citizenships within its boundaries. It did, however, establish certain limitations on their use for the purpose of discrimination. In fact, right from the beginning the ECSC Treaty imposed on Member States a prohibition of "any discrimination in remuneration and working conditions between nationals and migrant workers" (Article 69(4) Treaty establishing the European Coal and Steel Community of 18 April 1951). By conferring a right of free movement within the Union on workers, self-employed persons, and persons providing services, EU law (initially Articles 48, 52, 59 EEC Treaty, at present Articles 45, 49, 56 TFEU) further attenuated the

[2] See, for example Kochenov & Lindeboom (2020).

[3] Some outstanding examples of the many publications on EU citizenship are Azoulai (2010), Kochenov (2013), Schönberger (2005, 2007) and Weiler (1999), pp. 324–357.

exclusionary nature of national citizenship within the Union. Hence, at the foundation of EU law all citizens of the EU Member States were protected in all Member States against certain forms of discrimination and enjoyed certain (economic and social) rights. From 1979 on, this market-oriented process of transformation of national citizenship was extended into the political realm by the provisions on the election of the European Parliament: citizens of the Member States were entitled to vote and to stand as candidates across the Union. In order to consolidate and to amplify this unique status of citizens of EU Member States and to render the direct relationship between the Union and its citizens more visible, the EU Treaty of 1992 ('Maastricht Treaty') introduced a genuine concept of "citizenship of the Union." This quality no longer derives from specific economic or political activities of national citizens. It remains, however, closely interwoven with the citizenship of nationals of the Member States, since possession of the nationality of a Member State is its necessary precondition (*Treaty on the Functioning of the European Union* [TFEU], 2007, art. 20[1]).[4]

As a result, the prohibition of discrimination against citizens of other EU Member States under the general framework of EU citizenship radically changes the nature of national citizenship, since it loosens the traditional nexus between nationality and rights within a given polity, thereby reducing diversity within the Union. The corresponding gain in unity resulting from the additional common layer of citizenship is still fragile. It is based on a combination of a limited number of generally applicable rights with entitlements, valid "within the scope of application of the Treaties."

However, EU citizenship is not construed as a self-contained regime but rather as an evolutionary concept. To this end the second paragraph of Article 25 TFEU provides for the adoption of provisions intended "to strengthen or to add to" the rights listed at present in the EU Treaties. It follows that within the European Union the current balance of unity and diversity in matters of citizenship will remain in evolution.

[4] "Every person holding the nationality of a Member State shall be a citizen of the Union. Citizenship of the Union shall be additional to and not replace national citizenship."

## 7.1 The Legal Foundation of Citizenship of the European Union

According to Article 9 TEU and 20(1) TFEU, "[e]very person holding the nationality of a Member State" is per se considered to be a citizen of the Union. These provisions explicitly state that EU citizenship is not a substitute for national citizenship. EU citizenship confers rights and duties on persons holding the citizenship of a Member State (*TFEU*, 2007, art. 20[2]). While the rights are spelled out in Articles 21 to 24 TFEU and in Articles 15(2) and 39 to 46 of the Charter of Fundamental Rights of the European Union, no similar details are mentioned in the Treaties as far as duties are concerned. The power to lay down the conditions for national citizenship continues to be exercised exclusively by the Member States.[5] Moreover, rights and duties inherent in EU citizenship may overlap with similar conditions provided by national law. Yet the authority of the EU institutions to establish details by implementing legislation, to interpret and to provide for the protection of the above rights with effect throughout the Union, confers on EU citizenship a quality of its own, distinguished from parallel national citizenships. As the then Advocate General of the ECJ rightly stated: European citizenship

> presupposes the existence of a political relationship between European citizens, although it is not a relationship of belonging to a people. On the contrary, that political relationship unites the peoples of Europe. It is based on their mutual commitment to open their respective bodies politic to other European citizens and to construct a new form of civic and political allegiance on a European scale. It does not require the existence of a people, but is founded on the existence of a European political area from which rights and duties emerge. In so far as it does not imply the existence of a European people, citizenship is conceptually the product of a decoupling from nationality.[6]

Hence, citizenship establishes a genuine bond among its holders who continue to have different nationalities. It therefore provides a striking example of 'unity in diversity.'

[5] On the conditions governing and limits of the exercise of this power resulting from EU law see ECJ Case 135/08 (Rottmann), ECLI:EU:C:2010:104, para. 45.

[6] ECJ Case 135/08 (Rottmann), Opinion of AG Poiares Maduro, ECLI:EU:C:2009:588.

## *The Substance of EU Citizenship: Rights*

EU citizenship is a triple-layered concept that encapsulates entitlements vis-à-vis various categories of polities—different states within the EU, and the EU itself. It confers on nationals of a Member State rights in all or certain Member States and rights vis-à-vis the Union itself. At first glance the substance of EU citizenship does not seem to come from a comprehensive concept that encompasses the relationship between the Union and its citizens. It consists of a short and heterogeneous list of specific entitlements listed in the TEU, the TFEU, and the Charter, which in most cases codify previously existing rights introduced at different times into the Treaties without reference to a 'European' citizenship. Yet, the particular status resulting from this "interstate citizenship" (Schönberger 2005, 2007) is marked by a combination of three characteristic strands:

- rights that can be claimed against any Member State (*a*);
- rights against the Member State in which an EU citizen lawfully resides (*b*);
- rights against the European Union (*c*).

While the substance of the first two categories consists of a guarantee of limited equal treatment with citizens holding the nationality of the state in question and therefore largely (but not entirely) depends for that purpose on the specific national legislation, the substance of rights belonging to the third group is established at the level of the Union.

In addition, EU citizens enjoy fundamental rights, which are set out in the Charter in general terms (e.g. "every person" [*Charter of Fundamental Rights of the European Union* [CFR], 2000, art. 41], "everyone" [*CFR*, 2007, art. 2, 3, 6–8, 11, 12, 14, 15, 17, 20, 29, 34, 35, 47, 48]) without reference to the holding of a specific citizenship. Even if their scope extends further, they belong to the realm of EU citizenship.

Taken together, these rights offer throughout the Union a unique set of equal entitlements to their holders. Their particular feature is the fact that they are *common* to all citizens of the EU Member States and to that extent establish "the *fundamental status* of nationals of the Member States."[7]

[7]Rec. 1, European Council Directive 2015/637 on the coordination and cooperation measures to facilitate consular protection for unrepresented citizens of the Union. *Official Journal 2015* L106, 24 April, pp. 1–13. Less straightforward (before the entry into force of

### *Rights Which Can Be Claimed Against All Member States*

*Free Movement*

The strongest expression of unity inherent in European citizenship as a treaty-based promise is the right of free movement within the Union (*TFEU*, 2007, art. 21[1])[8] coupled with the prohibition of discrimination on grounds of nationality (*TFEU*, 2007, art. 18).[9] It does not, however, establish an unrestricted uniform status, which can be enjoyed equally by all citizens of all Member States, thus establishing full unity. With regard to residence, nationals of a Member State continue to enjoy in that state a privileged position compared with EU citizens of other Member States. This continuing diversity among EU citizens as far as the entitlement to free movement is concerned is compatible with EU law as it stands.

In fact, the guarantee of free movement for EU citizens within the Union and of equal treatment in law by the authorities of all Member States depends on *two conditions.*

The *first condition* requires that their situation has to fall "within the scope of the Treaty." Hence, the Treaty guarantee of equal treatment does not apply to matters purely internal to a Member State. However, this restriction does not exclude the applicability of the freedom of movement provisions to citizens within the Member State of their nationality.[10]

The exercise of the freedom to move and reside within the territory of the Member States, as conferred by Article 21 TFEU, belongs by definition to the scope of the Treaty. Any disadvantage resulting from national law because of the exercise of this freedom is to be considered a restriction that can only be justified where it is based on objective considerations and is proportionate to the legitimate objective of the national provisions.[11]

the Lisbon Treaty): ECJ Case 184/99 (Grzelczyk), ECLI:EU:C:2001:458, paragraph 31: "Union citizenship is *destined* to be the fundamental status of nationals of the Member States" (emphasis added).

[8] "Every citizen of the Union shall have the right to move and reside freely within the territory of the Member States." See also Article 20(2)(a); Article 4(1) in conjunction with Article 52(2) CFR.

[9] "Within the scope of application of the Treaties, and without prejudice to any special provisions contained therein, any discrimination on grounds of nationality shall be prohibited." See ECJ Case C-85/96 (Martinez Sala), ECLI:EU:C:1998:217, para. 62.

[10] ECJ Case C – 304/14 (CS), ECLI:EU:C:2016:674, para. 24.

[11] ECJ Case C-438/14 (Bogendorff von Wolffersdorff), ECLI:EU:C: 2016:401.

According to the *second condition*, the situation of a European citizen has to be compatible with the "limitations and conditions laid down in the Treaties and with the measures adopted to give them effect."[12]

The legal situation of EU citizens invoking a right to free movement derives directly from their status as EU citizens or is related to the exercise of a professional activity. The most important implementing act in this respect is Directive 2004/38 on the right of citizens of the Union and their family members to move and reside freely within the territory of the Member States (Guild et al. 2014).[13] It provides that "Union citizens shall have the right of residence on the territory of another Member State for a period of up to three months without any conditions or any formalities other than the requirement to hold a valid identity card or passport."[14] A right of residence on the territory of another Member State for a period of longer than three months is, however, subject to three alternative additional conditions:

- either status as a worker or self-employment in the host state; or
- having "sufficient resources for themselves and their family members not to become a burden on the social assistance system of the host Member State during their period of residence and have comprehensive sickness insurance cover in the host Member State"; or
- student status with comprehensive sickness insurance cover in the host Member State.[15]

These restrictions thus differ markedly to those of individual Member States where no such requirements exist.[16]

[12] See ECJ Cases C-391/09 (Runevič-Vardyn and Wardyn), ECLI:EU:C:2011:291, paragraph 61, and C-438/14 (Bogendorff von Wolffersdorff), ECLI:EU:C:2016:401, paragraph 29.

[13] Directive 2004/38/EC of the European Parliament and of the Council of 29 April 2004 on the right of citizens of the Union and their family members to move and reside freely within the territory of the Member States, *Official Journal* 2004, L158, 30 April, p. 77–123. On the free circulation of workers see European Parliament and Council Regulation 492/2011 on freedom of movement for workers within the Union (2011). *Official Journal* 2011, L141, 27 May, pp. 1–12.

[14] Art. 6[1], Directive 2004/38/EC.

[15] Art. 7[1], Ibid.

[16] See the contributions in: Bauböck (2019). See also the critical evaluation by Menéndez and Olsen (2020).

*Diplomatic Protection*
In addition to the rights enjoyed by EU citizens within the EU, there are a set of rights they enjoy in addition to their national citizenship outside the EU, as outlined in the TFEU and the Charter of Fundamental Rights (*TFEU*, 2007, art. 20[2][c]; *CFR*, 2007, art. 46). Unrepresented citizens of the Union enjoy the right of protection by the diplomatic and consular authorities of any Member State under the same conditions as nationals ("diplomatic protection").[17] The protection is to be offered on the same conditions as given to the nationals of that Member State. This applies, for example, to assistance in cases of arrest or detention, or to victims of crime.[18] In this situation EU citizenship does not lead to a uniform substantive status but only to treatment equal to that accorded to nationals of the Member State from which a person seeks assistance. Short of unity, the right of diplomatic protection of EU citizens establishes a common procedural minimum standard that maintains substantive diversity.

### *Rights Against the Member State in Which an EU Citizen Lawfully Resides*

*Participation in the Elections to the European Parliament*
The most important individual political right of EU citizens consists of the right to vote and to stand as a candidate in the elections to the European Parliament in the Member State in which he or she resides. This right can be exercised "under the same conditions as nationals of that State" (*TFEU*, 2007, art. 20[2][b]; *CFR*, 2007, art. 39[1]).

This guarantee is pivotal in giving shape to the particular combination of unity and diversity in the Union. It not only represents an individual entitlement and as such a guarantee for diversity but establishes a political bond with the sole institution of the Union, which has the task of representing the citizens of the Union (*Treaty establishing the European Union*

[17] The condition is that the Member State, whose citizen is in need of assistance, has no embassy or consulate in a specific third country, which is effectively in a position to provide consular protection in a given case Art. 2(1) European Council Directive 2015/637 on the coordination and cooperation measures to facilitate consular protection for unrepresented citizens of the Union. *Official Journal*, 2015, L106, 24 April, pp. 1–13.

[18] Art. 2[1], European Council Directive 2015/637 on the coordination and cooperation measures to facilitate consular protection for unrepresented citizens of the Union. *Official Journal* L106, 24 April 2015, pp. 1–13.

[TEU], 2007, art. 10[2]). It should be noted that the number of seats allocated to each Member State is "digressively proportional" to its population (TEU, 2007, art. 14[2]).[19] Hence, the number of seats is not calculated according to the number of nationals of a Member State but according to the number of its inhabitants—which includes foreign residents.[20]

The quality of unity symbolized by participation in the European elections is stressed by the guarantee by EU law of equal treatment with nationals of the State of residence. On the other hand, the method of allocation of the seats among the Member States raises questions as to the equality of votes, as discussed later in this chapter.

EU citizens may choose to exercise their right to vote either in the Member State of residence or in their home Member State.[21] If the law of the Member State of residence imposes that in order to vote or to stand as candidates, nationals of that State must have spent a certain minimum period as a resident in the electoral territory of that State, EU citizens shall be deemed to have fulfilled that condition as well when they have resided for an equivalent period in other Member States. Where in order to stand as a candidate nationals of the Member State of residence must have been nationals for a certain minimum period, citizens of the Union shall be deemed to have met this condition when they have been nationals of a Member State for the same period.[22]

Exceptionally, the voting rights of EU citizens in the host country may be restricted if, in a given Member State, the proportion of citizens of the Union of voting age among residents exceeds 20% of the total number of citizens. Moreover, such a Member State may take measures with regard to the composition of lists of candidates and which are intended in particular to encourage the integration of non-national citizens of the Union.[23]

[19] European Council Decision 2018/937 establishing the composition of the European Parliament, *Official Journal* 2018, L165, 2 July, pp. 1–3.

[20] Art. 2[c], European Parliament and Council Regulation 1260/2013 on European demographic statistics, *Official Journal* 2013 L330, 10 December, pp. 39–43.

[21] European Council Directive 93/109/EC laying down detailed arrangements for the exercise of the right to vote and stand as a candidate in elections to the European Parliament for citizens of the Union residing in a Member State of which they are not nationals, *Official Journal* 1993, L329, 30 December, pp. 34–38, as amended by European Council Directive 2013/1. *Official Journal* 2013, L26, 26 January, pp. 27–29.

[22] Ibid., Art. 3–5.

[23] Ibid. Art. 14.

*Participation in Municipal Elections*

The right of an EU citizen to participate in municipal elections in the Member State in which he or she resides (*CFR*, 2007, art. 40)[24] is similar to the right of participation in elections to the European Parliament, but expresses a different form of unity, since it does not derive from the election of members of a common institution. It is a direct consequence of the right of free movement. The unifying quality of this right articulates the common belonging and common responsibility for matters being decided by a local political entity where an EU citizen resides. It serves to promote integration in the host country.[25]

In providing that the right to vote and to stand as a candidate can be exercised by an EU citizen in the host state if he or she satisfies the same conditions in respect of the right to vote and to stand as a candidate as that State imposes by law on its own nationals, the Directive abolishes the nationality requirement to which most Member States made the exercise of the right to vote and to stand as a candidate subject. It does not, however, presuppose complete harmonization and maintains the diversity of electoral laws in the Member States.

Moreover, the Directive attenuates equality of voting rights in order to take account of specific circumstances in certain Member States. Similar to European Parliament elections, it authorizes Member States where the proportion of citizens of the Union of voting age who reside in it but are not nationals of it exceeds 20% of the total number of citizens of the Union residing there who are of voting age to restrict the right to vote and to stand as a candidate. The measures authorized consist in the introduction of a minimum period of residence and measures with regard to the composition of lists of candidates designed in particular to encourage integration (European Council Directive 94/80/EC, 1994, art. 12).

[24] "Every citizen of the Union has the right to vote and to stand as a candidate at municipal elections in the Member State in which he or she resides under the same conditions as nationals of that state."

[25] Detailed arrangements are laid down by European Council Directive 94/80/EC (1994), as amended by European Council Directive 2013/19. *Official Journal* 2013, L158, 10 June, pp. 231–233.

*Social Benefits*

If EU citizens have made use of their right to free movement, fulfilling the conditions of Directive 2004/38, their right of residence in the host Member State includes a "right to equal treatment with the nationals of that Member State" (European Parliament and Council Directive 2004/38/EC, 2004, art. 24[1]). This right includes inter alia an entitlement to social benefits. It is, however, subject "to such specific provisions as are expressly provided for in the Treaty and secondary law" and to conditions which are aimed at avoiding becoming "an unreasonable burden on the social assistance system of the host Member State."[26] A host Member State is not obliged to confer entitlements to social benefits on an EU citizen who is a national of another Member State, during a period of residence of up to three months, during which this right is guaranteed on condition that the EU citizen (and his or her family members) does not become an unreasonable burden on the social assistance system of the host Member.[27]

More problematic is the entitlement to social benefits when an EU citizen resides for longer than three months in a Member State other than that of his or her nationality, thus establishing a stronger relationship with the host country. In this situation workers, persons formerly working there, or self-employed persons acquire a right of residence, while for economically inactive EU citizens this right is subject to their having sufficient resources of their own.[28] It follows that a Member State has the possibility of refusing to grant social benefits to economically inactive EU citizens who have made use of their right to freedom of movement without qualifying for a right of residence.[29]

The details and limits of entitlement to social benefits of EU citizens who make use of their right to free movement are a matter of controversy that mirrors the tension between the right of free movement and the differences between the social systems of the Member States as well as the

[26] Rec. 10, Directive 2004/38/EG. The detailed conditions are laid down in Articles 7 and 24(2) of the Directive.

[27] See Art. 14(1), Ibid. and ECJ Joined Cases C-424/10 and C-425/10 (Ziolkowski and Szeja), ECLI:EU:C:2011, paragraph 39; and Case C-333/13 (Dano), ECLI:EU:2014:2358, paragraph 70.

[28] Directive 2004/38, Article 7(1)(b). See ECJ Case C- 67/14 (Alimanovic), ECLI:EU:C:2015:597.

[29] ECJ Case C-333/13 (Dano), ECLI:EU:2014:2358, paragraph 78.

variables of 'social solidarity.' More generally it symbolizes the limits to unity as regards free movement of EU citizens.[30]

### *Rights Which Can Be Claimed Against the European Union*

The abovementioned facets of EU citizenship all concern the specific situation of migrant citizens in Member States of which they are not citizens and apply in practice to a minority of EU citizens only. Rights against the Member State of their nationality have so far not been a part of EU citizenship. To this extent the unitary effect of EU citizenship is limited.

However, there is already another category of rights that applies without differentiating between nationality or residence to all EU citizens. These are the rights that can be invoked against the institutions of the European Union and which result directly from the EU Treaties or secondary legislation. In the case of the citizens' initiative, the exercise of this right consists of a combination of rights against Member States and against the European Commission.

#### *Citizens' Initiative*

The citizens' initiative is a unique entitlement of EU citizens that was established by the Treaty of Lisbon. It creates for all European citizens—irrespective of their residence—rights to the European Commission and, in an auxiliary way, against Member States.

Approximately one million citizens who are nationals of Member States may take the initiative of inviting the European Commission to submit draft legislative acts on specific issues (*TEU*, 2007, art. 11[4]). The exercise of this right is subject to several conditions. From the perspective of unity and diversity the most interesting is the need for support of such an initiative by "nationals of a significant number of Member States." Signatures have to come from citizens of at least one quarter of Member States.[31] Hence, a minimum degree of diversity in bringing forward such an initiative is required. Moreover, in at least one quarter of the Member States the minimum number of signatories of a citizens' initiative should correspond to the number of the Members of the European Parliament

[30] Among the contributions to the discussion of the inherent problems see de Witte (2015) and Kochenov (2016).

[31] Art. 3[1], European Parliament and Council Regulation 2019/788 on the European citizens' initiative. *Official Journal* 2019, L130, 17 May, pp. 55–81.

elected in that Member State, multiplied by the total number of Members of the European Parliament. These minimum numbers are set out in Annex I to the Regulation. The minimum number of signatories in the smallest states (Cyprus, Estonia, Luxembourg, Malta) is 4506, while in the state with the largest number of citizens (Germany) it is 72,096. A strict proportional ratio between the number of citizens of a state and the number of signatories would have required a significantly higher number of signatures in states with a larger number of citizens. This relative advantage of citizens of larger states can be interpreted as compensation for the opposite effect resulting from the distribution of seats among Member States in the European Parliament.[32]

The organizers of a citizens' initiative are entitled to request from the Member States that they verify the statements of support for an initiative submitted on the basis of appropriate checks, in accordance with national law and practice, as appropriate. On that basis, Member States are required to certify the number of valid statements in support (European Parliament and Council Regulation 2019/788, 2019, art. 12). To date, the right to submit a citizens' initiative may be regarded as the most consistent expression of unity inherent in EU citizenship. Yet the exercise of this right is subject to respect for the diversity resulting from the multitude of Member States.

*Right of communication with EU institutions*

Further direct links between individual citizens and their common institution at the level of the Union are established by the right to petition (*TFEU*, 2007, art. 20[2][d], 24, 227; *CFR*, 2007, art. 44) the European Parliament, to apply to the European Ombudsman (*TFEU*, 2007, art. 20[2][d], 24, 228; *CFR*, 2007, art. 43), and to address the institutions and advisory bodies of the Union in any of the Treaty languages and to obtain a reply in the same language (*TFEU*, 2007, art. 20[2][d], 24; *CFR*, 2007, art. 41[4]).

The common element of these rights is their full independence from any residence requirement or from the intervention of national authorities. Compared to all other rights attached to European citizenship they can be considered the most distinct symbols of unity.

[32] European Council Decision 2018/937 establishing the composition of the European Parliament (2018). *Official Journal* 2018, L165, 2 July, pp. 1–3. On the criteria for the distribution of seats see *supra*, 5.1.

*Access to EU Institutions (Transparency)*
The access for citizens to information held by EU institutions is part of their political rights against the European Union and a fundamental prerequisite to the democratic process within the Union. Any citizen of the Union (and any natural or legal person residing or having their registered office in a Member State) has a right of access to documents of the institutions and to bodies, offices, and agencies of the Union, whatever their medium (*CFR*, 2007, art. 42; *TEU*, 2007, art. 11[1]).

The conditions governing the limits on the exercise of the right make no distinction regarding the nationality of the person requesting such access.[33] While the right of access is not variable according to nationality, certain political rights inherent in EU citizenship lack an identical weight, with the paradoxical result of increasing diversity for the sake of promoting unity.

## 7.2 European Citizenship and the Equality of Political Rights

The composition of the European Parliament may raise questions as to the equality of political rights of EU citizens ("Representation of citizens shall be digressively proportional, with a minimum threshold of six members per Member State. No Member State shall be allocated more than ninety-six seats") (*TEU*, 2007, art. 14[2]).[34] In fact, the vote of an EU citizen residing in a smaller State has greater weight than the vote of a resident of one of the bigger States. A further distortion of proportionality results from the limitation of the maximum number of seats and the allocation of a minimum of seats to each State. Hence, in smaller States a relatively

[33] "Any citizen of the Union…." Art. 2, European Parliament and Council Regulation 1049/2001 regarding public access to European Parliament, Council, and Commission documents. *Official Journal* L145, 31 May 2001, pp. 43–48.

[34] See the definition given in Article 1 of the European Council Decision 2018/937 establishing the composition of the European Parliament. *Official Journal* L165, 2 July 2018, pp. 1–3: "Degressive proportionality is to be defined as follows: the ratio between the population and the number of seats of each Member State before rounding to whole numbers is to vary in relation to their respective populations in such a way that each Member of the European Parliament from a more populous Member State represents more citizens than each Member of the European Parliament from a less populous Member State and, conversely, that the larger the population of a Member State, the greater its entitlement to a large number of seats in the European Parliament."

higher number of representatives is elected than in the bigger States. Accordingly, while a member of the European Parliament who has been elected in Malta represents 68,833 residents, an MEP elected in Germany represents 821,232 residents, the average ratio being 664,575 inhabitants per seat in the European Parliament. The weight of votes cast in Malta is therefore 11 times higher than that of votes cast in Germany. Although within each Member State the right to vote can be exercised in an equal manner by all EU citizens residing in that State (see *TFEU*, 2007, art. 22[2]), the weight of the votes for the composition of the Parliament varies.

The equality of political rights of its citizens is essential for solidarity within any polity and for the legitimacy of its institutions. Restrictions on the equality of political rights might increase diversity at the expense of unity. One could therefore argue that the different weight of votes in the elections to the European Parliament, which results from the system of distribution of seats among the Member States, creates an obstacle to unity and even throws into question the legitimacy of this institution. This was indeed the position that the German Constitutional Court took in its Lisbon decision of 2009: "The European Union lacks, even after the entry into force of the Treaty of Lisbon, a political decision-making body which has come into being by equal election of all citizens of the Union and which is able to uniformly represent the will of the people."[35] However, this view represents a purely formal and national understanding of political rights, and does not take into account the specificities of European citizens' rights and the interplay of the Union's institutions. Such an argument is not able to perceive the fine balance between unity and diversity that the composition of the European Parliament and its mode of election represent.

Although the distribution of seats in the European Parliament is set out in the Treaty on the European Union according to criteria other than strict proportionality, thus creating unequal political rights for EU citizens, there is no infringement of equality as a principle of electoral law because differences in the possible influence of European citizens on the legislation are only part of a complex structure, which is intended to give a voice to citizens in their European, national, and regional identity. Only in combination do they convey a full picture of their representation in the Union. Three examples may give an idea of the multiple factors that

[35] BVerfGE 123/267 ('Lisbon'), 30 June 2009.

determine any assessment of 'equality' of EU citizens' political rights in the Union:

First, Members of the European Parliament act in full (legal) independence from the government of the State in which they have been elected. They are "not bound by any mandate" (Direct Elections Act, 1976, art. 6[2]) and hence are not delegates of a Member State and represent any citizen of the Union. Members of the European Parliament neither sit nor act together with the other Members who have been elected in the same country. Members exercise their mandate within a transnational political context, according to political affinities. Accordingly, the principal actors who prepare decisions of the European Parliament are the 'political groups.' Those groups can only be founded by at least 25 Members coming from at least 7 Member States (one quarter of the total number of Member States) (EP-Rules of Procedure 2019, art. 33[2]). The independence of EP Members from the State of their election is of legal significance in matters of enhanced cooperation. While the representatives of the States that do not participate in such cooperation are excluded from voting on issues related to that cooperation, the same issues are always decided by the entire European Parliament (see *TEU*, 2007, art. 20[3]).

The second example results from the fact that the number of inhabitants of each State is relevant for the composition of both branches of the legislative body. Articles 16 TEU and 238 TFEU apply a weighting factor to the votes of the Member States in the Council, which is based on the number of inhabitants of the State in question. Contrary to many national political systems, where the composition of only one chamber of the legislative institution is based on proportional representation of the citizens, the European Union model combines weaker proportionality with its broader application and is therefore equally well equipped for adequate representation of the citizens.

Third, another factor that contributes to the establishment of a category of political rights specific to the European Union results from the implementing mechanism introduced for the citizens' initiative (*TEU*, 2007, art. 11[4]).[36] Signatures have to come from "nationals of a significant number of Member States." The implementing legislation (see European Parliament and Council Regulation 2019/788, 2019) has taken as a reference for the calculation of the signatures required from each Member State the distribution of seats among the Member States in the

[36] See *supra* 5.1.

European Parliament. As a result, a (relatively) smaller minimum number of citizens' signatures is required in Member States with a larger number of inhabitants, Germany in particular. This in turn increases the weight of such signatures by citizens of bigger Member States.

Representation of citizens is not a static concept but a process whereby the will of the electors forms itself into the general interest of an entity.

The capacity of an institution to represent citizens for political purposes depends on multiple factors and has strong symbolic content. Formal or mathematical elements, such as a strictly proportional electoral system and the distribution of seats in proportion to the number of inhabitants of an electoral district, may contribute to the representativity of an institution. They are, however, neither the sole nor the decisive elements of the capacity of an institution to represent the electorate. Other values may appear relevant within a given entity, for example a pluralist composition of the legislative institution, which grants a more significant voice to minorities. Such a pluralist conception of representation can explain the present rules for materializing political rights of EU citizens within the political system of the European Union.

## 7.3 Accepting Citizenship

Citizenship is not merely a set of rights and duties, but also depends on the ways in which citizens engage with them and the extent to which the notion of citizenship becomes part of regular practices. Of course, many aspects of European citizenship are implicit and tied so closely to the individual Member State citizenship that individuals might not notice them or consider them specifically 'European.' However, European citizenship has become widely accepted among the population of the EU. Approximately 70% of citizens in a 2018 Eurobarometer poll identify (definitely or to some extent) as EU citizens, a number that was fairly stable throughout the 2010s, with the lowest point standing at 59% in Fall 2013. There is no single geographical pattern in terms of the countries of origin where the inhabitants do not identify strongly as EU citizens. Generally, this includes countries that joined the EU most recently (Bulgaria, Croatia, and Romania); in the Netherlands and France, two of the founding states, a larger than average share also do not see themselves as EU citizens. Overall, these were a minority in all countries as of 2018 (European Commission/Standard Eurobarometer 2018, pp. 29–30).

In terms of the hierarchy of citizenship, the notion of Europeanness has not just been a top-down phenomenon, but one adopted by a significant number of European citizens. Fifty-five percent of EU citizens according to Eurobarometer data view themselves first as a citizen of a Member State and then of the EU, whereas 6% reverse the hierarchy and only 35% give no weight to their EU citizenship. While it might only be a small minority of Europeans who identify as solely European (according to the 2018 Eurobarometer, 2%), still there are about the same number of Europeans as Greeks or Czechs in the EU and a larger number than citizens of 16 EU Member States. Considering the possibility of multiple identities, most Europeans see themselves as citizens of both their country and the European Union, all of which are trends that have increased during a period largely ascribed to be one of rising nationalism (European Commission/Standard Eurobarometer 2018, p. 35). While opinion polls only offer a snapshot and identification with a citizenship is highly contextual, one might consider voter turnout for European Parliament elections another dimension of exercising European citizenship. Here, turnout has ranged from 61.99% in the first elections in 1979 to the low point in 2014 with 42.61%, followed by an increase to 50.66% in 2019.[37] Initially, European elections were often described as second-order elections that citizens mostly consider less important than national elections, evidenced by lower turnout and often a greater vote for anti-systemic parties as protest votes (Hix and Lord 1997, pp. 87–90). Meanwhile, studies of the turnout suggest that it needs to be increasingly understood in European terms, that is, reflecting the importance voters attribute to European issues, both among pro-EU and Euroskeptic voters (Flickinger and Studlar 2007; Elsas et al. 2019). This is also reflected in the European public sphere. At first glance, it is easy to argue that in the absence of genuine European media, with a few exceptions such as *Euronews* and EU-specialized publications such as *Politico*, there is no Europe-wide public space. However, research on the European Public Sphere has focused less on unified European media and more on how Member State media adopted a more European outlook. One can thus speak of the Europeanization of the public space (Koopmans and Erbe 2004), and by extension the European public sphere "should not be seen as a coherent and unified space but more a result of the overlapping between national public spheres" (Nitoiu 2013, p. 35). Thus, just as European citizenship is linked

[37] https://europarl.europa.eu/election-results-2019/en/turnout/

and finds itself in a symbiotic and transformative relationship with Member State citizenship, the identification of citizens with the EU as part of their political identities mostly does not exist independent of national identity, but it is linked; Thomas Risse noted as early as 2010 that "Europeanized identities as "secondary identities" in the sense of inclusive nationalism…appear to provide the degree of diffuse support necessary to ensure the viability of the EU as a multilevel polity" (Risse 2010, p. 227). This support is not unconditional, nor is it permanent. As Brexit highlights, it can be challenged through a referendum, and Euroskeptic and far-right parties across the EU have been questioning the basic premises on which European citizenship rests.

## 7.4 European Citizenship: Prerequisite or Contribution to Balancing Unity and Diversity?

The effects of European citizenship may be limited in regard to rights and the impact of these rights on the life of the citizens of the EU Member States (European Commission/Eurobarometer 2016; Venables 2016, p. 63). Yet European citizenship demonstrates that it is conceptually and practically possible to be simultaneously entitled to rights which are offered and guaranteed by different—albeit connected and overlapping—polities.

However, European citizenship does not and should not establish absolute equality among its holders. Its quality consists precisely in its offer of limited rights that tolerate the parallel existence of different entitlements from other sources, that protect values of their own, and that therefore respect difference. It is therefore somewhat misleading to describe European citizenship as *the fundamental status* of nationals of the Member States.[38]

European citizenship is certainly not a tool for replacing national citizenship. Besides providing for certain specific rights, its core purpose consists of its transformation of an exclusive and exclusionary status to an open one, which enables its holders to rely on rights offered by different authorities that are meant to co-exist, by definition, with other authorities, equally guaranteeing rights to the same people.

[38] European Council Directive 2015/637 on the coordination and cooperation measures to facilitate consular protection for unrepresented citizens of the Union, preamble, Recital 1. *Official Journal* 2015, L106, 24 April pp. 1–13.

The continued existence of national and European citizenship offers a foundation for balancing unity and diversity in the quest for identity among European citizens. Achieving such a balance is a prerequisite for solidarity among the peoples of the European Union.

## References

Azoulai, L. (2010). La citoyenneté européenne, un statut d'intégration sociale. In G. Cohen-Jonathan, V. Constantinesco, & V. Michel (Eds.), *Chemins d'Europe: Mélanges en l'honneur de Jean Paul Jacqué* (pp. 1–28). Paris: Dalloz.

Bauböck, R. (Ed.). (2019). *Debating European Citizenship*. Cham: Springer Nature.

Bauböck, R., & Guirodon, V. (2009). Introduction, Realignment of Citizenship: Reassessing Rights in the Age of Plural Memberships and Multi-level Governance. *Citizenship Studies, 13*(5), 439–450.

Beiner, R. (Ed.). (1995). *Theorizing Citizenship*. New York: State University Press.

Benhabib, S. (2002). *The Claims of Culture*. Princeton: University Pres.

Elsas, E. J. v., Goldberg, A. C., & Vreese, C. H. d. (2019). EU Issue Voting and the 2014 European Parliament Elections: A Dynamic Perspective. *Journal of Elections, Public Opinion and Parties, 29*(3), 341–360.

EP-Rules of Procedure of 2019. (2019). *Official Journal* L302, November 22.

European Commission. (2016). Standard Eurobarometer 85. *European Citizenship*, May. https://ec.europa.eu/commfrontoffice/publicopinion/index.cfm/Survey/getSurveyDetail/instruments/STANDARD/yearFrom/1974/yearTo/2016/surveyKy/2130. Accessed 24 Apr 2020.

European Commission. (2018). Standard Eurobarometer 89. *European Citizenship*, March. https://ec.europa.eu/commfrontoffice/publicopinion/index.cfm/Survey/getSurveyDetail/instruments/STANDARD/surveyKy/2180. Accessed 24 Apr 2020.

Flickinger, R. S., & Studlar, D. T. (2007). One Europe, Many Electorates? Models of Turnout in European Parliament Elections After 2004. *Comparative Political Studies, 40*(4), 383–404.

Guild, E., Peers, S., & Tomkin, J. (2014). *The EU Citizenship Directive: A Commentary*. Oxford: OUP.

Harpaz, Y. (2019). *Citizenship 2.0: Dual Nationality as a Global Asset*. Princeton: Princeton University Press.

Heater, D. (1999). *What Is Citizenship?* Cambridge: Polity Press.

Hix, S., & Lord, C. (1997). *Political Parties in the European Union*. London: Palgrave Macmillan.

Joppke, C. (2007). Transformation of Citizenship: Status, Rights, Identity. *Citizenship Studies, 11*(1), 37–48.

Kochenov, D. (2013). The Essence of -EU Citizenship Emerging from the Last Ten Years of Academic Debate: Beyond the Cherry Blossoms and the Moon? *International and Comparative Law Quarterly, 62*(1), 97–136.
Kochenov, D. (Ed.). (2016). *EU Citizenship and Federalism: The Role of Rights.* Cambridge: CUP.
Kochenov, D. & Lindeboom, J. (eds). (2020). *Kälin and Kochenov's Quality of Nationality Index.* Oxford: Hart Publishing.
Koopmans, R., & Erbe, J. (2004). Towards a European Public Sphere? *Innovation: The European Journal of Social Science Research, 17*(2), 97–118.
Kymlicka, W. (1995). *Multicultural Citizenship.* Oxford: OUP.
Menéndez, A. J., & Olsen, E. D. H. (2020). *Challenging European Citizenship.* Cham: Springer Nature.
Nitoiu, C. (2013). The European Public Sphere: Myth, Reality or Aspiration? *Political Studies Review, 11*(1), 26–38.
Risse, T. (2010). *A Community of Europeans? Transnational Identities and Public Spheres.* Ithaca: Cornell University Press.
Schönberger, C. (2005). *Unionsbürger: Europas föderales Bürgerrecht in vergleichender Sicht.* Tübingen: Mohr.
Schönberger, C. (2007). European Citizenship as Federal Citizenship: Some Lessons of Comparative Federalism. *European Review of Public Law, 19*(1), 61–82.
Venables, T. (2016). *Piecing Together Europe's Citizenship.* Baden-Baden: Nomos.
Weiler, J. H. H. (1999). *The Constitution of Europe.* Cambridge: CUP.
Witte, F. d. (2015). *Justice in the EU: The emergence of Transnational Solidarity.* Oxford: OUP.

CHAPTER 8

# The Gradual Emergence of European Minority Rights

Minorities represent diversity within any given entity or group. The constitutional framing or at least the respect of their role is an important marker for a successful balance of diversity and unity. The acknowledgement of minorities is the litmus test of democracies.

The European Union is composed of minorities: none of its peoples or states holds a majority within the Union. Already for this reason, respect for and protection of minorities is part of the very nature of the Union. The mechanisms through which the resulting diversity of states and peoples is protected and balanced with unity have been discussed in previous chapters. However, another category of minority exists within and across peoples and EU Member States in the form of minorities within Member States. In this chapter we discuss the impact of recognition, protection, and integration of minorities at the level of Member States. The focus here is on national and ethnic minorities. One might also consider other minority groups, such as political, sexual, or religious minorities that share some features with national minorities: their protection is a defining feature of liberal democracies. Some minority categories are based on personal traits that are subject to little or no change, others might not be immutable but constitute an important feature of an individual's political and social identity. National minorities are given central attention, as their self-identification is closely linked to nations and states and thus to the core categories of diversity and unity on which the European Union is founded.



F. Bieber, R. Bieber, *Negotiating Unity and Diversity in the European Union*, Palgrave Studies in European Union Politics,
https://doi.org/10.1007/978-3-030-55016-5_8

Defining what constitutes national minorities has been elusive in scholarship and international law. The most commonly used definition was proposed by Francesco Capotorti, Special Rapporteur of the United Nations Sub-Commission on Prevention of Discrimination and Protection of Minorities in 1977: “A group numerically inferior to the rest of the population of a State, in a non-dominant position, whose members—being nationals of the State—possess ethnic, religious or linguistic characteristics differing from those of the rest of the population and show, if only implicitly, a sense of solidarity, directed towards preserving their culture, traditions, religion or language” (Capotorti 1977). While capturing much of the concept, even this definition is controversial and deficient in regard to minorities (Pentassuglia 2002; Jackson Preece 2005). As noted, it assumes the state as the unit of analysis. At the European level every citizen is a minority as no single majority exists. At the subnational level, local majorities might constitute national minorities. For example, Germans might constitute a local majority in Eupen or St Vith, but a small minority in Belgium; at the same time, however, they are part of the largest national group in the European Union. Being a minority is thus always relational. The EU as a polity creates an additional frame in which all are minorities of varying sizes. In addition, being a minority is based on voluntary identification with a nation. As many persons might be born to parentage from different countries, with multiple citizenship, languages, and national backgrounds, a mono-national self-identification might be simplifying social reality. Finally, the conventional understanding of minorities assumes citizenship. However, minorities can have a long-established residence in a country and still lack citizenship. This might be the result of exclusionary citizenship laws such as in Latvia or Estonia to exclude Russian speakers, or restrictive laws in immigrant societies such as Germany and Austria with the goal of preventing easy naturalization of immigrants and their decedents. Thus, national minorities are considerably more heterogeneous than often understood. The concept of what constitutes a minority has not been static: conventionally, national minorities are understood to be a traditionally settled group that is distinct from the majority population by identifying as belonging to a different nation or group. Some, like Hungarians in Central Europe, might have a kin state, whereas others might lack one, such as Catalans. It is these minorities that have been the focus of earlier minority rights protection and the main source of security concern in Central, Eastern, and Southeastern Europe in the 1990s. Another minority group often neglected in this understanding are the

Roma. Roma are not only the minority most widely subject to discrimination across the continent, but are also the largest transnational minority. With around 6 million members in the EU, the group is larger than 12 Member States in terms of inhabitants, and Roma live in nearly every EU Member State. Lacking a 'homeland' and some features of nationhood, Roma often have not qualified as a national minority, but are widely understood to be protected as minorities under European legal instruments. A further evolution in the understanding of national minorities can be found in regard to migrants. Established definitions of national minorities often require citizenship and long-standing ties to the country. While this might have been a possible criterion to set apart a national minority such as German speakers in South Tyrol from Turkish migrants to Germany in the past, the distinction has eroded. Millions of migrants have acquired citizenship across the EU and many have been long established for upwards of 50 years. As a result, the Framework Convention for the Protection of National Minorities (FCNM), through the work of the Advisory Committee, has included not only traditional minorities, but also migrants and individuals who might not fit the conventional understanding of national minorities (Ringelheim 2010, p. 99; ACFC 2016).

As outlined in Chap. 3, minorities can include EU citizens, their naturalized or bi-national descendants in other EU Member States, or those from third countries (Kochenov 2015). This does not mean that all those citizens who by background or citizenship are distinct from the majority population seek to enjoy specific minority rights. In fact, for most immigrant minorities, non-discrimination is critically more important than the use of language in education and media. At the same time, minorities often possess differentiated rights due to their citizenship, with Member State nationals advantaged in terms of political and other rights over nationals of another EU Member State and thus holders of European citizenship and with non-EU nationals generally further disadvantaged.

Conceptually, European integration has had an ambiguous effect on minorities. On the one hand, measures introduced at the level of the Union may strengthen minorities by offering stronger or additional protection against discrimination, thereby increasing diversity within the Union, even to the point of inadvertently encouraging separatist movements. On the other hand, the fact that such measures are common to minorities in most or all Member States may strengthen common values, and hence unity. This ambiguous effect explains (in part) why there are few explicit and clear protective mechanism adopted by the Union, as the

Union includes countries that offer extensive rights to national minorities and others who reject their very existence. The significance of the Union's policies toward minorities is mostly indirect.

In general, there are three approaches through which the Union has promoted the protection of minorities and diversity among its citizens. First, it adopted a set of anti-discrimination policies that requires Member States to adopt policies and laws to prevent minorities being subject to discrimination. Second, it includes policies of promoting mobility, reducing the relevance of national borders; defusing power of nation-states reduces the often rigid and hierarchical relationship between minorities and nation-states, thus blunting the sharp edge of the nation-states. Third and finally, the EU has drawn on the emerging minority rights tools of the Council of Europe and the Organization for Security and Cooperation in Europe (OSCE) and incorporated them into the accession process. Thus, the Union's use of international legal norms and soft law provisions helped significantly to bolster the post-1989 European minority rights system.

National minorities were not included in the initial conception of the European integration process. There were numerous reasons why minorities were not on the radar during the first four decades of European integration. At the level of international law and politics, minorities and their protection were a reminder of interwar Europe. The minority treaties in Central Europe—the product of the Paris peace treaties—offered little tangible protection and instead used by irredentist European states to advance their claims against neighbors. Meanwhile, nation-states saw minorities and the treaties that sought to protect them as a burden and an undue international imposition. Finally, Nazi Germany's instrumentalization of German minorities to justify occupation and war in Czechoslovakia and Poland implicitly justified the expulsion of German and other minorities at the end of World War II. After the war, the focus on minority rights shifted to the paradigm of human rights. International law focused on protecting individual rights rather than collective rights. As noted in Chap. 3, European countries also became considerably more homogenous after the war, so national minorities were at best a local issue of post-war Europe.

The nature of European integration in its initial stages also offered few points of reference to minorities, as Member State cooperation focused on eliminating discrimination based on nationality, that is, citizenship, and was not concerned with intrastate minorities. Although among the original six Member States minority demands for greater rights began appearing in the 1950s and 1960s (e.g. the demands for self-government in South

Tyrol/Alto Adige and in Flanders, and the demands of the Danish minority in the northern German state of Schleswig Holstein), many of these claims were restricted to the domestic sphere and had limited cross-border implications. Where there were cross-border negotiations, they often involved Member States and non-Member States. For example, the Bonn-Copenhagen Declarations of 1955 guaranteed the rights of the German and Danish minorities in the border region 18 years before Denmark joined the European Community. Italy reformed the autonomy for South Tyrol in 1972, and after a 20-year implementation period Italy and Austria declared their bilateral dispute resolved in 1992, three years before Austria joined the Union.

Minority rights thus could be easily ignored by the (then) European Community. With the growth of the EC, new minorities and conflicts entered the European projects, including those of Catalonia, the Basque Country, and Northern Ireland, but they still had limited significance for the Union. However, in parallel to this 'discovery' of the need for protection of human rights at the level of the European Union, the awareness *within* EU institutions of protection of minorities grew. According to Gabriel Toggenburg, one can distinguish three phases of the development of minority rights in the European Union.

During the first phase in the 1980s, the European Parliament dominated with a number of idealistic initiatives aiming to create a European system of minority rights protection. However, in the face of limited EC competencies, even less for the European Parliament, and resistance from key Member States, such a far-reaching system could not emerge.

The second phase is characterized by minority rights during enlargement, that is, the use of minority rights as a condition for EU accession, represented by the Copenhagen Criteria. Finally, the third phase marks the internalization of minority rights following the 2004–2007 enlargement, reflected in the Lisbon Treaty (Toggenburg 2018, pp. 365f.). Thus over four decades, minority rights moved from being marginal to being the field of idealistic experimentation to being an important part of the enlargement process to finally cautiously constituting part of the core Union values.

By the 1980s, the EC included a great variety of Member States, from those with no substantial minorities, such as the Netherlands, to diverse members such as Spain. Some countries were willing to grant minority rights and develop sophisticated self-rule and autonomy, such as Italy and Spain, whereas others, including France and Greece, denied the existence of any minorities. Among such a diversity of intra-state diversity and the range of state responses, minority rights were an unlikely field to become of concern for European integration.

The paradigmatic shift occurred after 1989. The Union successfully acquired new competences, and the dynamics of integration beginning with the Maastricht Treaty brought minorities into focus as well. The main catalyst was the end of the Cold War and the shift of integration toward Central and Eastern Europe that confronted the EU with new diversity.

The dissolution of multinational states like Czechoslovakia, Yugoslavia, and the Soviet Union and tensions between nation-states and minorities raised the awareness of minorities. The main advance in terms of minority rights in Europe occurred through the symbiotic relationship between the minority rights instruments developed by the Council of Europe and the politics of conditionality of the European Union. Whereas the Council of Europe began setting the legal standards for minority protection, the OSCE focused conflict management and diplomatic instruments to confront state-minority issues. Thus, within the span of a few years a new European framework emerged in the 1990s. In 1992, the European Charter for Regional or Minority Languages was adopted, and in 1994 the Committee of Ministers of the Council of Europe adopted the FCNM,[1] both coming into effect in 1998. In 1992, the OSCE established the High Commissioner on National Minorities (HCNM) as a diplomatic tool to intervene in non-violent conflicts between minorities and states.[2] Since then, the HCNM has also formulated numerous guidelines on minority rights and interethnic relations. These guidelines—a total of nine—were issued between 1996 and 2019, and highlight best practice in the OSCE area; they have made the High Commissioner a normative actor in articulating general principles of minority integration (Jackson Preece 2013).

The relevance of the EU in protecting minority rights consists of four distinct fields traced in this chapter, namely the indirect effects on minorities of European integration (such as the reduction of borders or new institutional opportunities), the impact of EU participation in the emerging European minority rights regime in the context of enlargement (in particular toward Central and Eastern Europe), the emerging

[1] Adopted on 1 February 1995.

[2] https://www.osce.org/hcnm

non-discrimination and minority rights standards within the EU since 2000, and the adverse effects of European integration on specific regimes toward minorities by some EU Member States.

## 8.1 Integration as a Tool to Accommodate Diversity

European integration as such has had a significant impact on addressing the position of minorities. To a large degree this could be described as not so much deliberate policy to improve minority rights, but rather a by-product of European integration. Of course, this outcome is not purely coincidental, but it is not primarily a policy for minorities. Integration, as a set of policies to diffuse tensions between minorities and nation-states, functions on several levels. The first dimension is that of reducing the importance of borders and thus reducing the relevance of living on the 'wrong' side of a border as a minority. The second dimension is reducing the symbolic monopoly of the nation-state and introducing symbolic pluralism that can incorporate minorities with greater ease. Finally, the EU has been diffusing minority—state tension by introducing another layer of decision-making, thus reducing potential contestation over decision-making and power at the level of the Member State. Finally, we also have to consider how integration and in particular the protection of unity in the European Union has at times come into conflict with minority rights. Thus, the indirect effects of European integration on minority rights are not exclusively positive.

### *Border Elimination Strategy*

An important aspect of the EU's direct and indirect strategies for minority inclusion has been the reduction of national borders and in particular the Schengen system. Whereas the reduction of border controls served the purpose of ensuring the freedom of movement of people and goods, it also impacted minorities, in particular those minorities separated from their kin state by internal EU borders. This includes German speakers in South Tyrol, Danes and Germans in the Schleswig/Slesvig German-Danish border region, Nationalists in Northern Ireland, and Swedish-speakers in Finland, to name just a few. Even minorities without a kin state, such as Basques in France and Spain, were disrupted in maintaining transnational ties by borders.

The creation of the Schengen Area and the elimination of border controls is not the only dimension in which the EU has shaped border regimes. In general, European integration has served to de-securitize borders within the Union. This has been particularly pertinent where cross-border minorities were viewed as a security concern by nation-states. A number of European initiatives instead promoted a variety of cross-border cooperation projects such as Euro-regions, INTERREG funds and the European Grouping of Territorial Cooperation. These highlighted the agency of subnational actors in engaging in cross-border cooperation (De Sousa 2013; Engl 2016). Even if many of these networks often remained limited in scope or weak, they still constituted one dimension in which borders were weakened, giving minorities a greater say in shaping these cross-border relations.[3]

The relevance of borders and EU integration for minorities became highly visible during the Brexit process in Northern Ireland. While neither the UK nor Ireland partake in the Schengen Area, EU membership for both countries allowed for the complete elimination of border controls. In the aftermath of the Good Friday Agreement, the border between Northern Ireland and Ireland became essentially invisible. Since the partition in 1920, there had been no formal immigration controls, but the border had become securitized in the context of the 'Troubles,' that is, the conflict between the supporters of Irish unification and those supporting Northern Ireland as part of the UK (Nash et al. 2013, pp. 109–140). A key concern during the Brexit negotiations was to ensure that border controls were not imposed between EU member Ireland and non-EU Northern Ireland, as such controls would undermine the freedom of movement in Ireland that constituted an important aspect of the Good Friday Agreement (Hayward and Murphy 2018). The conflicting goals of withdrawing from the EU and keeping the borders between Northern Ireland and Ireland open, emerged as the biggest difficulty in the Brexit negotiations.

Whereas European integration contributed to reducing the importance of borders among the Member States, the EU also reinforced the external borders of the EU and the borders of the Schengen Area. This has also affected minorities, as borders have become more rigid. For example, Hungarians living in Serbia or Ukraine or Russian speakers in the Baltic States have to cross an external EU border to maintain contact with their

[3] See for example in the case of the German-Danish border region, discussed in Malloy (2010).

kin state. This can make contacts more difficult, in particular when the bilateral relationship is volatile and antagonistic. Arguably these more rigid borders have encouraged kin states to offer easier access to citizenship to ethnic kin in neighboring countries to circumvent (or at least ease) any obstacles that the rigid division of the EU external borders creates (Tóth 2003). Croatia has been granting citizenship to Croats abroad, in particular in Bosnia and Herzegovina and Serbia, as has Hungary to Hungarians in Serbia and Ukraine. Bulgaria and Romania gave easy access to Macedonians and Moldovans respectively. While reducing the rigidity of external EU borders, they can also fuel tensions in minority—majority relations in those countries, as minorities are seen as having privileged EU citizenship; furthermore, the citizenship might facilitate outmigration into the EU.

The mitigation of minority-state tension through border elimination is fragile and reversible. Brexit brought risks to the foreground in regard to Northern Ireland, where after more than two decades of peace and an open border, the British departure from the EU now undermines the peace. Even without such a radical step as leaving the EU, these tools are vulnerable as they were not instituted to address minority rights and are easily reversed by unrelated considerations. This became apparent in the context of the so-called migration crisis after 2015, as intra-EU borders were subject to renewed controls and physical barriers, which made borders again visible. This was even more drastic in 2020, when the COVID-19 pandemic led to rigid border closures across the world and within the EU, limiting cross-border contacts.

### *Symbolic Pluralism*

Besides the mitigation of borders, the shift of decision-making to the EU can impact minorities even in seemingly irrelevant matters. Take the euro: with the adoption of this currency, currencies of the participating states disappeared, and with them the symbolic reminders of the nation-state. Currencies prior to the introduction of the euro depicted many "national heroes," for example Theodoros Kolokotronis, general and leader of the Greek war of independence on the 10,000 drachma note, or Douglas Hyde, the first president of Ireland and a key figure in the Celtic revival featured on the 50 Irish pound bill. Across the different currencies of the countries that joined the euro, national figures were featured in an example of banal nationalism (Billig 2005). By removing this daily reminder of nation-state from citizens' wallets, the new currency became less laden with national association (at least for minorities). The symbolic pluralism discussed previously in Chap. 5 also impacts the inclusion of minorities. With the use of the EU flag and symbols next to nation-state symbols, the symbolic monopoly of the nation-state is challenged. This might not mean that minority or regional symbols can be used without restrictions, but it does highlight that the nation-state is not the only authority able to display symbols traditionally associated with states. This symbolic pluralism once more diffuses the prevalence of the nation-state.

### *Institutional Diffusion and Inclusion*

While the structures of the European Union focus little direct attention on minorities, the layer of European institutions has a clear impact on minorities. As supranational institutions and rules, they diffuse the monolithic power of the nation-state. Scholars of multinational states and divided societies have noted that the diffusion of power can contribute to less contestation and greater distribution of access to power among different communities (Rothchild and Roeder 2005). In this sense, the EU constitutes another set of decision-making bodies that reduces the singular power of the state, in particular when the state is highly centralized and constituted as a nation-state.

Even more so, the EU is not another national layer of governance, but constitutes a level of decision-making that is multinational and, as a result, able to moderate different national perspectives in its decision-making. The impact is thus not just the diffusion and extension of centers of decision-making, but also the way in which Member State decision-making is co-shaped (Keating 2004). The European Union has been transforming the Member States. As discussed throughout this book, the Union is not just the institutions and the rules associated with the European Union conventionally, but also the ways in which the different levels of government of Member States are transformed by them. This process has often been described as Europeanization, although in recent decades, the term has been applied more in regard to the accession process in Central and Southeastern Europe.

New regionalism, promoting cooperation among subnational units and decentralization—including through such consultative bodies as the Committee of the Regions—has empowered regions. In addition, minority demands are often associated with particular territories and minority movements (whether they are secessionist or autonomist) and have often focused on claims based on a particular territory (Keating 2004). It is not clear-cut whether European integration moderates or potentially radicalizes minority party demands. On one hand, it offers new venues for addressing minority demands and reducing the power of the nation-state. On the other hand, regional parties have been using the EU to argue for independence while seeking to remain in the EU. The existence of an alternative polity might reduce the apparent cost of secession, as Catalan and Scottish parties and movements have argued.

Institutionally, the EU also provides new opportunities for minorities to organize transnationally, either to cooperate beyond national borders or to circumvent nation-state restrictions. For example, minority parties have been able to achieve representation and pursue their agenda at the European level. There are three relevant structures, namely, the political groups in the European Parliament, political parties at European level (*Treaty establishing the European Union* [TEU], 2007, art. 10[4]), and transnational NGOs or alliances of NGOs. These different mechanisms have enabled minorities to organize, more effectively pursue their agenda, and at times also circumvent a more restrictive environment within Member States. The main political party of minority representation is the *European Free Alliance*.[4] It was established first in 1981 to bring together minority and regional groups. As of 2020 it brings together some 46 nationalist, autonomist, and regionalist movements and parties, from the *New Flemish Alliance* (N-VA) or the *Republican Left of Catalonia* to the more obscure, such as the *Venetian Republic League*. It also includes members from non-EU countries such as the *Scottish National Party* (SNP) and the *League of Social Democrats of Vojvodina* (LSV) in Serbia. The EFA was registered in 2017 as a European Political Party.[5] The main challenge of the party has been its cohesion, as member parties cover an ideological spectrum from the left to the far right.

Within the European Parliament they have formed a common political group with the Greens.[6] Overall, the representation of minority and regionalist parties in the European Parliament is marginal and further weakened by the fragmentation across multiple parliamentary groups, as not all are aligned with the Greens. For example, the more conservative

[4] https://www.e-f-a.org/

[5] See the Register of Members, *Official Journal of the European Union* 2017, C 362/18.

[6] https://www.greens-efa.eu/en/

N-VA, while a member party of the EFA, belongs to the parliamentary group of European Conservatives and Reformists. As of February 2020, a total of twelve minority party MEPs (out of 705) consisted of four MEPs in the group of the Greens, four MEPs with the European Conservatives and Reformists, three MEPs who are unaffiliated, and one MEP who is in the European People's Party.[7]

The main European organization of minority non-governmental organizations, other than parties, is the *Federal Union of European Nationalities* (FUEN), established in 1949 as an international network of NGOs in the context of the formation of the Council of Europe.[8] It brings together 107 minority organizations in 35 countries. Although FUEN cannot be attributed to European integration, it is part of the larger development of global governance and civil society. Furthermore, it has used the instruments of the EU to advance minority rights, as will be discussed later in this chapter.

## 8.2 Externalizing Minority Protection

In addition to the indirect effects and institutions of integration that facilitated the improvement of minority—state relations in Member States, the EU adopted its first tentative steps to protect minority rights explicitly in the Copenhagen Criteria for accession to EU. This occurred in the early 1990s as part of a wider concern of international organizations with minority rights. The overlap with instruments of the OSCE and the Council of Europe resulted in a shared European minority regime with different international organizations mutually reinforcing each other (Galbreath and McEvoy 2012, pp. 112–141). In this emerging minority rights regime, the EU essentially externalized minority rights in two dimensions. First, externalization occurred by shifting the standard setting and monitoring to other organizations. The EU sought adherence to minority rights as a criterion among future members, but drew on the emerging legal standards and tools of others, in particular the FCNM. Second, it externalized minority rights by demanding them from aspiring members and also evoking minority rights in its nascent foreign policy, in particular in regard to the former Yugoslavia. However, this

[7] The departure of the UK reduced the number of minority party MEPs. In 2019, 6 of 73 MEPs were from minority and regional parties.

[8] https://www.fuen.org/

externalization meant that the Member States that had joined the EU earlier would not be subject to international minority standards. In particular, countries such as Greece and France that rejected the notion of national minorities were under no pressure to advance minority rights. These countries, together with Belgium and Luxembourg, are the only EU members not party to the Framework Convention and thus not subject to any reporting on minority rights.

As the EU lacked the legal and political framework for minority protection, not only because key members reject the existence of national minorities in their own countries (including Greece and France), the EU instead left minority rights protection to the Council of Europe and the OSCE and incorporated these only indirectly through the policy of conditionality during the EU accession process. This allowed the EU to require future members to safeguard minority rights, while avoiding opposition from Member States skeptical about this topic. It also reflected an East/West bias, as the urgency of advancing minority rights was triggered by repressive policies of late communist and early post-communist governments and tensions between majorities and minorities in Central and Eastern Europe. However, minority—state relations were not without friction in Western Europe either, and the level of violence was greater in several older EU Member States. In Spain a violent conflict in the Basque Country had continued after the end of the Franco regime; in France, Breton, Basque, and Corsican groups had demanded greater autonomy—including some using violence—and a low-level conflict persisted in Northern Ireland. In addition, non-violent yet politically potent tensions existed in Belgium as well. Thus, minority rights were not only on the agenda in new democracies in Central and Eastern Europe. However, the unique moment of large-scale enlargement shifted debates and norms on minority rights toward future members.

The enlargements after 1995 followed a different logic than the earlier wave of EU expansion. Unlike Austria, Finland, and Sweden that joined in 1995, the new applicants were recent democracies and engaged in multiple transformations simultaneously—political, economic, and social. While Spain, Portugal, and Greece had also undergone the transition from dictatorship to democracy prior to joining the European Community between 1981 and 1986, they did not need to fundamentally restructure their economic systems and joined the European Community before the major reforms of the early and mid-1990s.

The difference and the scale of the enlargement of the EU toward Central and Eastern Europe gave rise to a policy of EU conditionality during the accession process that focused not exclusively on the *Acquis Communautaire*, but also on democracy, human and minority rights, and, later in the case of the post-Yugoslav countries, cooperation with the International War Crimes Tribunal for former Yugoslavia as well. This package, which included minority rights, was advanced to prevent countries with serious internal problems from entering the EU and also used the leverage of EU membership to promote issues that were seen by many international actors as crucial from a position of both security and democracy. Countries that joined under the 1993 Copenhagen Criteria had to demonstrate their compliance with minority rights during the accession process. However, the EU also only held them to the minority rights standards of the Council of Europe as long as they were not members. Some critics have argued that this policy for imposing requirements on future EU Member States that earlier ones did not have to adhere to amounts to "do as I say, don't do as I do" (Johns 2003). However, this argument is only partially convincing. As membership is voluntary, the EU can set its criteria for membership without regard to whether current members adhere to the same criteria. While this might be perceived as unfair, in the case of minority rights there were a variety of reasons that justified them. Whereas some were based on East—West biases (Central and East European states are a greater threat to minorities), others were pragmatic (minority rights can either be promoted in Central and Eastern Europe or nowhere). Furthermore, the argument neglects that the accession process is always one-sided as the Union sets the criteria and measures compliance, and thus it is not a process of negotiation among equals. The inequality is thus not caused by the inclusion of minority rights requirements, but lies in the structural foundation of accession. Finally, countries achieve equality once they join the EU with earlier members, and the power asymmetry does not persist (Hillion 2004). Once Estonia, Croatia, and Bulgaria joined the EU, the new Member States were no longer bound by different criteria towards minority protection than old Member States, such as Greece or France.

Minority rights conditionality generally required aspiring EU members to join the FCNM.[9] The instruments of the Framework Convention entail regular state reports and monitoring. While countries are able to withdraw

[9] Not all Member States that joined in 2004 were party to the FCNM. Latvia signed in 1995, but only ratified the FCNM in 2005, that is, one year after joining the EU.

from the convention and there are no enforcement mechanisms, lowering standards drastically or withdrawing from the FCNM would draw the spotlight of international attention.

Moreover, the European Commission assessed the degree to which governments protected minority rights based on the Copenhagen Criteria, the implementation of the 2000 non-discrimination directive, and a Roma strategy, in countries where Roma were a sizable minority (Rechel 2008, p. 174).

Even during the accession process, when the EU was the most forceful in ensuring minority-friendly policies in the future Member States, the impact was limited. Whereas in many countries minority parties began participating in governing coalitions and comprehensive minority rights laws were passed, not everywhere was EU conditionality applied. In the Baltic states, many Russian speakers remained without citizenship of their country of residence and Roma remained marginalized and discriminated against in most of Central and Eastern Europe. The omissions were in part due to the fact that monitoring of minority rights conditionality was left to other organizations. Thus, the EU could use their assessments, but was not bound by them. As minority rights could not be assessed with firm criteria, but rather were subject to political judgment by the Commission, other criteria often trumped minority rights (Rechel 2008). Nevertheless, minority protection was considerably better-established in 2004–2007, when these countries joined, than it was a decade earlier. Most importantly, new Member States did not use the end of conditionality after joining to dismantle their minority rights regimes. While there were no firm legal safeguards, there were reputational costs. Severely curtailing previously established minority rights regimes might be possible, but would come at a cost, as it would draw international attention.

The course of events after the countries of Central, Southeastern, and Eastern Europe joined between 2004 and 2013 appears to confirm the "locking in" effect achieved through EU conditionality (Pridham 2008). Overall there has been no significant backsliding in terms of minority protection, despite the absence of both the scrutiny of the EU institutions and conditionality. This is not to deny some country-specific problems,[10]

[10] See, for example, in the case of Croatia, where the most important minority is the Serb minority, closely associated with the war. As the Advisory Committee of the FCNM notes in its 2015 report, "observers accredit this deterioration to a relaxation in external pressure following EU accession," ACFC (2015).

but overall the system has withstood the test of accession. Nevertheless, the stagnation in terms of minority rights also highlights that EU membership did not result in further advances in minority rights protection.

Considering the backsliding in other fields, such as democracy and rule of law in some countries that joined the EU in 2004 (such as Hungary and Poland), the preservation of the minority rights regime is not inevitable. The persistence of the minority rights regimes post-accession could be best explained by the reduced political polarization of majority—minority relations. Minority rights and the inclusion of minority parties in governments across the region meant that minorities were incorporated and at times co-opted into the existing political system and could no longer be credibly portrayed as a threat by nationalist majority parties. The main sites of political competition and contestations have shifted from national minorities to other 'threats' in the narratives of conservative and nationalist parties, including LGBT communities, migrants, and supposed liberal threats to the nation. It could thus be argued that the EU adoption of minority rights as an accession criterion and the delegation of standard-setting to the Council of Europe contributed to the emergence of a modest minority rights regime in Central, Eastern, and Southeastern Europe that, with all its limitations, became sufficiently accepted and robust to persist after accession.

Furthermore, the adoption of a minority rights system in new Member States shifted the balance of minority rights within the EU itself. Prior to the 2004–2007 enlargement, 4 of the 15 EU member states (27%) either did not ratify or did not sign the FCNM (France, Belgium, Luxembourg, and Greece). By 2020, the number of countries not participating in the FCNM stayed the same, yet membership nearly doubled. Thus, only 15% of Member States are not party to the FCNM. It could thus be argued that through the pre-accession conditionality in regard to minority rights, the overwhelming majority of EU Member States have become party to the FCNM and adhere to a European set of minority rights standards. One could therefore speak of a European minority rights consensus based on the FCNM, with few exceptions. This marks a fundamental shift from the early 1990s, when there were not only no Europe-wide instruments, but also not such a widely held position regarding the protection of minorities. The inclusion of minority rights in the Lisbon Treaty is not the only result of this process (Ringelheim 2010). As the next section will outline, the emergence of minority rights standards within the EU is largely a consequence of the Copenhagen Criteria and minority rights conditionality.

## 8.3 Increased Protection of Diversity Through EU Instruments

If the EU was long silent on minority rights and initially only indirectly acknowledged their importance during the 2004–2013 enlargement, over time they became more important. The accession of 13 countries meant that the balance shifted decisively toward minority rights in the EU as a large majority of EU Member States recognized minority rights, even if implementation was uneven. The evolution of international human rights also meant that minority rights were no longer marginal but gained prominence. The result has been a number of steps that introduced the protection of minorities into the core of the EU.

The first important step was the 2000 Race Equality Directive. The Council Directive 2000/43 is directed against racial and ethnic discrimination and became one important pillar of the EU *acquis* in the field of minority protection.[11] It does not envisage a state obligation to offer positive measures to protect and promote minorities, as the Council of Europe's Framework Convention does, but it prohibits direct and indirect discrimination. Indirect discrimination is particularly important, as this also includes "apparently neutral provision, criterion or practice [that] would put persons of a racial or ethnic origin at a particular disadvantage compared with other persons…."[12] However, the directive explicitly excludes different treatment on the grounds of citizenship.[13]

The Directive had important symbolic significance when it was passed. It was less aimed at protecting national minorities, and more at avoiding discrimination against EU citizens (and non-EU citizens) in the EU who hailed from a migrant background and had long been disadvantaged. The entry of the far-right Freedom Party (FPÖ) into the Austrian government that year highlighted the dangers of xenophobic policies and accelerated the adoption of the Race Equality Directive. It was also a great equalizer

[11] European Council Directive 2000/43/EC of 29 June 2000 implementing the principle of equal treatment between persons irrespective of racial or ethnic origin, *Official Journal* 2000, L180, 19 July, pp. 22–26.

[12] Art. 2[2][b], Ibid.

[13] Art. 3[2], Ibid.

as it highlighted that discrimination is an issue both in the West and the East of the EU. However, implementation initially lagged behind, and it appeared that the Directive was mostly of symbolic significance (Howard 2004). The provisions delegated much detail to the Member States and domestic processes that weakened the provision and reduced its effectiveness (Mason 2010; Lantschner 2019).

The Race Directive became part of the effort of the EU and its Member States to define notions of equality that reflect not just the greater concern at the level of the EU and other European instruments, such as those of the Council of Europe, but also reflect a changing understanding of what constitutes equality (De Witte 2010). Crucially, the Race Directive is limited by the competencies of the EU and is thus not applicable to all fields in which discrimination might take place (Watson 2012); however, it has a wider scope of application than other grounds for discrimination.

In terms of languages of minorities, the EU has been promoting diversity in terms of official languages, which has put languages of small EU members on equal footing with large languages. Thus, documents would be translated into Estonian or Maltese as much as English, French, or German. There is not complete equality, as working documents are generally available in fewer languages, usually English, French, and German. Non-state languages on the other hand do not enjoy official status, and Irish and Luxembourgish are also not treated equally to other Member State languages.

While not enjoying equal status, EU institutions have promoted minority and regional languages prior to even engaging with minority rights as such. This has led to multiple declarations of the European Parliament regarding the matter and the establishment of the European Bureau for Lesser Used Languages, a non-governmental organization initially funded by the EU and regional or local government organizations. In 2010 it was discontinued, and the European Language Equality Network took up its activities.[14]

The paradox of the EU and minority rights is that the EU lacks competences in the field and in the areas typically linked to minority rights, such as education, language policies, and political representation in the Member States. Yet more than 50 legislative acts of the EU refer to minorities, as Gabriel Toggenburg points out (Toggenburg 2018). In practice, minority

[14] https://elen.ngo/information/

protection in the EU has been mostly indirect and not universal (Ahmed 2011).

The EU lacks both the competences and definition of what constitutes a national minority. The latter is not unique to the EU, as there is no clear definition in international law of national minorities and even the Framework Convention does not offer a binding definition. However, this is less of an obstacle, as the work of the Advisory Committee shows, than the lack of competences (Kochenov 2015).

Even when it comes to monitoring, the means and mandate of the EU are limited. The Fundamental Rights Agency (FRA), established in 2007, is able to report on larger trends, but is not able to engage in the systematic monitoring and reporting the Advisory Committee of the FCNM has the mandate to conduct at regular intervals.[15]

A major turning point has been the Treaty of Lisbon (2007), which recognized and protected minority rights for the first time in the EU in numerous ways. The Treaty integrates minority rights into primary law by making the Charter of Fundamental Rights[16] a legally binding document and by authorizing the EU to accede to the European Convention on Human Rights the protection of minorities, which became integrated into the EU's DNA (Barten 2015).

Article 2 of the Lisbon Treaty mentions minority rights as a foundational value of the EU: "The Union is founded on the values of respect for human dignity, freedom, democracy, equality, the rule of law and respect for human rights, including *the rights of persons belonging to minorities.* These values are common to the Member States in a society in which *pluralism, non-discrimination*, tolerance, justice, solidarity and equality between women and men prevail."[17]

With the explicit reference to minorities, or rather persons belonging to minorities—avoiding any reference to collective rights—as well as pluralism and non-discrimination, the protection of minorities is inscribed as a fundamental value of the Union, de facto eliminating the divide between current and aspiring Member States.

[15] See, for example, the FRA European Union Minorities and Discrimination Survey, available at https://fra.europa.eu/en/publication/2012/european-union-minorities-and-discrimination-survey-main-results-report

[16] *Charter of Fundamental Rights of the European Union* (2007). *Official Journal* C83, 30 March 2010 pp. 389–403.

[17] Emphasis by the authors. Treaty of Lisbon (2007).

Furthermore, the Treaty places an emphasis on protecting diversity, which can also be seen as protecting minorities: it shall respect its rich cultural and linguistic diversity, and shall ensure that Europe's cultural heritage is safeguarded and enhanced (*TEU*, 2007, art. 3[3], par. 4).

It is important to note that none of these constitute collective rights, as only persons belonging to minorities and diversity in the abstract are protected, but not national minorities. Furthermore, Art. 2 emphasizes the respect for rights, including those persons belonging to minorities, but that does not mean that states have to institute minority rights; rather they must not breach the rights of minorities, in particular in regard to discrimination (Barten 2015, p. 79).

The inclusion of minority rights in the basic values of the EU also means that a breach by a Member State could trigger an Article 7 procedure, namely the suspension of voting rights and other sanctions. As highlighted by the efforts to evoke Article 7 in the case of Hungary and Poland over rule of law abuses, the threshold for this mechanism is high, and with several Member States currently not supporting the notion of minority rights, it is unlikely to be used for minority rights violations.

Although discrimination on the basis of language and membership in a minority group is prohibited in the EU due to the Lisbon Treaty and the Charter of Fundamental Rights, the Union lacks the competences in key areas to propose legislation to implement these fields, as noted earlier. As a result, the European Parliament has remained active in trying to advance minority rights at the level of the EU by adopting non-binding instruments, such as resolutions. In 2018, the European Parliament passed a resolution outlining "minimum standards for minorities in the EU" and calling on the European Commission to draft binding standards that build on the various hard and soft laws that emerged in the EU, during the accession process and by other European Organizations.

While non-binding, the large majority that supported it (489 to 112 and 73 abstentions) reflects that there is broad support in the parliament for EU-wide standards for minorities.[18] The resolution emphasizes that 8% of EU citizens belong to national minorities and 10% speak minority languages, and it argues for EU-wide minimum standards of minority protection. These rights are outlined in the resolution, which also draws on existing legal standards including the FCNM. While it reflects the more

[18] European Parliament Resolution of 13 November 2018 on minimum standards for minorities in the EU (2018). Document P8_TA(2018)0447.

idealistic approach of the European Parliament in advancing minority rights, it is also grounded in the existing minority rights system of the EU. It is unlikely to result in new EU-wide minority rights laws, but it does suggest that minority rights have become a central concern of the European Parliament. Furthermore, the resolution was a response to the EU-wide initiative "Minority Safe Pack" launched by FUEN with the support of a range of minority organizations and regional governments. This European citizens' initiative gathered more than 1.1 million valid signatures,[19] enough to trigger consideration by the European Commission, which declared it a valid initiative in January 2020.[20]

The proposal included nine measures—in particular focused on minority media—dealing with statelessness among Roma and some EU funding for minority cultures. More robust aspects, such as revising EU directives to take minority concerns into account and strengthening minority inclusion (in the European Parliament as well), were struck down by the European Commission ahead of the signature collections. Initially, the European Commission had refused the entire citizens' initiative on the grounds that it overreached by extending beyond EU competencies. However, following an appeal by the initiators at the European Court of Justice, the initiative could proceed (Bürgerausschuss für die Bürgerinitiative Minority SafePack—one million signatures for diversity in Europe vs. European Commission 2017). The decision of the ECJ in this case helped to advance the notion that the EU is able to take initiatives in the field that affect minority rights (Toggenburg 2018, pp. 379–383). The initiative only became possible through the European Citizens' Initiative, established in the Lisbon Treaty to encourage transnational grassroots activism at the European level. In this sense, the Minority SafePack is an example of bottom-up Europeanization, that is, the effort to create joint European rules and policies in the field of minority rights not based on a top-down, government-led initiative, but driven by minority organizations (Crepaz 2020, p. 29). However, it would be simplistic to ignore the involvement of Member States. The strong support by Hungary under the authoritarian government of Viktor Orbán tainted the initiative. Since he came to power in 2010, Orbán has strongly supported the rights of Hungarians in

[19] In total 1,215,879 signatures of support were gathered and the necessary threshold was crossed in 11 EU Member States; 1,128,385 were considered valid.

[20] For details see Minority SafePack – one million signatures for diversity in Europe, https://europa.eu/citizens-initiative/initiatives/details/2017/000004_en

neighboring countries, but has also instrumentalized them for his nationalist political rhetoric. Slovakia and Romania were thus reserved about the initiative and supported the EC's initial rejection at the European Court of Justice (Crepaz 2020, pp. 44–45).

Another similar citizens' initiative,[21] the "Cohesion policy for the equality of the regions and sustainability of the regional cultures," was submitted to the Commission in 2013 seeking to advance minority rights at the EU level by requiring cohesion policies of the EU to consider minorities in the distribution of cohesion funds.[22] The Commission similarly rejected it initially, due to lack of competencies. The decision was initially upheld by the ECJ, and the Commission was once more supported by Slovakia and Romania (as well as Greece), whereas Hungary supported the initiators, themselves members of the Hungarian minority in Romania.[23] However, upon appeal, the ECJ annulled the decision[24] of the Commission and paved the way for the initiative to gather signatures.[25]

Both initiatives highlight the restrictive approach of the Commission in permitting such efforts to expand minority rights protection at the European level, and how advancing minority rights pits Member States that are reserved about minority rights on the side of the Commission against each other, in particular Hungary, which has sought to promote the rights of ethnic kin in neighboring states. This demonstrates how the support for minority rights (or alternatively their rejection) is based on the particular country's position toward minorities, and essentially bilateral minority conflicts have become Europeanized. This is not inherently negative, as the citizens' initiatives had to be framed in a larger European context and the ECJ has given space for the initiatives to take place, despite Commission skepticism.

[21] https://eci.ec.europa.eu/010/public/#/initiative

[22] http://www.nationalregions.eu/index.php

[23] ECJ Case T-529/13 (Izsák and Dabi), Judgement, ECLI:EU:T:2016:282.

[24] ECJ Case C-420/16 Appeal (Izsák and Dabi), ECLI:EU:C:2019:177.

[25] Commission Decision (EU) 2019/721 of 30 April 2019 on the proposed citizens' initiative entitled "Cohesion policy for the equality of the regions and sustainability of the regional cultures" (notified under document C(2019) 3304), C/2019/3304, *Official Journal*, L122, 10 May 2019, p. 55–56.

## 8.4 Negotiating Between European Integration and Minority Rights

The ECJ has also been confronted with cases pertaining to minority rights. In particular, several cases have dealt with restrictions on EU nationals due to specific minority rights regimes and regional autonomies.[26] It has sought to reconcile the protection of minorities with the general principles of equality (Pentassuglia 2009, p. 132).

While overall the efforts to reduce the rigidity of the nation-state have provided minorities more space to maintain contact with their kin state or organize transnationally, they have also conflicted with minority rights. In particular, as the EU is focused on creating common rules within the Union, these can clash with specific arrangements negotiated between states and minorities (Kochenov 2015).

For example, the freedom of movement enshrined as one of the four freedoms might be restricted for the sake of minority rights. This was a central concern during the peace talks for Cyprus prior to accession as particularly the Turkish Cypriot side worried about free settlement of non-Turkish Cypriots in their region of control. The Annan Plan restricted the number of Greek and Turkish Cypriots who could settle in the other (respective) region to preserve the self-rule of the two communities. However, freedom of movement would have allowed Greek citizens, just like other EU citizens, to settle unrestricted in either part of the island. A similar concern emerged when Finland joined the EU, as the Swedish-speaking Åland Islands enjoy extensive autonomy and restricted settlement by Finns from Finland to preserve the minority culture on the island. On the other hand, for the EU, freedom of movement is central and generally only restricted by a transition period when a new country joins. Loosening the universality of freedom of movement would risk its undoing. As a result, the islands were granted a special status in the membership agreement to maintain the minority protection system.[27]

The European Union itself, with its aim to protect the internal market, thus might come into conflict with long-established minority rights. When

[26] See ECJ Case C-274/96 (Bickel and Franz), ECLI:EU:C:1998:563 and ECJ Case C-281/98 (Angonese v Cassa di Risparmio di Bolzano) ECLI:EU:C:2000:296.

[27] ACT concerning the conditions of accession of the Kingdom of Norway, the Republic of Austria, the Republic of Finland and the Kingdom of Sweden and the adjustments to the Treaties on which the European Union is founded, Protocol No 2—on the Åland islands, *Official Journal* C241, 29 August 1994, p. 352.

these two principles of the EU come into conflict, minority rights might be disadvantaged. As Kochenov has argued, "the ECJ applies a strict proportionality test to any such deviations, which means there is no guarantee that minority protection, however highly cherished, will actually prevail" (Kochenov 2015).

Diversity is a central value for the European Union, yet it has struggled to find a path to protection within Member States and in regard to national minorities. National minorities acquired the attention of the European Communities in the 1980s, but remained at the periphery as minority issues were not a central concern, but effect numerous (but territorially, clearly-defined) regions of old Member States. The new regional nationalisms, including Catalonia and Northern Ireland, were sometimes peaceful, at times violent, and often challenged the nation-state. This made the Member States of the (then) European Community reluctant to consider minority rights a topic to be protected at the EU level. Little attention was given in general to minority rights. Accommodating (or not accommodating) minority claims was mostly a matter of sui generis solutions. Only the end of the Cold War and the prospect of a great expansion of the Union eastward changed awareness of minority rights. The inclusion of minority rights in the Copenhagen Criteria was a product of its time, the concern about minority discrimination, and nationalist polarization and violence. With the parallel instruments of minority rights emerging in other European regional organizations, minority rights shifted from a marginal field to the center of EU expansion. This did raise the risk that minority rights would be the domain of Central and Eastern Europe, as had been the case in interwar Europe. The lack of universality contributed to their failure, as they were seen as being imposed by Great Powers on the weak and reluctant new states in Central Europe.

With the Lisbon Treaty (2007), minority rights have become part of the European Union legal framework, and thus now constitute a universal value of the Union. However, this legal status is not evidenced in clear and substantive rights in the EU, a reflection of the lack of competences in key areas and the resistance toward minority rights in principle by key Member States such as France. As outlined in this chapter, one needs to look beyond the formal minority rights framework of the EU in order to understand the much wider impact of the EU on minority rights in the Member States, as well as the improvement of majority—minority relations. The prevalence of the FCNM is largely due to EU conditionality during the accession process. Furthermore, a number of other strategies of the EU, in particular in terms of blunting the sharp edges of the nation-state, have eased the position of minorities in Europe.

Keeping in mind its doubtlessly positive impact on this level on the balance between diversity and unity, the EU remains a reluctant promoter of minority rights. The relationship between diversity and unity in regard to minorities in the Union results from three pillars: a) a symbolic commitment to diversity, b) accommodating specific policies and rules within Member States, and c) ensuring Union-wide non-discrimination of both migrant (from EU and non-EU states) and traditional national minorities, including transnational European minorities such as Roma (Kochenov 2015). Many of these commitments are largely declaratory as Member States are not always fully committed to minority rights and the EU itself is often blind to racial, national, and ethnic diversity.

## References

Advisory Committee of the Framework Convention on National Minorities (ACFC). (2015). *Fourth Opinion on Croatia Adopted on 18 November 2015*, ACFC/OP/IV(2015)005rev. https://rm.coe.int/CoERMPublicCommonSearchServices/DisplayDCTMContent?documentId=09000016806c268b. Accessed 22 Apr 2020.

Advisory Committee of the Framework Convention on National Minorities (ACFC). (2016). Thematic Commentary No. 4. "The Framework Convention: A Key Tool to Managing Diversity Through Minority Rights. The Scope of Application of the Framework Convention for the Protection of National Minorities".

Ahmed, T. (2011). *The Impact of EU Law on Minority Rights.* Oxford: Hart Publishing.

Barten, U. (2015). Minority Rights in the European Union After Lisbon. *Nordic Journal of Human Rights, 33*(1), 74–94.

Billig, M. (2005). *Banal Nationalism.* London: SAGE.

Capotorti, F. (1977). Study on the Rights of Persons Belonging to Ethnic, Religious and Linguistic Minorities. *United Nations*, E/CN.4/Sub.2/384/Rev.1, para. 568. Available at: https://undocs.org/en/E/CN.4/Sub.2/384/Rev.1

Crepaz, K. (2020). The Minority Safepack Initiative: A European Participatory Process Supporting Cultural Diversity. *European Yearbook on Minority Issues, 17*(2018) (Brill), 23–47.

De Sousa, L. (2013). Understanding European Cross-Border Cooperation: A Framework for Analysis. *Journal of European Integration, 35*(6), 669–687.

de Witte, B. (2010). From a "Common Principle of Equality" to "European Antidiscrimination Law". *American Behavioral Scientist, 53*(12), 1715–1730.

Engl, A. (2016). Bridging Borders Through Institution-Building: The EGTC as a Facilitator of Institutional Integration in Cross-Border Regions. *Regional & Federal Studies, 26*(2), 143–169.

Galbreath, D. J., & McEvoy, J. (2012). *The European Minority Rights Regime: Towards a Theory of Regime Effectiveness*. Basingstoke/New York: Palgrave Macmillan.

Hayward, K., & Murphy, M. C. (2018). The EU's Influence on the Peace Process and Agreement in Northern Ireland in Light of Brexit. *Ethnopolitics, 17*(3), 276–291.

Hillion, C. (2004). Enlargement of the European Union: The Discrepancy Between Membership Obligations and Accession Conditions as Regards the Protection of Minorities. *Fordham International Law Journal, 27*(2), 715–740.

Howard, E. (2004). The EU Race Directive: Its Symbolic Value—Its Only Value? *International Journal of Discrimination and the Law, 6*(2), 141–163.

Jackson Preece, J. (2005). *Minority Rights: Between Diversity and Community*. Cambridge: Polity Press.

Jackson Preece, J. (2013). The High Commissioner on National Minorities as a Normative Actor. *Journal on Ethnopolitics and Minority Issues in Europe, 12*(3), 77–82.

Johns, M. (2003). "Do as I Say, Not as I Do": The European Union, Eastern Europe and Minority Rights. *East European Politics and Societies, 17*(4), 682–699.

Keating, M. (2004). European Integration and the Nationalities Question. *Politics & Society, 32*(3), 367–388.

Kochenov, D. (2015). The European Union's Troublesome Minority Protection: A Bird's-Eye View. In J. Boulden & W. Kymlicka (Eds.), *International Approaches to Governing Ethnic Diversity* (pp. 79–101). Oxford: Oxford University Press.

Lantschner, Emma. (2019). *Reflexive Governance in the Enforcement and Promotion of the Right to Equality and Non-Discrimination: Relevance for the EU Enlargement Context and Beyond*. Unpublished Habilitation, University of Graz.

Malloy, T. H. (2010). Creating New Spaces for Politics? The Role of National Minorities in Building Capacity of Cross-Border Regions. *Regional & Federal Studies, 20*(3), 335–351.

Mason, L. (2010). The Hollow Legal Shell of European Race Discrimination Policy: The EC Race Directive. *American Behavioral Scientist, 53*(12), 1731–1748.

Nash, C., Reid, B., & Graham, B. (2013). *Partitioned Lives: The Irish Borderlands*. London/New York: Routledge.

Pentassuglia, G. (2002). *Minorities in International Law: An Introductory Study*. Strasbourg: Council of Europe Publishing.

Pentassuglia, G. (2009). *Minority Groups and Judicial Discourse in International Law: A Comparative Perspective*. Leiden: Brill.

Pridham, G. (2008). The EU's Political Conditionality and Post-Accession Tendencies: Comparisons from Slovakia and Latvia. *Journal of Common Market Studies, 46*(2), 365–387.

Rechel, B. (2008). What Has Limited the EU's Impact on Minority Rights in Accession Countries? *East European Politics and Societies, 22*(1), 171–191.

Ringelheim, J. (2010). Minority Rights in a Time of Multiculturalism: The Evolving Scope of the Framework Convention on the Protection of National Minorities. *Human Rights Law Review, 10*, 99–128.

Rothchild, D. S., & Roeder, P. G. (2005). Dilemma of State-Building in Divided Societies. In P. G. Roeder & D. S. Rothchild (Eds.), *Sustainable Peace: Power and Democracy After Civil Wars* (pp. 1–25). Ithaca/London: Cornell University Press.

Toggenburg, G. N. (2018). The European Union and the Protection of Minorities: New Dynamism via the European Citizen Initiative? *Europäisches Journal für Minderheitenfragen, 11*(3–4), 362–391.

Tóth, J. (2003). Connections of Kin-Minorities to the Kin-State in the Extended Schengen Zone. *European Journal of Migration and Law, 5*, 201–227.

*Treaty of Lisbon amending the Treaty on European Union and the Treaty establishing the European Community* (2007). Official Journal C306, 17 December.

*Treaty on European Union* (2007). Official Journal C202, 7 June, pp. 13–46.

Watson, P. (2012). Equality Between Europe's Citizens: Where Does the Union Now Stand. *Fordham International Law Journal, 35*(5), 1426–1484.

CHAPTER 9

# Conclusions

Negotiating a balance between unity and diversity has been part of the DNA of the European Union since its founding. As the Union grew in terms of Member States and competences, it has been constantly recalibrating this balance, thus reflecting its quality as a constantly evolving project rather than a set structure. The commitment toward 'an ever closer union,' had been made in the Rome Treaties in 1957 and reaffirmed in a solemn declaration by heads of state and government in 1983, as well as in the Maastricht Treaty and finally in the Lisbon Treaty.[1]

Over the past decade it is true that many Member State governments have implicitly or explicitly ruled out the idea of a closer union. Open objections to this commitment have been used as an argument by supporters of Brexit in the United Kingdom and have also fueled criticism and challenges in the light of the failure of the Constitution for Europe, which ironically did not contain such a promise. Irrespective of the merits of such a position, it would be an error to conceive the commitment as a description of a final condition to be reached. Treaty changes have not been on the agenda since the Lisbon Treaty, following nearly 25 years of intense

[1] Preamble, Treaty establishing the European Economic Community, 25 March 1957, Solemn Declaration on European Union. European Council, Stuttgart 19 June 1983, Treaty on European Union, 7 February1992, Treaty of Lisbon amending the Treaty on European Union and the Treaty establishing the European Community, Lisbon, 13 December 2007.



F. Bieber, R. Bieber, *Negotiating Unity and Diversity in the European Union*, Palgrave Studies in European Union Politics, https://doi.org/10.1007/978-3-030-55016-5_9

constitutional and institutional evolution from the Single European Act signed in 1986, to the Lisbon Treaty of 2009.

There is no definitive balance between the unity and diversity. It could also be argued that all states that seek to accommodate difference have to constantly recalibrate their approaches, in particular in decentralized and federal states, but the EU possesses a number of additional particularities that set it apart from other diverse polities. By allowing states to join and also Member States to leave, it is more flexible than most states. This brings about greater dynamism that extends to the balance of diversity and unity. In addition, it is continuously tested and advanced through crisis. The multiple crises at the European and global level, in particular since 2008, have required joint action but have also often underlined the lack of consensus among the Member States and the EU institutions. Yet the Union has been able to find tools and mechanisms of cooperation that have endured amid the crises. Thus, the EU appears to remain functional despite serious internal tensions and externally imposed crises. Majority decisions aside, the Union is a consensus-seeking structure that often succeeds in and through last minute compromises. As a result, it can also exist with significant ambiguity and internal tensions that most polities would struggle with. However, this ambiguity is not constructive in all cases. The decline of democracy in Hungary since 2010 and to a lesser degree in Poland since 2015 highlights the limited ability and willingness of the EU and its Member States to confront countries that are undermining the values of the Union for the sake of maintaining consensus (and other factors) and their tendency to paper over this.

The experience of negotiating diversity and unity in the European Union, with all the difficulties implied by this process, highlights the centrality of two concepts that are often neglected in the study of multinational states. The combination of responsibility and solidarity of the Member States and citizens represents a critical aspect of negotiating the balance between unity and diversity examined throughout the chapters of this book. Both have been evoked repeatedly during the crises of the past decade, be it in calling on the solidarity for Southern European countries in the Eurozone crisis, or assuming responsibility during the migration 'crisis' or solidarity during the COVID-19 pandemic. What is easily a simplistic slogan or appeal for one or the other, or both, is in fact a central feature of the European Union.

Responsibility is first of all an ethical notion.[2] It can, however, be found in many normative contexts of national[3] and international law. In the former, it refers to specific obligations of the State. In the latter, the notion comprises two different meanings. In its traditional (narrow) sense it refers to the *liability* (of States) for breach of an obligation under international law (Pellet 2010), while more recently it has acquired a meaning that refers to substantive obligations to act, for example to protect people (ICISS 2001).[4]

At its core, responsibility consists in the behavior of an individual or an entity that takes into account the implications of that behavior not only for one (itself) but also for others. In its minimal form it seeks to avoid any damage, or even the threat of damage, to the existence of others. Responsibility establishes a limited amount of unity between different actors. Responsibility unfolds independently from any hierarchy between its bearers. It does not aim at absorption or domination. In the context of a common project undertaken by individuals or entities, which can only be achieved if a minimum amount of *unity* can be found, responsibility extends further to include consideration for the capacity of the others to reach the common goals. Yet both situations presuppose the continued existence of all the other actors, hence, *diversity*. In a social context, responsibility relates to 'others.' If this context consists of a common project, it relates to the capacity of all participants to achieve the common goals and to maintain and promote the agreed project.

In practice, this requires mutual attention among all participants, a willingness to take stock of the situation, the essential conditions, and the capacity of the others to achieve the common goal. More generally, as the philosopher Jürgen Habermas called it, "the inclusion of the other" (Habermas 1998, p. 56). Inclusion in this sense entails an active interest in information about others and a willingness to act accordingly, including the prevention of danger and general support. At this point, responsibility condenses into solidarity. In his book *The Imperative of Responsibility* the philosopher Hans Jonas notes (Jonas 1984, 94):

[2] The subsequent section draws on Bieber (2020).

[3] For example, German Basic Law of 1949, preamble ("Conscious of their responsibility before God and man"); Article 20a ("Mindful also of its responsibility towards future generations, the state shall protect the natural foundations of life and animals …"); Art. 23 § 6 ("…responsibility of the Federation for the nation as a whole.").

[4] See also Wolfrum and Kojima (2010).

> It is not entirely clear whether responsibility in the strict sense can exist between fully equal. Cain's counterquestion to God's query concerning Abel 'Am I my brother's keeper?' rejects—not quite wrongly—the (pretended) imputation of responsibility for the independent equal. There certainly are what can be described as relations of mutual responsibility, such as in a dangerous team enterprise (like mountain climbing).

Mountain climbing is a metaphor for a social situation marked by a more intense relationship between the participants than mere 'belonging' to a group. It is characterized by a bond, resulting from a situation common to them all, and a joint endeavor where the behavior of one shapes the fate of others.

In this particular case, the responsibility of all participants relates to each member's capacity to achieve the common goal.[5] Responsibility between equals is therefore reciprocal. Yet, in any group, whether consisting of individuals or States, participants are equal in a formal sense only. States vary in size, in economic, technological, and military power, in natural resources, and in their climatic conditions. Therefore, the duties of responsibility that arise may vary between the actors according to their capacities.

The preamble to Regulation 2018/1475 on the European Solidarity Corps offers the following definition of solidarity and responsibility:

> solidarity may be understood as *a sense of responsibility on the part of everyone with regard to everyone to commit oneself to the common good,* which is expressed through concrete actions without consideration of return service.[6]

Whether such relations may exist among (formal) equals (like States) is not obvious. In fact, on an individual level, self-responsibility is an expression of liberty. At the level of States, it characterizes sovereignty. To this extent, conceptually, common responsibility represents the opposite to the principle of non-intervention in the domestic affairs of States in international law (*Charter of the United Nations*, 1945, art. 2[7]). Yet States do

[5] Other forms of responsibility, resulting from a specific relationship, for example of states with citizens, are not discussed in this context. See, however, infra, note 9.

[6] European Parliament and Council Regulation 2018/1475 laying down the legal framework of the European Solidarity Corps. *Official Journal* 2018, L250, 4 October.

not operate in isolation. Their sheer existence entails effects on other States, in particular on their neighbors. Therefore, as in any social system, some form of structured co-existence, or cooperation, is required. If effective, in its minimal form such cooperation is grounded in respect for the continuing existence of other States, their people, and their borders. Over and beyond such minimal responsibility, modern international law doctrine acknowledges a requirement of further responsibility in specific situations, for example a threat to the physical existence of groups of people (the principle of a "responsibility to protect") or a common responsibility for certain natural resources.[7] Some authors note, in certain situations, a "duty to intrude" (Nicolaidis and Viehoff 2012, p. 40).

Referring to the European Union, in 2019 Advocate General Sharpston argued in the Court of Justice:

> Sharing in the European 'demos' is not a matter of looking through the Treaties and the secondary legislation to see what one can claim. *It also requires one to shoulder collective responsibilities* and (yes) burdens to further the common good.[8]

Responsibility—or, more precisely, responsible behavior—is indeed instrumental within any given system for maintaining a balance between diversity and unity. This concept of responsibility is echoed in the "Sibiu Declaration," adopted by the Heads of State and Government of the EU Member States meeting in the European Council on 9 May 2019, in commemoration of the Schuman Declaration of 1950:

> We will stay united, through thick and thin. We will show each other solidarity in times of need and we will always stand together. We can and we will speak with one voice.
>
> We will always look for joint solutions, listening to each other in a spirit of understanding and respect.
>
> We will continue to protect our way of life, democracy and the rule of law. The unalienable rights and the fundamental freedoms of all Europeans were hard fought and will never be taken for granted. We will uphold our shared values and principles enshrined in the Treaties. (European Council, *Sibiu Declaration*, 2019).

[7] For details see the contributions of Crawford et al. (2010).

[8] Opinion of Advocate General *Sharpston*, European Court of Justice (ECJ), Case C - 715/17 (Commission/Poland), ECLI:EU:C:2019:917, paragraph 253, emphasis added.

This commitment refers simultaneously to elements of unity and diversity within the European Union. Responsibility is instrumental in establishing a balance between the two notions when accepted not only as an ethical principle, but also as a legal and political concept, from which rights and obligations follow. Mutual (or peer) responsibility within the meaning discussed here is encapsulated in the founding concept of the European Union, which is spelled out in the introductory "common provisions" of the EU Treaty, in Article 1 in particular: "By this Treaty, the HIGH CONTRACTING PARTIES establish among themselves a EUROPEAN UNION, hereinafter called 'the Union', on which the Member States confer competences to attain objectives they have in common." The Union was established to realize common objectives. All Member States are bound by an obligation to contribute to the achievement of those objectives. As Article 4(3) TEU states, this obligation also applies to relations *between* Member States: "… the Union and the Member States shall, in full mutual respect, assist each other in carrying out tasks which flow from the Treaties."[9]

This provision encapsulates at the same time *diversity* ("mutual respect"), a common goal, *unity* ("carrying out tasks which flow from the Treaties"), and *responsibility* ("assist each other"). A failure by one Member State to fulfill its duty to contribute may put the entire project at risk. This is true, in particular, when—as is the case with the EU—no Member State may be expelled from the Union. Therefore, all participants in the common project by definition have an interest in the capacity of all participants to contribute to the achievement of the common goals. That 'interest' is not restricted to the role of a benevolent observer; it requires acceptance of an active role in the protection of the functioning of the Union by way of an active interest in the other States' conditions of existence. An example of the meaning of responsibility—an active mutual interest in the situation of other Member States—can be found in the Treaty establishing the European Stability Mechanism of 2012, which was created outside (yet closely connected to) the EU Treaty by certain EU Member States. It is aimed at "fostering *fiscal responsibility and solidarity* within the economic

[9] See Opinion AG Bot in ECJ, case C-364/10 (Hungary/Slovak Republic): "commitment to maintain good-neighbourly relations consubstantial with their decision to join the Union," ECLI:EU:C:2012:124, paragraph 59. See also ECJ, case C-457/18 (Slovenia/Croatia), ECLI:EU:C:2020:65, paragraph 109.

and monetary union."[10] To this extent the term refers to the substantive behavior of Member States in fiscal matters with the aim of reaching a common goal, the Economic and Monetary Union.

In the European Union, peer responsibility therefore means the acceptance of Member States' autonomy by Member States of the Union, who are at the same time responsible for the use made by each Member State of its autonomy, so that the general interest of the Union is promoted and the common aim achieved.

Thus, the responsibility of Member States in respect to the functioning of the European Union as well as in respect to the capacity of each to fulfill its obligations is a "general principle" of European law (Lenaerts and van Nuffel 2011, p. 851) that belongs to what the ECJ calls

> a structured network of principles, rules and mutually interdependent legal relations linking the EU and its Member States, *and its Member States with each other*, which are now engaged, as is recalled in the second paragraph of Article 1 TEU, in a 'process of creating an ever closer union among the peoples of Europe.'[11]

It is therefore possible to infer the existence of a general horizontal duty between EU Member States to behave responsibly, which may require action or abstention from adopting certain acts.

A specific case of transnational responsibility consists of the Member States' obligations resulting from EU citizenship—for example, the obligation to afford diplomatic protection in third countries (*TFEU*, 2007, art. 23). This obligation is not, however, strictly between States as equals, since it results from an entitlement of citizens.[12]

The various forms of solidarity in EU law are to be understood as resulting from the general principle of responsibility between Member States, comprising simultaneously solidarity and the duty of sincere cooperation. In fact, the treaties refer to solidarity in a number of places with differing substance. Solidarity is, for example, described as a criterion for decision-making within the EU (*TFEU*, 2007, art. 80, 194), as a criterion for positions to be taken by the Member States (*TEU*, 2007, art. 24[3]),

[10] *Treaty Establishing the European Stability Mechanism*, 2012, preamble, rec. 5, emphasis added.

[11] ECJ opinion 2/13, ECLI:EU:C:2014:2454, paragraph 167, emphasis added. See also ECJ, opinion 2/17, ECLI:EU:C:2019:341, paragraph 109.

[12] See Chap. 7 and Haag (2019).

and as a description of certain social rights (*Charter of Fundamental Rights of the European Union*, 2000, art. 27–38). Therefore, solidarity, as it is understood in the EU Treaties, has different meanings, serves different purposes, and does not cover all the duties resulting from mutual responsibility between Member States.

The principle of *sincere cooperation* describes a legal obligation concerning the manner in which the Member States accomplish the tasks resulting from the Treaties. The obligation comprises a variety of activities or to abstain from them. According to the ECJ, for example, it implies "mutual trust" between Member States.[13] Yet again, like solidarity, sincere cooperation (loyalty) has a narrower scope within the meaning of the Treaties than responsibility. Especially in "horizontal" relations involving Member States only—without any direct implication of the EU institutions—responsibility may extend beyond the "tasks which flow from the Treaties." Such a situation could occur, for example, in regard to a member state's activities, which, though located outside the field of application of Union law, might have an impact on the functioning of the Union.

Therefore, responsibility, loyalty, and solidarity form a hierarchically structured set of duties of the EU Member States that applies between the States. They also apply to relations between the EU institutions and the Member States.

*Responsibility* is the overarching principle that applies independently of a particular task or act of implementation and includes all situations where Member States' acts or abstinence from acts may have direct or indirect implications for the fulfillment by other Member States of duties resulting from the EU Treaties. *Loyalty* (or sincere cooperation) describes a general duty as to the manner in which obligations spelled out in the Treaties are to be implemented. *Solidarity* requires, in the particular cases where it is mentioned, more intense attention–and ensuing action–that acknowledges the interests of other Member States. The European Union is composed of States which continue to exist as autonomous actors and whose identity has to be respected (*TEU*, 2007, art. 4[2–3]). At the same time, it was established in order to realize common goals and to bring about common values. This structure is built on the assumption of the simultaneous and permanent presence of unity and diversity, two opposing principles.

[13] ECJ, Case C-359/16 (*Altun* et al.), ECLI:EU:C:2018:63, paragraphs 40, 42, emphasis added. See also Case C-620/15 (*A-Rosa*), ECLI:EU:C:2017:309, paragraphs 39, 40. Earlier, in a similar vein, ECJ, Case C-178/97 (*Barry Banks*), ECLI:EU:C:2000:169, paragraph 39.

Responsible behavior aims to take into account the otherness by establishing bridges to the other. These 'bridges' presuppose the continuing existence (the 'otherness') of the bearers of responsibility. Moreover, they operate in both ways: responsibility is reciprocal. In the context of the European Union, responsibility between its Member States is of fundamental importance for maintaining its unique quality. Responsible behavior, which takes into account the other Member States' identity, their existential needs, and specificities, is instrumental to achieving unity while respecting diversity. The core concepts of responsibility, loyalty, and solidarity take a less central role than diversity and unity in the European integration, but are their core features. In a polity based on the negotiation and re-negotiation of difference to build a joint political, legal, and economic project, these principles are central. The ability to exit the Union highlights that the shared project is based on the voluntary association and thus the shared understanding that the commitments undertaken are based on free commitment of the Member States and their citizens. With the commitment to democracy, the European Union is not just ensuring the democratic governments of its own institutions, it is also ensuring that the Member States are able to represent citizens and thus reflect the shared commitment of state and citizens to the principles of loyalty, solidarity, and responsibility. Thus, the EU does not offer a simple blueprint for complex states or how to build polities to confront and accommodate differences. It is not free of its own difficulties; while this book has argued that the EU has been able to balance diversity and unity, there have been numerous challenges. Furthermore, it does have a number of features that make it difficult to compare or emulate.

## 9.1 Final Considerations

Combined with the aforementioned qualities, three features characterize the EU: the democratic nature of the Member States, the possibility of a voluntary exit, and the absence of hegemon, all of which are interconnected. These set them apart from previous multinational polities, as discussed in Chap. 2.

First, democracy is a core principle of the EU and of its Treaty: the EU is defined as a representative democracy (*TEU*, 2007, art. 10[1]) and essentially also assumes that the institutions of the Member States are democratic (*TEU*, 2007, art. 10[2]). In order to join the EU, respecting the values of the EU, which include democracy (*TEU*, 2007, art. 2), is a requirement (*TEU*, 2007, art. 49). Democracy is thus understood as the political system that defines the Union and its Members. The very fact that the Treaty offers no mechanisms for expelling Member States and only allows for suspension of voting rights if a Member State breaks the values of the EU (*TEU*, 2007, art. 7) suggests that the EU assumes (as it turns out wrongly) that democracy within the EU is consolidated.

This assumption has proven problematic, as some Member States—most notably Hungary under the government of Prime Minister Viktor Orbán (since 2010) and Poland under the rule of the Law and Justice Party (PiS) of Jarosław Kaczyński (since 2015)—have experienced a serious decline in democracy. Hungary is no longer considered a liberal democracy by various scholars and global and regional indices of democracies (Freedom House 2020; V-Dem Institute 2020). This decline of democracy in some Member States has repercussions for the EU itself. The institutional setup of the EU has become more democratic over the decades, but it is a consensus democracy, that is, based on the attempt to seek as broad an agreement as possible. Thus, the EU is not a majoritarian democracy by its institutional setup and practices. The consensus-seeking approach stands in stark contrast with the anti-democratic populism in some Member States, where checks and balances have been dismantled and the ruling majority present themselves as the will of the people against previous elites, foreign enemies (including the EU itself), and independent institutions. As such, populism, in particular when it dismantles liberal democratic institutions, is incompatible with the institutional and ideational logic of the EU that seeks compromise and consensus, and gives room to checks and balances. To draw on the terms used in this book, populists and their autocratic regimes reject diversity and instead claim to be the sole legitimate representatives of unity—a unity of a particular people, often defined in exclusively ethnic terms. Paradoxically, the EU as a consensus-seeking polity is largely immune to populism and majoritarianism, as the institutional setup, the diversity of its Member States, and other factors outlined in this book prevent it. However, it is also ill-prepared to confront such patterns among its Member States, as it is founded on the assumption that all its constituent units are committed to liberal democracy, as well as checks and balances.

Second, voluntary exit is a right few states afford their units. When such provisions exist, they are often declaratory, rather than substantive, as they were in several socialist federations. In other cases, such as the Scottish referendum on independence, the right to vote on exit was negotiated with the central government and was offered not as a permanent right to leave the Union, but as a special case. Elsewhere, central governments reject the right of units to determine their own status and leave. The Catalan referendum in 2017 that was prohibited by the Spanish authorities and the numerous civil wars around the world based on the secessionist claims of a unit are examples of when governments reject exit. Even federal states that are based on the gradual and voluntary association of their units, such as Switzerland and the United States, have fought civil wars over secession. In this sense, the EU constitutes an exception in safeguarding the right of all Member States to leave the Union. Demonstrating that this provision was not just declaratory has been the departure of the United Kingdom from the EU in 2020, based on the 2016 referendum and the United Kingdom invoking Art. 50 of the TEU in March 2017, which triggered the formal process of exiting the EU. Whereas Brexit preoccupied the EU for several years and constituted a serious loss in terms of its size, economic might, and reputation, the EU survived the departure of its third largest Member State and the ability to leave was never contested.

Third, the absence of a hegemon in the EU set it apart from most other polities that are structured around diversity. That hegemon might be a dominant ethno-national or linguistic group, like in most nation-states, or a dominant territorial unit in a federal or decentralized state. As discussed in Chap. 2, most polities that have sought to balance diversity and unity have often had a center, dominant group or unit, such as the German speakers in the Habsburg Monarchy, Serbs in Yugoslavia, or the initial English and protestant majority in the United States. Even in polities where one group might not dominate politically, such as Belgium or Bosnia and Herzegovina, there are clear majorities, and the anxiety of being outvoted, marginalized, or becoming a minority is central to political competition and polarization. The EU lacks such a dominant actor. While Germany is often described as the most important or dominant Member State, its population accounts for less than 20% of the EU total, and the German share of the EU GDP is just below a quarter. Beyond the numbers, in terms of decision-making, Germany can be outvoted, and other Member States cannot be ignored by Germany. It has been argued that the economic and political weight of Germany makes it a "reluctant hegemon" in the EU (Bulmer Paterson 2018). While this might apply to some policy areas, such as the Eurozone, it is less clear in others, such as foreign policy. Overall, despite its size and weight, Germany is unable (and unwilling) to dominate the EU. As a result, the EU, despite having a great variety of Member States ranging from Malta (with 0.01% of the EU population) to Germany, is a non-hegemonic polity. This reduces the majoritarian temptation that a dominant unit could seek to outvote the interest of others.

## 9.2 Implications for Multinational Polities

What does the EU tell us about balancing diversity and unity? The starting point of this book is that the experience of the EU in balancing diversity and unity is specific, but not unique. Multinational federations, power-sharing systems, and other political systems that seek to accommodate diversity—often divisive and at times antagonistic—all pursue these two core principles of the EU. In this sense, the EU has been developing responses to these demands as other polities have. The EU does not offer an easy institutional blueprint. Beyond the observation of scholars of institutional design that (generally speaking) there are no one-size-fits-all blueprints,[14] there are a series of specific reasons that make it a difficult model to emulate. The EU has grown over the decades in terms of population and Member States, nearly tripling in terms of inhabitants from 167 million in 1957 to 446 million in 2020, and growing nearly five-fold in terms of membership. Few polities have grown so rapidly in peace time. The United States, which has also grown substantially since its founding, did so through conquest and immigration rather than solely through voluntary association (and conquest). The EU has also been undergoing substantial institutional and legal evolution that is structurally engrained in the Union. The EU thus never just is, but is always becoming. Of course, all states change—the gradual shift of competences from the states and cantons of the United States and Switzerland attest to that—but the shifts in the EU have occurred voluntarily, in peaceful times and to a much greater extent over a shorter period of time.

It is beyond doubt that negotiating diversity and unity is fragile, reversible, and subject to exogenous and indigenous shocks. The tempting answer to the challenges the EU has had to face over the past 15 years was to call for either its abandonment (as supporters of Brexit and all its counterparts in other Member States have argued) or, at the other end, a European Republic. This book has sought to show that negotiating diversity and unity is one of the strengths of the Union, even if it is making it a more 'difficult' polity than conventional states. The intricate tension of

[14] While scholars of power-sharing propose different models, these are not set blueprints, but principles on how to arrange the institutional structure of a given polity. McCulloch (2020); Jakala et al. (2018); Schneckener (2002).

the Union makes its 'incomplete' nature a virtue—a need for citizens and Member States to recast, develop, and reimagine the Union. This evolutionary nature of the Union is its greatest asset that has allowed it to evolve and respond to new challenges. Of course, it also highlights its own unfinished nature, opens it up to criticism, and makes it harder to identify with. The argument is not that the status quo or European integration can adequately respond to all the difficulties the Union is facing, ranging from democratic decline in some Member States to the lack of solidarity and the contestation of the European institutions by national institutions. Instead, it suggests that a patient, gradual process can best accommodate difference.

## References


Bieber, R. (2020). Wechselseitige Verantwortung der Mitgliedstaaten – ein Rechtsprinzip der Europäischen Union? *Festschrift Georg Ress*. Baden Baden: NOMOS.

Bulmer, S., & Paterson, W. E. (2018). *Germany and the European Union. Europe's Reluctant Hegemon?* London: Red Globe Press.

*Charter of the United Nations* (1945). https://legal.un.org/repertory/art2_7.shtml. Accessed 15 May 2020.

Crawford, J., Pellet, A., & Olleson, S. (Eds.). (2010). *The Law of International Responsibility*. Oxford: OUP.

Freedom House. (2020). *Nations in Transit 2020: Dropping the Democratic Façade*. https://freedomhouse.org/sites/default/files/2020-04/05062020_FH_NIT2020_vfinal.pdf. Accessed 15 May 2020.

Haag, M. (2019). *A Sense of Responsibility: The Shifting Roles of the Member States for the Union Citizen*. Unpublished Ph.D. thesis, EUI Florence.

Habermas, J. (1998). *Die Einbeziehung des Anderen* (English translation: *The Inclusion of the Other*). Frankfurt/M.: Suhrkamp.

Jakala, M., Kuzu, D., & Qvortrup, M. (Eds.). (2018). *Consociationalism and Power-Sharing in Europe: Arend Lijphart's Theory of Political Accommodation*. Basingstoke: Palgrave Macmillan.

Jonas, H. (1984). *The Imperative of Responsibility*. Chicago: University of Chicago Press.

Lenaerts, K., & van Nuffel, P. (2011). *European Union Law*. London: Sweet & Maxwell.

McCulloch, A. (2020). Confronting the Empirical and Normative Challenges to Power-Sharing Governance. *Ethnopolitics, 19*(1), 85–87.

Nicolaidis, K., & Viehoff, J. (2012). The Choice for Sustainable Solidarity in Post-Crisis Europe. In G. Bajnai, T. Fischer, H. Fischer, et al. (Eds.), *Solidarity for Sale?* (pp. 23–40). Gütersloh: Bertelsmann.

Pellet, A. (2010). The Definition of Responsibility in International Law. In J. Crawford, A. Pellet, & S. Olleson (Eds.), *The Law of International Responsibility* (pp. 3–16). Oxford: OUP.

ICISS (2001). Report of the International Commission on Intervention and State Sovereignty. *The Responsibility to Protect*. Ottawa. http://responsibilitytoprotect.org/ICISS%20Report.pdf. Accessed 15 May 2020.

Schneckener, U. (2002). Making Power-Sharing Work: Lessons from Successes and Failures in Ethnic Conflict Regulation. *Journal of Peace Research, 39*(2), 203–228.

*Treaty Establishing the European Stability Mechanism* (2012). https://www.esm.europa.eu/sites/default/files/20150203_-_esm_treaty_-_en.pdf. Accessed 15 May 2020.

V-Dem Institute. (2020). *Autocratization Surges – Resistance Grows: Democracy Report 2020*. https://www.v-dem.net/media/filer_public/f0/5d/f05d46d8-626f-4b20-8e4e-53d4b134bfcb/democracy_report_2020_low.pdf. Accessed 15 May 2020.

Wolfrum, R., & Kojima, C. (Eds.). (2010). *Solidarity: A Structural Principle of International Law*. Heidelberg: Springer.

# Epilogue

This book began its life in the aftermath of the global economic crisis 2008–2009, large parts were drafted during the Brexit referendum and its aftermath, and it was completed during the COVID-19 pandemic. Crises of the European Union and the wider world have accompanied it over a decade. The COVID-19 pandemic might become the biggest test for the EU yet. In a matter of days the borders between Member States were closed and the freedom of movement that many Europeans have become accustomed to ceased for weeks and months.

At first, the government responses to the pandemic appeared to fulfill the demands of populists and nationalists that have argued for closed borders, suspicion toward the outside world, and deglobalization. In fact, Nigel Farage, the long-standing far-right advocate of Brexit and leader of UKIP and later the Brexit Party, claimed in March 2020 that "We are all nationalists now" (Farage 2020). However, the deglobalization that occurred during the first response to the pandemic was not voluntary isolationism, but rather part of an attempt to stem the disease and control people's movement where it was easiest, at national borders. However, the economic crisis and isolation experienced by citizens of the EU highlights rather the degree of integration that most had taken for granted and the challenges of its disruption. In fact, the criticism directed at the EU during the crisis has been not that it was overreaching or intruding into citizens' lives—the classic theme of Euroskepticism—but rather that it had not done enough, ignoring the lack of competences of the Union.



F. Bieber, R. Bieber, *Negotiating Unity and Diversity in the European Union*, Palgrave Studies in European Union Politics,
https://doi.org/10.1007/978-3-030-55016-5

Being limited in terms of competences the field of public health, the EU could at first offer little assistance to Member States that especially struggled with the pandemic, such as Italy and Spain. Solidarity among Member States did emerge as Germany, Luxembourg, Austria, and other states less hard hit by the disease offered hospital beds to patients from countries more overwhelmed, and EU Member States provided medical supplies to each other. However, the first shock of the crisis, when many Member States first looked after their own interests, left its mark. This failure was acknowledged by European Commission President Ursula von der Leyen, who apologized to Italy, noting that "[t]oo many were not there on time when Italy needed a helping hand at the very beginning" (Henley 2020). The reservations of several EU Member States towards so-called Coronabonds, a jointly issued public debt instrument backed by all Eurozone countries, also gave the impression that solidarity within the EU was limited. In the first response, skepticism towards the EU, in particular in Italy, rose sharply (Johnson et al. 2020; Coratella 2020). In the midst of the pandemic, the long-term consequences for the EU are impossible to assess. Yet, the difficulty of managing an emergency has been apparent not just in the EU, but in a variety of different polities. Federal and decentralized polities are often struggling more in responding quickly and coherently as they test solidarity among the sub-units, be they states in the United States, Länder in Germany, or Member States in the EU. Furthermore, they require coordination and agreement, where such institutional mechanisms and political consent might be lacking. The variety of responses to the pandemic by different states (and at times by counties) in the United States has been greater than among the Member States of the EU, as has the level of antagonism and the severity of the pandemic.

The pandemic threw a light on the difficulty of negotiating diversity and unity in a polity like the EU. It is based on the voluntary and consensual cooperation and support of the Member States and citizens, and thus always up for being challenged and renegotiated. This has allowed the Union to adapt and change to a degree that states are often unable to do. On the other hand, it is also met by many who might doubt its *raison d'être* and reject it. This is not the fate of states. So, if the government of a particular state responds badly to crises like the COVID-19 pandemic, few citizens will question the state; instead, they might question the government or the policy. In debates about the appropriateness or competences of decision-making of the EU, not only is the response versus competence in the era often ignored, there is also little distinction made between the decision-makers in the EU, particular policies or ideologies, and the EU as a polity itself.

The EU has survived multiple crises, in particular since 2008, be they economic crises, crises of solidarity and values, or disasters. This does not mean that this is inevitable, but merely that the EU has been able to adapt and respond to these challenges. More importantly, it also highlights that the Union responds to a genuine need of citizens and the Member States of the EU, even if often slowly and in a piecemeal fashion.

# References

Coratella, T. (2020). The Dangers of Crisis Diplomacy: Italy, China, and Russia. *European Council on Foreign Relations*, April 17. https://www.ecfr.eu/article/commentary_the_dangers_of_crisis_diplomacy_italy_china_and_russia

Farage, N. (2020). Coronavirus Has Shown We Are All Nationalists Now. Does Boris Johnson Realise That? *The Daily Telegraph*, March 12. Available at: https://www.telegraph.co.uk/politics/2020/03/12/coronavirus-has-shown-nationalists-now-does-boris-johnson-realise/. Accessed 6 Apr 2020.

Henley, J. (2020). EU Offers 'Heartfelt Apology' to Italy over Coronavirus Response. *The Guardian*, April 16. Available at: https://www.theguardian.com/world/2020/apr/16/eu-offers-heartfelt-apology-italy-coronavirus-response-herd-immunity

Johnson, S. F., & Chazan, G. (2020). Coronavirus: Is Europe Losing Italy? *Financial Times*, April 6. https://www.ft.com/content/f21cf708-759e-11ea-ad98-044200cb277f. Accessed 8 April 2020.



F. Bieber, R. Bieber, *Negotiating Unity and Diversity in the European Union*, Palgrave Studies in European Union Politics,
https://doi.org/10.1007/978-3-030-55016-5

# Index[1]



[1] Note: Page numbers followed by 'n' refer to notes.



F. Bieber, R. Bieber, *Negotiating Unity and Diversity in the European Union*, Palgrave Studies in European Union Politics,
https://doi.org/10.1007/978-3-030-55016-5

The manufacturer's authorised representative in the EU is Springer Nature Customer Service Centre GmbH, Europaplatz 3, 69115 Heidelberg, Germany. If you have any concerns regarding our products, please contact ProductSafety@springernature.com

Printed and bound by CPI Group (UK) Ltd, Croydon, CR0 4YY
30/09/2026
02225452-0001